T0331985

Ethical Business Cultures in Emerging Markets

Previous research on corporate cultures and ethical business cultures has focused almost exclusively on studies of multinational corporations from a handful of developed countries. This book addresses the intersection of human resource development and human resource management with ethical business cultures in the five BRICS (Brazil, Russia, India, China, and South Africa) and three other fast-growing emerging economies: those of Mexico, Indonesia, and Turkey. The book compares managers' and employees' perceptions of ethical business cultures in these eight countries, and discusses the economic and sociocultural context and current research on business ethics in each of the countries. The scholarly discussion, presented in country-specific chapters, is complemented by chapters based on contributions by industry practitioners. This significant study will appeal to scholars, researchers and students in business ethics, management, human resource management and development, and organization studies, and addresses issues faced daily by business executives and practitioners working in emerging market countries.

DOUGLAS JONDLE is a consultant with Bains Jondle & Associates LLC, which fosters ethical cultures in a global economy, and is a former research director of the Center for Ethical Business Cultures (CEBC) at the University of St. Thomas (UST). His research includes modeling ethical organizational culture, evaluating organizational cultures multiculturally, the development of the Ethical Perception Index, and modeling ethical risk management (a cooperative research project between CEBC and UST's Veritas Institute), and he previously co-edited the *Ethics* volume of the Wiley Encyclopedia of Management.

ALEXANDRE ARDICHVILI is Professor and Hellervik Endowed Chair in Leadership and Adult Career Development at the University of Minnesota. He is President of the University Council on Work and Human Resource Education, past editor-in-chief of *Human Resource Development International*, and Fellow of the Center for Ethical Business Cultures. Dr. Ardichvili has published 3 books, 70 peer-reviewed articles, and numerous book chapters related to international HRD, leadership development, entrepreneurship, business ethics, and knowledge management.

Ethical Business Cultures in Emerging Markets

Edited by

DOUGLAS JONDLE

Bains Jondle & Associates LLC

ALEXANDRE ARDICHVILI

University of Minnesota

CAMBRIDGE
UNIVERSITY PRESS

CAMBRIDGE
UNIVERSITY PRESS

University Printing House, Cambridge CB2 8BS, United Kingdom

One Liberty Plaza, 20th Floor, New York, NY 10006, USA

477 Williamstown Road, Port Melbourne, VIC 3207, Australia

4843/24, 2nd Floor, Ansari Road, Daryaganj, Delhi – 110002, India

79 Anson Road, #06-04/06, Singapore 079906

Cambridge University Press is part of the University of Cambridge.

It furthers the University's mission by disseminating knowledge in the pursuit of education, learning, and research at the highest international levels of excellence.

www.cambridge.org
Information on this title: www.cambridge.org/9781107104921
DOI: 10.1017/9781316225165

First published 2017

Printed in the United Kingdom by Clays, St Ives plc

A catalogue record for this publication is available from the British Library.

ISBN 978-1-107-10492-1 Hardback

Contents

Figures and Tables

Contributors

Mesut Akdere
Purdue University, USA

Alexandre Ardichvili
University of Minnesota, USA

Edgard Cornacchione
University of São Paulo, Brazil

Ahmet Coskun
Istanbul Commerce University and Erciyes University, Turkey

Douglas Jondle
Bains Jondle & Associates, LLC, USA

Liliane Klaus
University of São Paulo, Brazil

Emery Koenig
Former Chief Risk Officer and Vice Chariman of Cargill, Incorporated

Jessica Li
University of Illinois, USA

Jane Maringka
GCM Advisory Pty Ltd, Australia

Noor Rahmani
Gadjah Mada University, Indonesia

Kelsey-Jo Ritter
Manchester University, USA

Deon Rossouw
Ethics Institute of South Africa, South Africa

Martha Sañudo
Instituto Tecnológico y de Estudios Superiores de Monterrey (ITESM),
Mexico

Thomas Thakadipuram
St. Claret College, India

Jack Wiley
Manchester University, USA

Foreword

THE INDIVIDUAL VERSUS THE COLLECTIVE

As the final preparations for the submission of this book to the publisher were underway, I reflected on recent experiences during the 41st Ryder Cup, a golf sporting event between the United States and Europe held every other year that attracts a huge global audience. Representatives consisting of twelve players from each side compete in two-person teams for two days and a singles format on the third and final day with a goal of securing enough points to win and/or retain the Ryder Cup until the next competition. Winning the Ryder Cup is a tremendous honor and brings great pride and "bragging rights" to the team and their respective country (or countries).

Despite having players ranked higher in golf standings, an overall team considered consistently stronger, and a history of dominating the event, the US team had lost the last three Ryder Cups, six of the last seven, and eight of the last ten. The performance of the United States had become so concerning that a task force made up of former Ryder Cup US captains, US players, and US golf officials was convened to address the pattern of losses and create a new trajectory.

It is interesting to note that other than the Ryder Cup event (and a companion event called the President's Cup contested in alternate years from the Ryder Cup featuring the United States against *non-*European countries from around the world), *professional golf is very much an individual sport*. Players train, practice, and compete as individuals to win first place in tournaments that bring fame, lucrative financial rewards, and endorsement contracts. They also work to compile an annual record that positions them to compete in a season-ending series of playoff tournaments that brings the individual winner the distinction of being the best in the world, along with well over ten million dollars in prize money. They are incentivized to act and compete as individuals, with all of the rivalry and frailties of temperament that come with intense individual competition.

But for the Ryder Cup, once every two years, the European team, made up of players from all over Europe, have found a way to rise above the individual rivalry, to bond, and to function as a *team of one* united with a common goal of defeating the United States. And by functioning as a *team of one*, the Europeans have given greater meaning to the phrase, *the whole can be greater than the sum of its parts if we work together as a team.* Working as a team, they have built strong relationships and camaraderies that significantly lift the spirit and the level of play of their fellow teammates, allowing them to outperform higher-ranked opponents on the US team. *The spirit of the collective becomes greater than the spirit of the individual.*

FORMAL OR INFORMAL – RELATIONSHIPS MATTER

In my role as President and CEO of the Center for Ethical Business Cultures, I have had the honor and good fortune to work with multiple organizations intensively building a global footprint to reach new markets with their products and services as well as benefit from the utilization of global workforces supplying goods and services.

The best organizations devote attention to answering three questions: *why* – why are we here (purpose – mission and vision); *what* – what is it we are trying to accomplish (strategy, goals, and objectives); and *how* – how do we go about accomplishing the "why" and the "what" (setting behavioral expectations through clearly defined values, ethics, and compliance standards of conduct).

Often organizations concentrate on the "why" and the "what" assuming everyone understands the "how." But failure to devote balanced attention to the "how" can lead to a culture of achieving the goal "by any means necessary" – *the ends will justify the means.*

In global settings, this becomes even more complex because the "how" takes on different interpretations and meaning based on the culture of the country one is doing business in. One cannot assume that the behavioral standards and expectations of the "home country" (where the business is headquartered) are transportable and acceptable to the "host country" (where the business is actually being conducted). And if there are differences, failure to understand, internalize, and operationalize these differences can lead to a breakdown in the organizational culture and ultimately a failed realization of mission, vision, strategies, goals, and objectives.

As an example, in certain countries, particularly developed economies, business relationships are more formal and centered on the nature of the business that is being conducted. These business relationships are often codified in formal contracts, memorandums of understanding, or letters of agreements, often enforceable by law. Any social or personal relationships are secondary and may evolve as the business relationship matures.

In other countries, including emerging economies, business relationships are informal and based on social, familial, clan, or political networks. Formal instruments to codify the relationships are viewed as flexible, allowing interpretation and adaptation to accommodate the particular situation. And it is the social, familial, clan, or political relationship that is primary and ultimately determines the nature of the business relationship.

Imagine the conflict that arises when one party assumes business decisions are being made based on formal agreements and the other sees the formal agreement as flexible – being able to be adapted the particular situation at hand.

WHY DOES THIS MATTER

Individual versus collective, informal versus formal, professional versus personal relationships – why should these or any other differences in cultures or countries matter? As many have written, we have clearly entered a new era of global economic interconnectedness with shifting leadership roles among countries. The rules of engagement have been determined by those with economic power, primarily developed economies. Likewise, the standards of behavior – the "how" – have also been determined by developed economies.

But there are many countries with emerging economies that will over time surpass the economies of the developed countries. And as this unfolds, we will need to pay just as much attention to "how" we work together in this new environment of developed and developing economies as we do to "what" we do together to realize the economic opportunities for all. We need to understand and appreciate the differences, seeing them as opportunities to build better relationships and strengthen the performance of organizations within differing cultural settings.

This book is an essential ingredient to advance the conversation about our differences and similarities. We must learn to understand, appreciate, and incorporate practices that respect our similarities and our differences as we learn to work together to ensure successful outcomes. And it is better to have the conversations as we are going through the shifts in economic power than to wait until we are facing a crisis. Because if we wait until a crisis occurs, the conversation becomes much more complex and complicated. Individuals revert to what works best in their culture or country, which can lead to tacit agreements, misunderstandings, or, at its worst, polarization.

This book brings together the voices of business practitioners, business consultants, and leading academics to explore the differing approaches to ethics in a global setting. With practical examples, stories, research, and firsthand insight into differing cultures from those who have experienced it, this book broadens our perspective and helps us learn to understand and appreciate how we work together.

Ron James
President and Chief Executive Officer
Center for Ethical Business Cultures

Preface

The legitimate peculiarity of each person, which formerly had troubled and irritated Pierre, now constituted the basis of the sympathy and interest he took in people.

Leo Tolstoy, *War and Peace*

THE STORY OF A YOUNG MANAGER: A CASE STUDY IN CULTURAL EXCHANGE

It was September 1989. Recently conferred a PhD, I had just been asked if I would be on a research team created as part of a joint corporate venture in the Soviet Union. I was a graduate of the University of Wisconsin–Madison (UW), with a degree in plant breeding and plant genetics, with no administrative training or corporate experience. In June 1989, I assumed the title and role of corn breeder and research station manager in a small town in southern Minnesota, and immediately became responsible for supervising five full-time employees, more than 20 seasonal workers, and a budget of $300,000.

After three months on the job, the vice president of research for the United States asked if I was interested in traveling with him to the Soviet Union the following spring. The company had just entered into a joint venture agreement with the All Union Research Institute (the Institute) in Dnipropetrovsk, Ukraine. Up until recently, Dnipropetrovsk had been a closed city to foreign travelers due to the extensive military and space industry located there. The company would develop business relationships with emerging market countries through its seed division. The thought was that everyone needs to eat, and providing seed technology was a means of feeding a hungry population. Once the seeds business was established, it would not be that difficult to open other distribution channels within the country to bring in other products behind the goodwill provided by seeds.

Accepting the offer meant traveling twice a year, for a week or more at a time, to Ukraine, once each in the spring and the fall. I would reciprocate, and host my Soviet peers once a year during the summer. The purpose of the visits to Ukraine was to consult among peers and to travel the countryside, from *kolhoz* (communal state-run farm) to *kolhoz*, extolling the greatness of the joint venture and the advantages of our product over others, which were mostly locally produced. On occasion we partnered with other Western companies to jointly promote products such as our seeds and their farm machinery. Beyond the face-to-face contact, my joint venture responsibilities included evaluating both the germplasm coming from and going to the Institute.

International travel had never been a projected strength of mine. Prior to this opportunity, I had only traveled outside of the United States twice, once to Cancun, Mexico, and a second time to Canada. Either hardly resumé builders.

In March 1990, I made my first of eight trips to the Soviet Union. Accompanied by vice presidents of both US and International Research, I sat in Logan International Airport's lounge in Boston, all of us completing our final prep before boarding the flight to Moscow. While my contribution of personal perspective was fairly weak and insignificant, the two VPs were rich sources of personal international experiences and a wealth of information that quickly negated the significance or importance of the briefing material I had received from the company in the form of a 1975 CIA report. Within months, due to political volatility and economic turmoil within the Soviet Union, the republics that comprised the country were clamoring for independence. In my travels that followed, the emphasis quickly shifted from the Soviet Union to the newly independent countries of Ukraine and Russia.

Arriving in Dnipropetrovsk, we were met at the airport by Pavel and Boris, senior scientists at the All Union Research Institute in Dnipropetrovsk and my research peers. Typical of our visits to the Institute, we spent the greater portion of the trip discussing the exchange of germplasm, touring the Institute's numerous research nurseries, observing hybrid yield trials throughout the region, visiting with officials at *kolhozy*, and, most importantly, discussing how to spend the $125,000 budgeted to the research project. Ultimately, how best to spend the money was my responsibility.

Pavel and Boris immediately identified two large purchase items as "must-haves," and earmarked several smaller ones as necessities, such as pollinating supplies, seed counters, and electronic scales. The large items were a 15-passenger van and a specialty combine to mechanically harvest hybrid research plots.

Working from the perspective that I knew what was best for the program (after all, the money was being provided by the company), we agreed that the first item to procure was a gasoline-fueled Ford van. First of all, it was needed to pick up and transport visiting international guests (myself included) and be at their disposal during their visit. Second, it would be used to transport supplies and personnel to and from the fields. This was all regardless of the fact that gasoline (versus diesel) was both expensive and scarce, and the van was not known for having great gas mileage. Nevertheless, one of my first orders of business upon returning home was purchasing and arranging for the shipment of a white Econoline Ford van to the Ukraine. Thirty-five thousand dollars spent. It arrived in the country in good shape, being available for the next visit. Needless to say, its availability was not always guaranteed. More times than not, the van was not available. Reasons varied, but most followed two lines of reasoning: (1) it was too expensive to run, or (2) the newly installed country manager, an expat from Western Europe, needed it in Kiev for nonresearch functions, much to the ire of the Institute. Regardless, after a while I never saw the van again.

Now moving onto the combine. Spending the remaining budgeted dollars became problematic. In part because the combine (specifically designed and built as a research plot combine) that both Pavel and Boris were interested in was made in West Germany, while I was favoring purchasing a used field combine and modifying it in the

United States for plot work. Being fairly easy to transport overland to its delivery point at the Institute, the research combine was a brand new combine. Purchasing it meant using all the remaining available cash, maybe more. From my personal experience, Option B was a better deal. For less than half the cost, a used field combine could be secured in the United States, it could be specially modified for small plot work, and shipped overseas. After all, I had just gone through a refitting of a combine for my own research station. However, Pavel and Boris were not having it. They wanted the new combine.

Pollinating supplies required to carry out controlled pollinations in the breeding nurseries were in chronic short supply for the Institute. The Institute barely had enough supplies each year to complete the needed number of pollinations. While not the most glamorous of purchases, it was evident that they were vital for the success of the project. To make matters worse, they needed to be ordered a year in advance and shipped. The problem was that Pavel and Boris still wanted the new combine. On the other hand, after purchasing the van, the decision in my mind became clearer. The only option was to secure the pollinating supplies and to find a used combine in the United States and ship it to Ukraine. And that is what I did.

Good plan. Made sense.

Everyone was happy.

No, not Pavel and Boris.

The pollinating supplies were ordered in time to arrive for use during the next growing season. The research combine was built from a used Allis Chalmers F2 Gleaner Combine and was ready for shipment the next spring, with arrival in time for use in the next harvest season. Enough money was saved, even with international shipping costs factored in, to include key spare parts, like belts, gears, and filters.

The combine arrived as scheduled at the port of Odessa on the Black Sea. It never arrived at the Institute as planned.

I later discovered that the Institute had no way of picking up the combine once it arrived at port. How did I not know this? The combine stayed at portside all winter, unprotected from the elements. Finally, the Institute took delivery of the combine the following spring. The combine had suffered severe damage as the result of being left outside, portside in the damp, salty air. More damage was sustained as it was driven overland back to the Institute some 470 km.

Arriving that fall with the director of information technology, we were taken to what remained of the combine. It had been parked unceremoniously, outside again, in a corner of the maintenance yard in the mud. One of the large front-drive tires was flat. The gears that ran the corn-harvesting head were rusted fast. The computerized weighing system that measured each research plot's yield and other agronomic data was corroded and shorted out by saltwater. After an hour assessing the damage, our attempt to breathe any life into the combine was futile. We pronounced it unsalvageable. A loss of $75,000.

Making mistakes is easy and learning is not always pretty, but it can be and usually is messy. So, at the end of the day – $125,000 later – the only purchases that provided any real value to the project were the pollinating supplies – and they were only a one-year supply and a seed counter.

As an inexperienced research station manager given significant attention and responsibility, important decisions were made based on cultural *naiveté* and lack of or limited situational experience. *Arrogance*, or superiority over peers, created an aura of power and control that led to the practice of limiting information, poor analysis of situations, and snap decisions. *Indifference* in entertaining alternate points of view established a rigid path to uncompromising results – room to maneuver for change was stifled. Intense and excessive pride (*hubris*) played a crippling role in fostering a path to poor results and hard feelings between parties.

I recall from nearly the start of my experience having an unfounded feeling of power and control over the agenda and my peers. This stemmed from the fact that of the joint venture partners, it was the company, after all, that was bringing with it the capital and other business acumen for the benefit of the Institute. I considered the Institute as inferior, both as a business and research partner. I did not view my peers as equals. I truly felt that, as an American, I held both the morally superior ground and the more capable intellect.

This bluster was totally unfounded. My peers received comparable training, more professional vetting and accreditation, and certainly had more practical experience. They had more travel experience internationally, and were more culturally astute. My arrogance and self-assurance were grounded in the belief that, as an American, trained in an American school, I possessed the superior capability to make the strategic decisions. This feeling of overconfidence and preeminence was amplified all the more when, after the third trip, I was traveling without the vice president of US Research to Ukraine. Surely this was a nod to his confidence in me and my personal feeling of having control over the situation.

From a business perspective, there was truth in the ability of the company to wield significantly more clout in the international business arena than the Institute. After all, the company was a well-established and respected international player in the global business community. The Institute, on the other hand, had traditionally been focused on local interests, and was certainly more isolated by the political situation in the Soviet Union at the time. Funding was drying up, as the result of economic hardships within the old Soviet Union, and further erosion of monies was the result of Ukraine declaring independence in 1991. The company certainly was looked upon as a white knight from the Institute's perspective, with the potential to infuse vitally needed capital and business know-how.

As long as I was part of the project, I never truly appreciated the opportunities it presented for me to grow personally – to better understand that the world is a really small place. And in that small place what is needed to be successful is for people of differing abilities, interests, and values to work together as a team, where no one member dominates the decision-making process or the moral high ground. I needed to learn that in order to continue to innovate, there needs to be a continual embrace of different things, an injection of variability, and an assurance that with change comes improvement.

The breakdown in the ability of a leader to recognize his own shortcomings, fed by ambition and blinded by his own cleverness, clouds a true understanding of the situation at hand and shields him from the inevitabilities of change and innovation. These attitudes can only be a long-term hindrance to cultural integration, social harmony, and a realization of the true meaning of business.

Hubris, naiveté, arrogance, and indifference – these are not the characteristics that one wishes to employ when building lasting and healthy relationships with business associates. It is not how a culture and its leaders demonstrate cultural empathy and social tolerance. It is certainly not how management creates a culture for a business that is based on ethical and profitable behavior – a business culture that espouses a fundamental understanding of what is right and what is wrong, and subscribing to this as a minimal standard of how to conduct business. When all options seem right, it is up to management to make decisions that reach for the higher ground. Even in the face of short-term monetary loss, following through with the more righteous act will reap long-term advantage and reward.

Now, upon reflection some 25 years later, would I act the same, make the same or different decisions? Does the distance of time and a greater wealth of perspective and experience sharpen my capacity to make important decisions free from cultural bias or personal prejudices? How influenced am I when it comes to my cultural intelligence?

I might still make the same decisions as I did the first time, but experience has taught me that they would be based on a far broader perspective, with a better understanding of cultural differences. I would hope not to be predisposed to a particular viewpoint or hastily made decision. While age played a role – I was twenty years Pavel and Boris's junior – I feel I was more influenced by the fact that I was an American, representing a very large and successful corporation that was well respected the world over, and I was chosen to represent that corporation. I just knew better.

Many cultures outside of the United States place a premium on relationships among family, friends, and business peers, as will become evident in the pages that follow. A crucial mistake that I made back then was not taking advantage of numerous opportunities to build on the personal relationship between me and my peers to examine my biases that stemmed from being an American. Our "relationships" were mostly built around business opportunities. I spent five years traveling back and forth to Russia and Ukraine several times a year, and Pavel and Boris traveled to the United States once a year during that period. Plenty of opportunity to get to know someone on a more personal level. On numerous occasions, I was invited to visit with them at their dacha and dine with their families. And we spent an inordinate amount of time traveling by car to research stations, farm shows, and government farms. These were all opportunities with plenty of time to foster deeper understandings of just who we were as persons. But most of the time was either spent in silent thought or talking business.

My point in all this is, in business transactions it is all too easy and may be an expectation that most or all of your time should be directed understanding the mutual business at hand. It is certainly not efficient or relevant to the business deal to talk about family, friends, or politics with your business peers. Nonsense! I contend that in part my business decisions would have been better informed if I had had a better understanding of who my partners were, what made them act the way they did. It would have been more important to know them as a person, not as a transaction that needed to be completed. This, I believe, is all the more important and relevant when operating in other cultures that are different from your own.

There is another point to make, the one about the importance of diversity or variability (my geneticist voice), and ultimately change, being an asset rather than a detriment. Diversity needs to be embraced, not shunned out of fear. We must not shelter ourselves from diverse thought, experiences, and cultures.

In plant breeding, a basic tenet is that to effect change, in order to improve the performance of an existing hybrid or variety, you need genetic variability or a diverse population of individuals. I would argue the same tenet applies in business. In order to effect progress and performance within an organization, you need to have and take advantage of diversity in the workforce and in the pool of customers you serve. Operating in the global markets serves this purpose. No one person possesses the mind-set or skill-set to account for all specialties of ability. You need a blending of many minds with varying backgrounds and experiences to maximize change that leads to innovation that leads to sustained business performance. Furthermore, it is of utmost importance to acknowledge that all of this needs to be accepted as an integral part of and nurtured through the building and sustaining of ethical business cultures.

Douglas Jondle

Acknowledgments

We would like to thank the Center for Ethical Business Cultures and its staff (Terri Hastings, Ronald James, Judi Olson, David Rodbourne, and Robert Shoemake) for their support of the research that lead to this book and all the encouragement as the book was being written. Along the road to publication the Center hosted the Building Ethical Business Cultures in Emerging Markets: Challenges and Risks Conference in September 2015 in Minneapolis, Minnesota. The conference brought together the book's authors from all over the world for a full-day conversation with executives from leading local business organizations. Doing away with the traditional presentation-based session format, the conference organizers created an interactive forum based on a dialogue between scholars and practitioners. The conference was funded through the generous support of the conference sponsors. Based on the lessons learned at the conference, the focus of the book was sharpened to address important challenges business practitioners face in conducting business on a global scale.

We would like to thank the James A. and Linda Mitchell Foundation for its support of the book. In addition, it was on Jim's foresight and vision of the importance of ethical business cultures that the research at the Center was based.

We also would like to thank Paula Parish, our commissioning editor at Cambridge University Press, who first approached us to write the book and for all her encouragement and support following.

Introduction: Business Ethics and Ethical Cultures in Emerging Markets

Alexandre Ardichvili and Douglas Jondle

As the economies of Brazil, Russia, India, China, South Africa (BRICS), and other emerging market countries continue to grow, and multinational corporations originating in these countries become major players in global markets, questions pertaining to trust, integrity, and standards for ethical business behavior become important concerns for stakeholders. Will norms that shape current acceptable business behavior be challenged by the growing influence of stakeholders within the emerging market countries? What competing values and behaviors will business practitioners/executives have to reckon with as they conduct business in a shifting paradigm, fueled by the inherent variability of differing cultural norms that influence behavior within emerging market countries? How will governments define and regulate ethical behavior, and how will businesses be accountable to their stakeholders for ethical behavior when the foundations on which compliance and ethics programs have been built are subjected to competing norms?

Whether or not managers and employees behave ethically depends largely on how ethical behavior is perceived in various cultures, and how it is shaped by organizational cultures and national institutional environments. Issues around managing corporate cultures have long been a central concern of executives around the world. The discussion of *ethical* corporate cultures has become more prominent both in business ethics and human resource development (HRD) publications in recent years (Ardichvili et al., 2009; Goodpaster, 2007). One of the reasons for the growing interest in understanding what makes organizational cultures ethical was the realization that the global financial and economic crisis of 2008–2009 was triggered,

I

among other things, by major ethics violations at multinational corporations (MNCs) and financial institutions. Furthermore, recognition is growing that corporations governed by questionable business ethics are much more likely to behave in socially irresponsible and unsustainable ways.

Previous research on corporate cultures and ethical business cultures has focused almost exclusively on studies of MNCs from a handful of developed countries. At the same time, the importance of understanding and promoting ethical cultures in large business organizations from emerging economies cannot be overstated. In 2001, Goldman Sachs projected that by 2050, combined gross domestic product of four BRIC countries (Brazil, Russia, India, and China) alone will be larger than that of the seven largest developed economies of the world (G7) (Goldman Sachs, 2001). South Africa was added to the list soon thereafter, and the group became known as BRICS. In 2005, Goldman Sachs has created an additional list of fast-growing emerging countries, calling them The Next Eleven. This group of fast-growing and influential emerging markets includes Bangladesh, Egypt, Indonesia, Iran, Mexico, Nigeria, Pakistan, the Philippines, Turkey, South Korea, and Vietnam (O'Neill et al., 2005). Furthermore, multinationals from BRICS and other emerging countries are playing a major role in shaping the way business is done globally.

This book fills two gaps in the current business ethics and ethical business cultures literature. First, it discusses attributes of ethical business behavior and ethical business cultures in firms from emerging market countries. Second, the book provides executives from the United States and other developed economies with a better understanding of how to succeed in doing business in emerging markets, and it offers suggestions for practitioners on ways to approach complex ethical dilemmas arising from cultural clashes and perceived differences in ethical business values of organizations from different countries.

The book is structured as follows. In Part I, Chapters 1 through 8 are devoted to eight emerging market countries. Given space limitations, we had to make difficult choices when deciding which countries to include in this volume. In addition to all five BRICS (Brazil, Russia, India, China, and South Africa) nations, we selected three countries that have recently gained prominence as some of the largest and most influential in their part of the world: Mexico, Indonesia, and Turkey. This choice allowed us to include three important geographical regions not covered by BRICS: North and Central America, Southeast Asia, and MENA (Middle East and North Africa). These eight chapters are contributed by leading scholars residing in or originating from the countries in question and representing the disciplines of management, organization development, human resource development, and business ethics. Each chapter provides an overview of the sociocultural and economic background of the country, discusses the distinctive characteristics of each country's culture, and then provides an analysis of the attributes of ethical business cultures and ethical behaviors in business organizations, operating in and originating in the said country.

Part II is devoted to the practice of building and sustaining ethical business cultures. In Chapter 9, Jack Wiley discusses the results of a large-scale, longitudinal, survey-based study of the opinions of thousands of managers and employees from 22 developing and developed countries, comparing perceptions of what constitutes ethical business behavior in these countries to indexes of Employee Engagement and Performance Confidence. In Chapters 10 and 11, the scholarly discussion, presented in previous chapters, is complemented by practitioner perspectives. Chapter 10 is based on a keynote address, given by Emery Koenig, former Chief Risk Officer and Vice Chairmen of Cargill. In it, Koenig discusses Cargill's unique approach to building ethical business culture in the largest privately held company in the United States, and its relentless effort to ensure that organization's ethical values serve as guiding principles for its work in all 67 countries of the world in which Cargill has substantial business presence. Chapter 11 reports the results of interviews with business executives from the United States and several emerging market economies. We use the five characteristics Model of Ethical Business Cultures (MEBC), developed at the Center for Ethical Business Cultures, to demonstrate how organizations can build and sustain ethical business cultures in the long term. Extracting themes from our interviews of business practitioners, we overlay their comments with the five elements of the MEBC, thus bringing an empirically validated academic model (Jondle et al., 2014) to life through story and personal experience and providing tangible and actionable examples of practiced ethical business culture to both practitioners and academics.

This book is intended for both scholarly and practitioner audiences. We assume that the book will appeal to both academics and practitioners not only in the countries discussed in this book, but that the information will be extrapolative to the many other developed and emerging economies.

The scholarly audience includes academic instructors and researchers, students in business ethics, management, human resource management and development, and organization studies. The book can be used as the main or a supplemental text in graduate courses related to business ethics and organizational culture.

An important audience for the book will be business executives and practitioners working in the areas of business ethics, corporate social responsibility (CSR), HRD, and HRM, and anyone involved in global and international work.

REFERENCES

Ardichvili, A., Mitchell, J., & Jondle, D. (2009). Characteristics of ethical business cultures. *Journal of Business Ethics*, 85, 445–451.

Goldman Sachs. (2001). The world needs better economic BRIC. Goldman Sachs, Global Economics Paper No. 66, New York.

Goodpaster, K. E. (2007). *Conscience and corporate culture*. Malden, MA: Blackwell.

Jondle, D., Ardichvili, A., & Mitchell, J. (2014). Modeling ethical business culture: Development of the ethical business culture survey and its use to validate the CEBC model of ethical business culture. *Journal of Business Ethics*, 119(1), 29–43.

O'Neill, J., Wilson, D., Purushothaman, R., & Stupnytska, A. (2005). How solid are the BRICS? Global Economic paper #134. Goldman Sachs. Retrieved from www.goldmansachs.com/our-thinking/archive/archive-pdfs/how-solid.pdf

PART I Ethical Business Cultures: Country Perspectives

I Ethical Business Culture in Brazil: Advantages and Obstacles of National *Jeitinho*

Edgard Cornacchione and Liliane Klaus

ABSTRACT

Doing business in Brazil requires a thorough understanding of what ethical business culture means in the country and how this culture is related to the inherent threats and opportunities in the Brazilian business environment, stressing the private and public connection, as many economic crises have had their origins in corruption scandals and ethical deviations. Historical and cultural factors such as *jeitinho* (a specific Brazilian approach to circumventing bureaucratic barriers and solving problems using informal networks of relationships and favors) still permeate social and business behavior, hindering the development of a more professional and ethical business culture for both private and public enterprises and impairing a more consistent national growth. Despite progress, made recently, changing a traditionally paternalist, personalist, and impunity-based business culture is neither easy nor automatic. Merely adopting codes of conduct has proven to be insufficient to transform Brazilian business culture, which is typically characterized by power concentration, paternalism, personal loyalty, and conflict avoidance. We explore this context behind the Brazilian model of ethical business culture and invite investors to cautiously enter the market, consciously preparing to both face it and help with the required change.

INTRODUCTION

Brazil is a federal, presidential, constitutional republic based on representative democracy organized into one federal government, the states, the federal district, and the municipalities. The supreme law governing the country is the Federal Constitution, based on a multiparty system and on fundamental principles such as morality, publicity, legality, neutrality, and efficiency. A young democracy, Brazil is still learning to listen to multiple and diverse opinions within its society and adapt to the challenges of a new global community.

A key player in Latin America and globally, Brazil has advanced through a myriad of challenges throughout its history. With its colonization background, largely connected to Portuguese culture and values, Brazil has also been influenced by other European countries (especially Germany, Italy, Spain, France, and the Netherlands), Japan, and African countries. During the initial stages of the country's development, the economy relied mostly on natural resources and agricultural products (e.g., gold, coffee, and sugarcane). More recently, industrial, political, and social developments led to the emergence of a nation that is more powerful and willing to become a global player, both politically and economically. A young democracy that emerged in 1986 with the end of the military dictatorship, Brazil has seen two decades of the reorganization of the political system and macroeconomic environment (e.g., political system and inflation). Brazilian society has had to cope with a number of major challenges as the result of government-led restructuring.

A wide gap in wealth distribution is still present within Brazil. Government-led assistance programs were successful in enabling the direct transfer of wealth to families and individuals in deep need. For example, the government programs *Bolsa Familia* and *Bolsa Escola* have helped keep millions of K–12 kids in school and provided financial resources to their families at the same time. Other government initiatives that have helped increase the level of well-being of the poorest parts of the population were the introduction of the universal health care system and the general public pension system. However, at the same time, a complex and massive taxation system was introduced, which imposes a heavy tax burden on businesses and individuals. A myriad of political, social, and fiscal elements – such as government interference and inefficiency, bureaucracy, tax burden, demographics, urbanization, to mention a few – has a direct impact on the size of Brazil's informal economy, which already encompasses 16.1 percent of the country's gross domestic product (GDP), according to the Shadow Economy Index (HEI) (Forte, 2014).

With about one-third (204 million people in 2015, according to the *CIA World Factbook*) of Latin America's population and about 40 percent (US$ 2.4 trillion in 2014, according to the International Monetary Fund [IMF]) of its GDP, Brazil could soon overtake the United Kingdom and France in GDP to become the fifth largest economy in the world. Brazil's demographics are very different from the developed countries of Europe, North America, and Japan, with their aging populations and declining share of working-age population. Over two-thirds of Brazilians are in the age range between 15 and 64, and a total of 7.3 million students are enrolled in the Brazilian post-secondary education system.[1]

Doing business in Brazil requires a thorough understanding of what ethical business culture means in Brazil and how this culture is related to the inherent threats and opportunities in the Brazilian business environment, as many economic crises have had their origins in corruption scandals. Macroeconomic elements, such as fiscal and monetary policies, along with tariffs and exchange rates, are other factors that affect business decisions and catalyze business operations. The Brazilian economy spans a wide continuum, from producing fruit juices to building jets. Natural resources and agriculture continue to feature heavily in Brazilian trade. Engines, cars,

---

[1] Information as of 2013, according to *Instituto Brasileiro de Geografia e Estatística* (IBGE) and *Instituto Nacional de Estudos e Pesquisas Educacionais Anísio Teixeira* (INEP). It is noteworthy that as of 2013, 40 percent of post-secondary enrollment was in the social sciences, business, and law (IBGE, 2013).

trucks, houses, and jets are examples of manufactured goods exported by Brazil. The influential role of family business in Brazil also needs to be taken into account. Of the ten largest conglomerates in Brazil, six are family controlled (as of 2013, according to *Exame Magazine*). Another important component in the global expansion of Brazilian multinational corporations is the role of external mergers and acquisitions. Mergers involving the companies Inbev (with the world's second-largest global beer conglomerate SABMiller) and América Latina Logística (with rival Rumo Logistica) are notable examples.

Within the business environment, the financial infrastructure of Brazil is very strong, mainly due to the necessary regulations put into place during and after the period of high inflation (1980–1994). Key variables, such as interest rates and exchange rates, are tied into this infrastructure. The Brazilian financial market had to evolve in order to cope with rapid changes in the purchasing power of the population. Banking systems and government markets became well established in advance of most developed economies. Improvements in telecommunication systems, energy sources, and, more recently, basic infrastructure goods, such as water, became critical to guarantee development.

A country poised for stable growth and with abundant opportunities, Brazil is not the easiest place to do business, according to the World Bank. A recent global study, conducted by the World Bank, illustrates how difficult it is for a local entrepreneur to open and run a small business or medium-size firm while complying with relevant regulations. The World Bank (2015) has comparatively analyzed regulations affecting 11 areas in the life cycle of a business: (1) starting a business, (2) dealing with construction permits, (3) getting electricity, (4) registering property, (5) getting credit, (6) protecting minority investors, (7) paying taxes, (8) trading across borders, (9) enforcing contracts, (10) resolving insolvency, and (11) following labor market regulation. With a possible ranking between 1 and 189, Brazil was placed 120th, suggesting that the country has plenty of room to improve. This challenging situation can also be observed in the Brazilian tax system, characterized by federal, state, and municipality-regulated taxes. With approximately 90 complex taxes, duties, and contributions, the country has been ranked the most time-consuming nation in the world in which to do business by a study called "Paying taxes," issued in 2014 by PricewaterhouseCoopers (PwC, 2014[2]). Supported by the World Bank and the International Finance Corporation (IFC), PwC compared tax systems in 189 economies worldwide, analyzing not only overall complexity and tax rates but also the time required to comply with tax codes and the number of payments.

In Brazil, where tax professionals were said to spend 2,600 hours per year in 2014 in order to comply with the Brazilian Tax Code, it's common for firms to recur to intermediate professionals called "despachantes" (bureaucracy facilitators) to cope with ever-changing tax laws, to record the differences between the accounting and tax bases,[3] to provide reams of complex data, and finally, to handle time-consuming compliance procedures. This artifice may sometimes involve the use of illegal methods, such as the corruption of public officials through the giving of bribes. This kind of flexibility in solving problems has been present in the country since its early years of colonization. The good news is, as PwC (2014) argues, the enactment of Law 12,973 in 2014, which aligned tax legislation with the new Brazilian International Financial Reporting Standards (IFRS)-based accounting standards, should help reduce some of the tax bureaucracy. In general, the adoption of IFRS is meant to target accounting practices, such that the current system of multiple concurrent sets of accounting books and systems will no longer exist. However, this system is currently in transition.

Nonetheless, historical and cultural factors such as *jeitinho* (meaning the behavioral characteristic to use – often illegal – tricks to bend the rules, discussed in more detail later in this chapter) still

---

[2] www.pwc.com/gx/en/paying-taxes/assets/pwc-paying-taxes-2014.pdf

[3] This relates to the difference between corporate accounting standards (formal accounting rules) and tax rules (which are determined by national public policies and do not necessarily match formal accounting rules).

permeate social and business behavior, hindering the development of a more professional and ethical business culture for both private and public enterprises. Exploring the context behind the Brazilian model of ethical business culture will enable investors to not only cautiously enter the market but also appreciate how local business men and women apply local business processes in dealing with changing social attitudes toward corruption. Recent political events (corruption scandals, such as Mensalao in 2005 and Car Wash in 2015–16) at the very top of Brazilian power structures (the executive, legislative, and judiciary) are the latest damning evidence.

GEOGRAPHICAL, HISTORICAL, AND CULTURAL HERITAGE: THE BAD SIDE OF *JEITINHO*

Brazil, with more than 8.5 million sq. km, represents about 45 percent of Latin America's landmass (World Bank, n.d.[4]). The country emerged as an independent state in 1822 after more than 300 years of colonization by Portugal. The colonization process led to the civil law approach in Latin America, mostly based on the legal systems of Portugal and Spain. As civil law is primarily based on legislation (rules, codes) while common law, used in the United States and United Kingdom, is based on court decisions (essence, jurisprudence), this orientation has important implications for international business transactions between Brazilian companies and their foreign counterparts. With the globalization of business and the harmonization of accounting rules among countries, the impact of legal systems on business conduct, from contracting to commercial disputes, is key to comprehending the expanding Brazilian and Latin American business environment.

Having to adapt to the demands of international markets, often with higher ethical business standards, Brazilian private businesses have reacted quicker than the government, which only reactively issued an anti-corruption law applicable to enterprises and

---

[4] www.worldbank.org/en/region/lac/overview

their leaders following massive protests in 2013. Often under pressure from headquarters or clients located in Europe or the United States, firms started to produce codes of ethics and auditing procedures which could attest to international partners and buyers that Brazilian-based firms were able to provide products of fair origin as required by consumers from more developed countries. Moreover, guaranteeing ethical business procedures became not only a question of legal protection and conscious sustainable development but also an essential tool for marketing and corporate reputation. To this end, Brazilian firms have been investing both time and money into complying with international transparency and ethical standards in order to be competitive in the international business environment (Ardichvili et al., 2012). Although the number of firms that have codes of ethics has been growing since the enactment of the anticorruption law, there seems to have been little change in the real world, as is shown by a report from the BBC:

> "Unfortunately, despite the importance and the recurrence of the subject, ethics is not yet in fact valued by a large number of companies operating in Brazil," says Douglas Linhares Flinto, founder and president of the Brazilian Institute of Business Ethics. Mr Flinto adds: "Many businesses can talk about ethics, and even highlight it in the list of the company's values hung on the wall and emphasized on the website. However, corporate actions prove that ethics is not a value to be pursued and used on a daily basis. And this is the biggest problem of the business world – the inconsistency in which many companies preach and act." (Bowater, 2015)

Changing a traditionally paternalist, personalist, and impunity-based business culture (Gorga, 2003) by injecting ethical values is neither easy nor automatic. Merely adopting codes of conduct has proven to be insufficient to subdue Brazilian business culture, which is typically characterized by paternalism, power concentration, passivity, flexibility, personalism, formalism, impunity, personal loyalty, and conflict avoidance, as described by Barros and Prates (1997) (cited by Capobiango et al., 2013). The authors argued that clientelism and patrimonialism are products of both Brazilian colonization – based on slavery and exploration – and of Brazilian industrialization processes, which evolved from newly abolished slavery and not from free work, as happened in Europe. Two periods of dictatorship, under President Vargas (1930s) and the military dictatorship (1960s to early 1980s), have permeated the private and public national environment, seeding authoritarianism (submission) and clientelism (exchanging favors) practices, which survived the development strategies that followed in the 1970s. Such elements characterized Brazilian management systems up until the end of World War II, when imported management models started to be used in the country. More rational management models started to be preferred, and work and production flexibility were introduced. But until globalization emerged, with its requirements for standard business practices from international clients and partners, ethical models in management were never a priority.

Based on Martins (2007) and Caldas (2007), Capobiango et al. (2013) concluded that an authoritative and clientelist cultural heritage still exists within Brazilian social and economic culture. Even with the ratification of the new Brazilian Federal Constitution in 1988, which established basic ethical principles to be followed by firms and citizens, clientelist practices were used to guarantee public employment to a particular group without due competition. This is reflective of the national *jeitinho*, a strategy of flexibility for dealing with bureaucracy derived from Brazilian cultural development and that has been extensively discussed by scholars.

Duarte (2006, pp. 512, 513) studied the historical roots of *jeitinho*, acknowledging that it "emerged as a response to the excessive legalism and formalism of Brazilian society inherited from its Portuguese colonizers," which accompanies Brazilian society's personalism. Citing the work of Rosenn (1971), Duarte explained that *jeitinho* goes back to the 17th century, when Portuguese kings ruled within an authoritarian, paternalistic, particularistic, and ad hoc political system, which generated "an unnecessarily complex, confused and rigid legal system" full of different rules, laws, and decrees so numerous and so complex that it made the normal lives of citizens very difficult. This system, characterized by excessive formalism, has survived into the 21st century. *Jeitinho* emerged as a natural solution to getting things done and to avoid time-consuming form-filling, hours of queuing, or months of waiting for the right procedure to work.

Duarte compared *jeitinho* with similar reciprocity (relationship-binding) strategies (e.g., rooted in clientelism) in other countries and considers *jeitinho* to have the unique characteristic – as Brazilians view it – of a valid problem-solving strategy with heavy social weight. She argues that for *jeitinho* to succeed, there must be a relationship of sympathy and affinity between the involved parties so that the favor can be offered or requested. While *jeitinho* was originally a necessary, almost naïve, strategy to get things done in a timely manner, it has quickly evolved into a way of escaping rules applicable to all and to enable corruption, since it often comes with some kind of bribe or counter-favor.

Rodrigues et al. (2011) confirmed this view through a qualitative research study based on interviews in which the authors identified *jeitinho* as an indigenous psychological construct concerning a problem-solving strategy that involves social and cunning tricks to break formal rules. For example, it may involve contracting with intermediaries who have personal relationships with bureaucracy officials who may accelerate one's problem resolution through the payment of bribes or favors exchanged. Brazilians view the *jeitinho* term dichotomously, positively or negatively, depending on the context and on the people involved. It is seen more as a rule-breaking trick by younger people than by older ones. For investors and practitioners this can be an interesting element, as older people, as defined by Rodrigues et al., will require a more personal relationship to engage into the *jeitinho* practice. So avoiding a too personal relationship with business partners may eventually help investors avoid being asked favors.

In identifying the common conceptualizations of *jeitinho* by Brazilians, the authors found seven relevant themes: "sympathy, harm to others, 'malandragem' (cunning), disregard for social rules, innovative processes, power relation, and compensation" (Rodrigues et al., 2011, p. 32). In general, interviewees understood *jeitinho* as a problem-solving strategy that "(1) requires skills (sympathy, malandragem, innovation/creativity), (2) has an impact on others and the social order (harm to others, disregard for social rules), (3) works as a tool to challenge hierarchical relations and social hardship (power relation, compensation), and (4) is seen as both positive and negative." These representative perceptions of *jeitinho* give practitioners and investors another puzzle to solve. It follows that Brazilians will be inclined to apply formal ethical rules according to what they see as a necessary context, and will also be inclined to break them, despite their awareness that such rule-breaking is associated with causing harm to others. As previously discussed, in the worst-case scenario, it can be associated with corruption.

Puffer et al. (2013) seem to confirm these findings. The authors compared academic research on the practice of favors in BRIC (Brazil, Russia, India, and China) countries, including *jeitinho* in Brazil. They concluded that favor practices in the countries analyzed involved bribery and corruption. In Brazilian business culture, favors granted by *jeitinho* were found to be frequently illegal and involved much more than simply giving the parties involved an easy life, but rather enriching them to the detriment of the well-being of the firm and the employees. Even if the favor is legal, because of its informal, non-traceable nature, there is no way of making granters or grantees accountable for their actions, which makes *jeitinho* incompatible with modern national and international legal requirements for ethics and transparency in doing business. Moreover, as administration is becoming more technically advanced, formalism is being increasingly eroded, and the argument for placing one person's rights ahead of the rights of another person cannot be sustained in a democratic society. So, a challenge for practitioners will be that while *jeitinho* is a principle that is deeply rooted within Brazilian society, it does not fit with the desirable notion of Brazilian business culture nor the international ethical requirements (i.e., regulating agencies, citizens, or consumers), which Brazil can no longer afford to ignore.

The good news is that Brazilian society as a whole is starting to change, at least on the surface, despite the historical passivity of its citizens toward politically corrupt behavior. A small glimmer of hope arose following the Vinegar Uprisings involving common people against government, which started in 2013. They focused on the following themes: lack of services, underrepresentation, high taxation, and public sector corruption (expected to destroy circa 10 percent of national GDP). The media drew attention to the inefficiency and incompetence produced as the externalities of corruption hindered innovation, production, and performance. Although journalists asserted that "the giant is awakened" (referring to the traditional passive cordiality of Brazilian nationals) and despite the fact that citizens, to some extent, are becoming more aware of their rights and the lack of governmental transparency, corruption is still a big problem in a country where its citizens in their own small circles often behave outside the moral code (Klaus, 2016), following the *jeitinho* strategy. The consequences of this approach can be dire for local business culture and business practices. Gorga (2003, p. 76) has explained how Brazilian culture constrains corporate governance and economic performance. According to Gorga, in the Brazilian capital markets, "the Directors considered independent tend to be not so independent in practice," "society does not strongly condemn self-dealing practices," "there is little risk of liability," and "the courts lack sophistication ... judges are not prepared to understand complex business transactions." He explains that despite the many scandals, dishonest executives still seem to behave with impunity.

BRAZILIAN MODERN BUSINESS CULTURE: THE
OPPORTUNITIES OF *JEITINHO*

Despite the corruption-enabling, deep-rooted principles of *jeitinho*, Brazilian business culture can be seen to be moving toward some positive outcomes. Brazil is, after all, a country where informal relationships rule, and verbal communication easily takes place, making negotiations more flexible and creative. Brazilian people are considered to be cordial (Holanda, 1975), exhibiting sincerity, hospitality, and generosity. Véras and Véras (2011) have discussed the differences between the cultures when doing business in China and in Brazil. The authors pointed out the micro-cultural aspects when building more effective business relationships, such as preferring face-to-face meetings to written communication and using informal greetings (handshaking for men and kissing for women), all prioritizing individual empathy (see Duarte 2011 on the concepts of charm and empathy) rather than an institutional approach. These elements showcase the more personal and informal way in which Brazilians do business in order to maximize efficiency and reduce risk.

These interpersonal and communication skills, which are commonly associated with creativity, teamwork, and flexibility, are considered by Oxford Economics (2012) to be valuable skills for enterprising future managers and leaders under pressure from continuous and radical market changes. The study identified a shift from traditional "command-and-control" structures to intercultural and globalized contexts where "a more fluid and collaborative style" fosters networking, consensus, and collaboration. Ardichvili et al. (2012) have pointed out the benefits of the flexible Brazilian business culture, acknowledging that the country has recovered from the 2008–2009 economic crisis more quickly than other more developed countries because of its resiliency features.

Véras and Véras (2011, p. 81) have classified Brazilian cultural characteristics through the lens of Hofstede's dimensions,[5]

---

[5] Power Distance, Individualism, Masculinity, Uncertainty Avoidance, and Long-Term Orientation. See Hofstede (2001) and Hofstede and Hofstede (2004) for more information.

acknowledging that the country's "low level of tolerance for uncertainty is the country's most prominent characteristics" and that "strict rules, laws, policies, and regulations are adopted and implemented in order to minimize or reduce this level of uncertainty." Also, the low level of individualism that leads people to loyally protect their groups, although not lower than Chinese business culture, reveals that the ultimate goal is to avoid the unexpected and to maximize success. Kuchinke and Cornachione (2010) produced similar results, also based on Hofstede's cultural dimensions, when researching the meaning of work and performance-focused work attitudes among mid-level managers in Brazil. The authors identified power, masculinity, uncertainty avoidance, and long-term orientation as key Brazilian characteristics. Having also noticed that Brazilian business culture is more prone to group orientation and collective behavior, which can lead to nepotistic practices and to the merging of personal and group interests as well, O'Keefe and O'Keefe (2004) have relativized the masculinity dimension. The authors argued that Brazilian firms may have a more feminine than masculine dimension, being more cooperative and facility oriented, but not at all altruistic. Nepotistic practices, although illegal, are still socially accepted and valued and are considered to bring benefits to both sides: to firms and to working families.

Given that scholars associate Brazil with Hofstede's dimensions of "collectivism" and "femininity," the country's ethical business culture can seem old-fashioned and inappropriate to new global standards. This gap is not due to the different levels of internationalization of the firms (operating in different countries and employing staff from different cultures), but more as a result of an inherited and colonial cultural heritage, which is difficult to neutralize. Gutterman (2010) has tried to describe some elements of Brazil's current organizational culture as a long-lasting product of the country's colonial, agricultural, and latifundium past that still remains (according to a study performed by CEBRAP in 2012, almost one-third of all its arable land is owned by 0.8 percent of landowners, while two-thirds of the agricultural areas occupied between 2003 and 2010 were in the hands of large landowners). Citing Vizeu (2011) and Islam (2010), Gutterman argues the protectionism that still characterizes Brazilian business relationships, which is based on political influence and privileges given to the rich, making it difficult for the country to adapt to global competition. Investors will, then, find many firms where a patriarchal, personalistic structure exists: one in which family ties, formal authority, and property rights dictate the functioning of a firm rather than technical competence, such as solid practical experience or educational background. From this paradoxical coexistence between high deference to formal authority, tendency to creative improvisation, and the disjunction between authority and technical expertise, inefficiency will prevail. However, Gutterman points out that there seems to be a growing difference between government and corporate organizational cultures, as corporations are usually more open to external influences and are currently more interested in modernizing work practices than the government.

The impetus to change cultural models has often come from the outside, even if adapted and modified, as Gutterman points out. However, these tendencies have usually been incipient, as group and personal loyalty and the certainty of impunity are more valued than organizational ethics itself. The lack of support for whistle-blowing cases and the nonexistence of self-corruption reporting by Brazilian companies seem to support this. Sampaio and Sobral (2013, p. 372) explained that whistle-blowing seems to be a taboo for Brazilian organizations and that "some cultural aspects highlighted by scholars, such as high power distance, high uncertainty avoidance, overreliance on interpersonal relationships, aversion to conflict, a spectator attitude and having an affective nature may hinder whistleblowing and reinforce the perception of disclosure acts as deviant behaviors."

As regards organizational ethics and related policies, it is not unrealistic to assume that they are simply imposed from outside, from the firm's headquarters, or just copied from the next best competitor. It is advisable for investors to identify and understand this fact, and to trigger an improved process, by revising documents that are not consistent with ethical standards and will not, therefore, be accepted by business partners. Despite its mostly imported content, the Anti-Corruption Law promulgated in 2012 places the responsibility of unethical behavior with executives and their firms, and the design of effective ethical codes has since gained traction. According to Ardichvili et al. (2012, p. 425), the imported model still seems to prevail as "there is evidence of growing convergence between USA and Brazilian practices on the use of codes of ethics," due not only to business connections but also to the influence of North American universities on Brazilian managers.

Investors and businesspeople should be aware that in Brazil, relationship management (Davel and Vergara, 2005) and personal ties may make it difficult to adopt formal ethical rules and to report misconduct. Much effort is still needed to change this strong colonial culture. While scholars usually recommend that the content of such codes should be based on transformational styles, there is no consensus. Gutterman argues that there is an emphasis on reward and training practices among private companies, a practice that is consistent with Klaus' (2015) suggestions to improve ethical behavior in Brazilian governmental organizations, even in environments where authority is more centralized or hierarchically established. According to Klaus (2016), a nation's unethical moral vision can hinder well-intentioned executives from fighting a national culture where corruption is traditionally taken for granted.

Based on Sanchez et al. (2008), this appears to be the case for Brazil, where the tolerance of bribery can be rationalized through some of the cultural values that characterize Latin American countries, such as collectivism, particularism, subjugation to nature, and high-power distance. They argue that other factors that sustain tolerance of bribery include relationship orientation and historical political and business domination by large families. Other studies (e.g., Fine, 2010) consider such elements as determinants of a greater tolerance for misconduct. To help organizational leaders in the difficult task of improving ethical standards in Brazilian governmental organizations, the author suggests the use of punishment-based transactional styles related to authority, rather than to modern charismatic or transformational styles; a strategy that is naturally compatible with the traditional functioning of Brazilian firms. Klaus (2015) adds, however, that authority alone will not oblige subordinates to behave ethically and that duty or legal obligation to obey will not override people's personal moral standards. Klaus cites Skitka and colleagues' (2008) research which argued that "authorities' ability to lead rather than simply coerce compliance is tied closely to subordinates' perceptions of whether authorities share their moral vision" (Klaus, 2015, p. 87). According to this line of thought, leaders in globalized Brazilian firms seeking to show commitment to business ethics will have to embody their moral identity toward subordinates, rather than just saying they possess adequate ethical values. They will have to operationalize this ethical leadership not only by giving employees the conditions and tools to act on these values but also by rewarding ethical behavior, as well as punishing any counterproductive behavior.

CONCLUSIONS

All generalizations are difficult (try to generalize a trait of an organization and its employees). Even more complex are country-wide generalizations. In this chapter, we built on a series of facts and impressions based on hard evidence, mixed with a critique from our own personal standpoint. Because of the aforementioned deeply rooted Brazilian cultural values and practices, international firms and consultants aiming to work in Brazil, or with Brazilian organizations, are advised to consider the following suggestions:

1. Walk the talk: You will not be able to impose ethical rules if you do not follow them yourself. First, set an example to others, and then require respect for ethical rules. Remember that, as a new trendsetter, you are being observed, and behaviors must follow through into your

private life. Consistency in ethical behavior will smooth the compliance officer's path.

2. Do not think "imperialistically," imagining you are going to arrive, give orders, and everything will change. Communication is a very important skill in Brazilian society, and you will be more effective if you blend and convince, instead of isolate and impose.

3. The ethical message conveyed by international compliance officers will only have an impact on Brazilian businesspeople – no matter whether they are located in or outside of Brazil – if punishment systems exist and work effectively. History and scientific research have shown that formal ethical standards and codes of conducts alone will not perform miracles. Request ethical behavior sensitively and kindly, but enforce rules and punishments with transparent fairness and strength.

REFERENCES

Ardichvili, A., Jondle, D., Kowske, B., Cornachione, E., Li, J., & Thakadipuram, T. (2012). Ethical cultures in large business organizations in Brazil, Russia, India, and China. *Journal of Business Ethics*, 105, 415–428.

Bowater, D. (2015, September 16). Brazil's continuing corruption problem. Retrieved from www.bbc.com/news/business-34255590

Capobiango, R. P., Nascimento, A. L., Silva, E. A., & Faroni, W.. (2013). Reformas administrativas no Brasil: Uma abordagem teórica e crítica. *REGE Revista de Gestão*, 20(1), 61–78,

CEBRAP (2012). The real Brazil: The inequality behind the statistic. Retrieved from www.christianaid.org.uk/images/real-brazil-full-report.pdf?awc=3927_ 1450211905_85619f8662ccb7e1b555a39bdd0ae89c&approachcode= A018279&_$ja=tsid:56802&utm_source=affiliate&utm_medium=Deep_ link&utm_campaign=awin

Davel, E., & Vergara, C. S. (2005). Desafios relacionais nas práticas de gestão e de organização. *RAE – Revista de Administração de Empresas*, 45(1), 10–13.

Duarte, F. (2006). Exploring the interpersonal transaction of the Brazilian Jeitinho in bureaucratic contexts. *Organization Articles*, 13, 509–527.

Duarte, F. (2011). The strategic role of charm, simpatia and jeitinho in Brazilian society: A qualitative study. *Asian Journal of Latin American Studies*, 24 (3), 29–48.

Fine, S. (2010). Cross-cultural integrity testing as a marker of regional corruption rates. *International Journal of Selection and Assessment*, 18(3),

251–259. Retrieved from http://onlinelibrary.wiley.com/doi/10.1111/j.1468-2389.2010.00508.x/abstract

Forte, J. (2014, June 26). Informal economy in Brazil worth R$826 billion in 2014. *The Rio Times*. Retrieved from http://riotimesonline.com/brazil-news/rio-business/brazils-informal-economy-was-worth-r826-billion-in-2014/#

Gorga, E. C. R. (2003, May). Does culture matter for corporate governance? A case study of Brazil. Stanford Law School. John M. Olin Program in Law and Economics Working Paper 257.

Gutterman, A. S. (2010). Trompenaars and Hampden-Turner's seven dimensions of culture, in organizational management and administration: A guide for managers and professionals. Retrieved from http://alangutterman.typepad.com/files/oc---dimensions-of-oc.pdf(updated version as of 2015).

Hofstede, G., & Hofstede, G.-J. (2004). *Cultures and organizations: Software of the mind*. New York: McGraw-Hill.

Hofstede, G. (2001). *Culture's consequences: Comparing values, behaviors, institutions, and organizations across nations*. Thousand Oaks CA: Sage Publications.

Holanda, S. B. (1975). *Raízes do Brasil*. Rio de Janeiro: Livraria José Olympio.

IBGE (Brazilian Institute of Geography and Statistics) (n.d.). Education and work indicators. Retrieved from www.ibge.gov.br/home/estatistica/populacao/condicaodevida/indicadoresminimos/suppme/default_educacao.shtm

Islam, G. (2010). *Between unity and diversity: Historical and cultural foundations of Brazilian management. Insper Working Paper*: 218/2010. Sao Paulo: IBMEC.

Klaus, L. C. O. (2015). Tone of the top at hierarchical institutions: A cannonball to fight military corruption in Latin America. *Scientia Militaria, A South African Journal of Military Studies* 43(2), 79–111.

Klaus, L. C. O. (2016). *The citizen-advocacy approach: For a new Governmental PR Theory in times of open governance*. Postdoctoral Thesis. University of Sao Paulo, Brazil.

Kuchinke, K. P., & Cornachione Jr., E. B. (2010). The meaning of work and performance-focused work attitudes among midlevel managers in the United States and Brazil. *Performance Improvement Quarterly*, 23(3), 57–76.

O'Keefe, H., & O'Keefe, W. M. (2004). Business behaviors in Brazil and the USA: Understanding the gaps. *International Journal of Social Economics*, 31(5/6), 614–621.

Oxford Economics (2012). *Global talent 2021: How the new geography of talent will transform human resource strategies*. Retrieved from www.oxfordeconomics.com/Media/Default/Thought%20Leadership/global-talent-2021.pdf

Prates, M. A., & B. T. Barros (1997). O estilo brasileiro de administrar. In F. P. Motta and M. P. Caldas (eds.), *Cultura Organizacional e Cultura Brasileira* (pp. 55–69). São Paulo: Editora Atlas.

Puffer, S. M., McCarthy, D. J., Jaeger, A. M., & Dunlap, D. (2013). The use of favors by emerging market managers: Facilitator or inhibitor of international expansion? *Asia Pacific Journal of Management* 30(2), 327–349. doi:10.1007/s10490-012-9299-3

PwC (2014). Paying taxes. Retrieved from www.pwc.com/gx/en/paying-taxes/assets/pwc-paying-taxes-2014.pdf

Rodrigues, R. P., Milfont, T. L., Ferreira, M. C., Porto, J. B., & Fischer, R. (2011). Brazilian jeitinho: Understanding and explaining an indigenous psychological construct. Revista Interamericana de Psicología/Interamerican. *Journal of Psychology*, 45(1), 27–36.

Sampaio, D. B. D., & Sobral, F. (2013). Speak now or forever hold your peace? An essay on whistleblowing and its interfaces with the Brazilian culture. *BAR*, 10 (4), 370–388.

Sanchez, J. I., Gomez, C. and Wated, G. (2008). A value-based framework for understanding managerial tolerance of bribery in Latin America. *Journal of Business Ethics*, 83 (2), 341–352.

Skitka, L. J., Bauman, C. W. and Lytle, B. L. (2008). Morality as a foundation of leadership and a constraint on deference to authority. In D. Forsyth & C. Hoyt (Eds.), *Social psychology and leadership* (pp. 300–315). Westport, CN: Praeger Press.

Véras, E. Z., & Véras, D. B. (2011). Cultural differences between countries: The Brazilian and the Chinese ways of doing business. *Journal on Innovation and Sustainability*, 2(2), 77–83.

Vizeu, F. (2011). Rural heritage of early Brazilian industrialists: Its impact on managerial orientation. *Brazilian Administrative Review*, 8(1), 68–85.

World Bank (n.d.). Latin America and Caribbean: Overview. Retrieved from www.worldbank.org/en/region/lac/overview

World Bank (2015). Doing business 2015 Brazil. Socio-economy profile 2015. Retrieved from www.doingbusiness.org/data/exploreeconomies/brazil

2 Business Ethics and Ethical Business Cultures in the Russian Federation

Alexandre Ardichvili

ABSTRACT

Ethics and ethical cultures in business organizations are influenced by numerous contextual factors, including national and organizational cultural characteristics and norms, regulatory frameworks, and political and socioeconomic climates. Identifying all the important contextual influences can be a daunting task in any society. However, Russia presents an especially challenging case, since this country went through several fundamental transformations of its social structure and institutional environment in recent history. This chapter uses the institutional theory framework to discuss major regulatory, normative, and cultural factors that shape the current environment for business ethics in Russia. The historical development of business ethics and its current state are examined, and implications for managers and professionals from other countries working in Russia and/or with Russian companies operating internationally are formulated. Specifically, the chapter demonstrates that the current regulatory framework is characterized by weak legislative structures, ambiguous economic legislation, and growing power of the central government and of a handful of business groups aligned with the presidential administration. This creates opportunities for corruption among government officials at various levels and conditions under which businesspeople are forced to engage in unethical behaviors, ranging from bribes to using informal connections within the government elite to secure preferential treatment. Furthermore, a combination of cultural dimensions of power distance and paternalism suggests that employees are not likely to report ethical violations committed by their superiors, tend to shift the responsibility for making ethical decisions to the boss, and are not likely to question these decisions.

Russian managers and employees differ from their Western counterparts in that they are likely to be more particularistic than universalistic when solving ethical dilemmas. Thus, Russian managers would be more inclined to apply situational decision rules when solving ethical dilemmas and feel that being loyal to their in-group is a sign of ethical behavior, even if general societal rules are violated. Finally, under the Russian system of reliance on informal networks in business dealings (*svyazi*), managers tend to consider the exchange of favors with their informal network of business connections as part of standard and ethical business practices.

THE RUSSIAN ECONOMY AND BUSINESS ENVIRONMENT

Having experienced a significant plunge in economic activity after the breakup of the Soviet Union in 1991, Russia went through radical market reforms, two major economic crises, and a period of rapid expansion during the first decade of the 21st century. In 2015, with GDP of US$3.47 trillion (at purchasing power parity), Russia was the seventh largest economy in the world (Central Intelligence Agency, 2016). The country is among the world's three largest exporters of oil and gas and one of the largest producers of steel and aluminum. It also has a full range of industry sectors, from consumer goods to aerospace, information technology, and software engineering. However, many Russian manufacturing enterprises are not globally competitive and mostly serve the domestic market as well as markets of the former Soviet states that still maintain close economic ties with Russia. The government finances and the health of the economy overall are heavily dependent on revenues from exports of mineral resources. Nevertheless, Russian multinational companies (MNCs) continue to expand their presence in Central Asia, Europe, the Middle East, North Africa, and Latin America. Some Russian companies have joined the ranks of the largest firms in the world. The largest among them, Gazprom, was listed as the 17th largest company in the world in 2014 (Fortune, 2014).

INSTITUTIONAL FRAMEWORK FOR THE ANALYSIS OF BUSINESS ETHICS: REGULATORY, NORMATIVE, AND CULTURAL FACTORS

To analyze the most important factors shaping business ethics in contemporary Russia, we will rely on institutional theory and, in particular, Scott's (2014) three-pillar institutional framework. According to Lawrence and Suddaby (2013), "Central to both theoretical and empirical examinations of organizational phenomena that adopt an institutionalist perspective is the idea that there are enduring elements in social life – institutions – that have a profound effect on the thoughts, feelings, and behavior of individual and collective actors" (p. 216). The Nobel Prize-winning economist Douglass North defined institutions as "the rules of the game in a society" (North, 1990, p. 3), and "humanly devised constraints that structure political, economic, and social interaction" that "consist both of informal constraints (sanctions, taboos, customs, traditions and codes of conduct) and formal rules (constitutions, laws and property rights)" (p. 97).

Scott's (2014) framework for institutional analysis consists of three "pillars": regulatory, normative, and cultural. The first type of institutions include "regulatory structures, government agencies, laws, courts, and professions" (Oliver, 1991, p. 147). According to Scott (2014), governments play three main roles: "referee, rule maker, and enforcer" (p. 62). Institutional sociologists point out that governmental agencies are rarely objective and dispassionate rule makers. Therefore, when examining the regulatory "pillar" of the institutional framework, self-interest and power issues need to be taken into consideration.

The normative pillar includes formal and informal norms of behavior, developed by the society and various professional associations and interest groups. For example, at the societal level, there are norms for behavior in the marketplace that are common to all business organizations in a certain country or region. At the same time, other norms are specific to certain sectors of the economy. These norms are, as a rule, formalized through codes of conduct developed by professional associations or other industry groups. Finally, there are also norms of behavior specific to individual organizations, reflected in organizational codes of conduct or codes of ethics.

The regulatory and normative pillars are heavily influenced by cultural values and assumptions that are common to a national culture or an ethnic group. According to Scott (2014), in Western countries, cultural norms of competitive individualism have been institutionalized and shape both individual and organizational behavior. In contrast, in many other countries of the world, where collectivism is one of the defining cultural characteristics, business organizations function as networks of interdependent (and mutually constrained) actors. Among some of the salient cultural differences that affect business behavior and norms are collectivism and individualism, high versus low power distance, uncertainty avoidance, and indulgence versus restraint (Hofstede et al., 2010).

Russian Regulatory and Normative Frameworks in the Pre-reform Period

To better understand the current regulatory and political frameworks in Russia, we need to start with a brief historical excurse. For approximately 50 years, between 1861 and 1914, Russia went through a series of economic and political reforms aimed at introducing a less authoritarian and more democratic and market-oriented economy and society. In the late 19th century, the country's economy started to expand rapidly, and by the beginning of the 20th century, Russia was one of the 10 largest economies in the world. However, the process of democratization and the development of market-based economic mechanisms came to an abrupt end after the Bolshevik Revolution of 1917. The democratic institutions that had emerged during the reforms were dismantled. Private ownership of the means of production was abolished, enterprises were nationalized, and business activity and all aspects of the private lives of individual citizens were strictly controlled and regulated by the government.

The socialist regime lasted for more than 70 years, from 1917 to 1991. During this time, the state and the Communist Party were inseparable, and any opposition to the will of the party elite was crushed by the state apparatus of surveillance. The key element of the regulative framework was the five-year economic development plan of the country, approved by the Central Committee of the Communist Party and legislated by the central government. The main economic regulatory agency was the Central Planning Committee (Gosplan) that was in charge of setting production targets and making detailed resource allocation decisions for all enterprises in the country. A key institution in the sociopolitical and economic sphere was the *nomenklatura* – cadres of high-level administrators who represented the party in managing all key organizations, ranging from government ministries, industrial enterprises, law enforcement agencies, and the military, to hospitals, schools, and colleges.

As regards the normative framework, the first code of ethics for businesspeople was published by a national committee of representatives of Russian commerce and industry back in 1912 (Association of Independent Directors, 2004). The code was called Seven Principles of Business Conduct in Russia. It is interesting to note that the very first of these principles was "Respect the authorities." The other elements of the code were "Be honest and truthful," "Respect private property," "Love and respect human beings" (with an explanation that an entrepreneur's love and respect for his workers will create an atmosphere of harmony and conditions for human flourishing), "Be true to your word," "Be frugal and live according to your means," and

"Be goal oriented" (with a clarification that the pursuit of business goals should not overshadow moral values).

During the Soviet period, the normative framework was shaped by Communist ideology (Kornai, 1992), and societal norms were dictated by the Communist Party. The party promoted an idealized image of a "Soviet man," who was presumed to be a standard-bearer of loyalty to the party, setting an example of a high work ethic and dedication to the goal of building the Communist utopia.

Central planning has replaced market-based pricing as the major mechanism for regulating economic activities. The extreme centralization and attempts to micromanage all aspects of supply and demand have produced an unexpected side effect: shortages of goods and materials at all levels. The main reason for these shortages was the inability of central planners to accurately predict the demand for resources and goods from enterprises and consumers (Kornai, 1992). As a result, a parallel shadow economy has emerged, providing alternative avenues for procuring and distributing goods needed by individual consumers and industrial enterprises. Shortages forced enterprise directors to circumvent official channels and engage in informal bargaining for resources with suppliers. At the same time, individual citizens had to look for consumer goods on the black market. Personal networks became more important than access to official channels. A whole new category of professionals had emerged who acted as intermediaries in unofficial negotiations and as "resource scouts." Needless to say, the existence of this large shadow sector of the economy, unsanctioned by the state, provided a fertile ground not only for individual initiative and entrepreneurship but also for violations of ethical standards, bribery, and corruption.

In the normative sphere, a dual framework existed that included a set of officially endorsed norms of behavior of a "Soviet man" and unofficial norms, based on the exchange of favors. The latter norms were unspoken but were followed in practice by a large number of managers and employees. A normative institution, called "blat," had emerged; it involved the exchange of favors among members of informal professional networks and friend- and family-based in-groups (McCarthy & Puffer, 2008; McCarthy et al., 2012). This duality of norms resulted in significant ambiguity in societal perceptions of the ethicality of business and entrepreneurship. Any innovative and independent business activity was perceived to be illegal and, thus, labeled as unethical. Both independent business operators and those state enterprise managers who were creative in finding ways of increasing production levels found that the quality of their goods was viewed with suspicion, and they were seen as profiteers, or even criminals. These negative societal attitudes toward business and entrepreneurship persist to this day.

In addition, the discrepancy between overinflated state production targets and the much more modest reality of resource availability and productivity resulted in cynicism and an atmosphere in which both managers and workers were forced to misrepresent their work results on a regular basis by producing misleading financial statements and output reports and hiding earlier obtained supplies and resources (to avoid their arbitrary reallocation to other enterprises). Thus, the acceptability, or even necessity, of deceiving the authorities became a societal norm. Furthermore, since private ownership of the means of production was abolished, and all equipment and resources became property of the state, many managers and workers developed a notion that it was acceptable to use company resources for private gain and consumption. Taking home office supplies, or using company phones to make long-distance calls to family members, was not regarded as stealing from the organization.

The Regulative and Normative Environment for Business Ethics after the Dissolution of the Soviet Union (1991 to Present)

Since the fall of Communism, the Russian regulatory, political, and normative institutional environment has changed radically. This change amounts to what Newman (2000) called "institutional upheaval": "A rapid and pervasive change in the norms and values that underlie and legitimate economic activity, which results in fundamental changes in a society's political system, its legal and regulatory frameworks, its economic system, and its financial infrastructure" (p. 603). The institutional upheaval that followed the dissolution of the Soviet Union resulted in a situation in which the institutional framework "no longer provided organizing templates, models for action and known sources of legitimacy" (Newman, 2000, p. 605), because "the underlying assumptions about the purpose of economic activity were destroyed or significantly changed within a short time" (p. 602). Furthermore, according to Roth and Kostova (2003), while the central planning regime was dismantled, new institutional forms were slow to emerge, and many of the existing institutions were incapable of adequately supporting the functioning of the market-based economy.

The period of institutional upheaval began in 1991, when the first legitimately elected Russian president, Boris Yeltsin, started political and economic reforms. During the first years of Yeltsin's rule, the command-and-control institutions were largely dismantled, price controls lifted, and the majority of industrial enterprises privatized. But some key conditions for a successful transition to a market economy were not met. First, strong and transparent property laws were not created. Second, privatization turned into an appropriation of huge amounts of assets by a small group of former party officials and black market operators. Third, the economic changes were not accompanied by the creation of strong democratic institutions. As a result, corruption became endemic and the economy stagnated.

In 1998, Russia was hit by the global financial crisis and fell into a deep recession. The economic recovery started at the turn of the century, after Boris Yeltsin was replaced by Vladimir Putin. Putin's government has introduced a number of fairly significant reforms, reducing subsidies to state companies, deregulating trade, liberalizing the tax code, and introducing the new Civil Code. This period was also characterized by a rapid growth in demand for Russia's main sources of export revenues – oil and gas. All these factors resulted in an impressive economic expansion (Aslund, 2007). However, what seemed to be the dawn of a new era of democratization and economic freedom proved to be short-lived. A major consolidation of power in the hands of central government began toward the end of Putin's first term in office. The power of the parliament was curtailed, opposition parties and movements were marginalized or banned, and most of the media came under the control of the government or oligarchs associated with the government. In the economic sphere, a re-nationalization of strategically important industrial enterprises took hold, and large state-owned (or majority state-owned) companies like Gasprom, Rossneft, and Russian Railways monopolized key industrial sectors. Aslund (2007) wrote that during this time, "Putin accomplished an amazing de-institutionalization, leaving the presidency as the only institution of relevance" (p. 278). By 2007–2008, a new corporate-statist model was created, characterized by the dominance of the authoritarian state and large state-controlled companies. The institutional mechanisms crucial for free markets, such as property rights and contract laws, were never properly developed, and corruption started to grow again.

Today, the Russian institutional environment can be described as consisting of weak institutions, but a powerful state. Various authors point out the absence of strong regulative frameworks that would enforce the primacy of private property and inviolability of contractual agreements, while strengthening the financial markets and pricing mechanisms. At the same time, the state structures are amassing even more power and influence. A combination of weak regulatory frameworks, curtailed economic freedom, and a strong executive power at the federal level creates conditions conducive to unethical behavior on the part of businesspeople and employees (Kantemirova, 2004; Matolygina & Ruglova, 2012; Visokov, 2013).

When considering the normative framework for business ethics in Russia, it is important to discuss the role of the Orthodox Church and Russian Orthodoxy as an ideology and normative institution. As pointed out by Clendenin (2003), "For Russians ... Orthodoxy is an entire way of life and culture.... Imagine living in Italy without understanding Catholicism, traveling to Kuwait and ignoring Islam, or trying to understand the people of Utah without ever studying the history of Mormonism. That will give an idea of catastrophic results of attempting to engage Eastern Europe and the former Soviet Union while neglecting the role of Orthodox Christianity" (p. 21).

There are two conflicting points of view on the impact of Orthodox thinking on attitudes toward business in general, and business ethics in particular. Some researchers point out that, unlike its Catholic and Protestant counterparts, the Orthodox Church has never developed a set of prescriptions for behavior in industry and commerce. Furthermore, compared to other religions, the Orthodoxy is the least adaptable to the desires to acquire "earthly well-being" (Bazunov, 2009; Zhuravlev, 2004). Thus, Feldman-Leibovich (1995) argued that work and the pursuit of material well-being were not important for Russian workers, since Orthodoxy "celebrated the eternal life of heaven and declared earthly existence as transitory and meaningless. Salvation and absolute good, the meaning of life and human activity, were attainable in the heavenly kingdom alone" (p. 2). According to Zhuravlev (2004), the Orthodox Church is more interested in the moral and spiritual development of an individual than in developing his ability to achieve economic independence or prosperity. At the same time, the Orthodox often tend to believe that there is such a deep divide between the temple and the marketplace that overtly pious behavior can easily coexist with unethical conduct in business.

On the other hand, in recent years numerous articles have appeared in practitioner-oriented publications and online forums suggesting that it is possible to apply Orthodox principles in the business sphere, including business ethics. The argument is that Orthodox values, such as love for one's neighbor, selfless service for the benefit of others, frugality and self-restraint, and truthfulness, can form a solid foundation for promoting business ethics and building ethical corporate cultures (Baranova, 2013). Some outside observers (e.g., Frank, 2012) also point out that principles of moral business behavior in Russia can be further developed on the dual foundation of collectivist assumptions, rooted in the prerevolutionary Russian institution of *obzhina* (collective), and the Orthodox idea of *sobornost* (spiritual unity of members of the society, centered around the Orthodox faith).

In addition to formal and informal norms, the normative pillar includes normative documents issued by various governmental and nongovernmental organizations. Normative documents that affect ethics in the Russian business community can be classified into three categories: (a) international norms that are widely discussed in Russian business circles and are perceived as obligatory to follow if a Russian company wants to join the global business community; (b) codes and normative documents developed by various governmental agencies or independent professional groups and associations; and (c) codes of conduct created by individual enterprises.

Among the international codes of ethical business conduct, those most often discussed in the Russian academic literature and industry publications are the 1994 Caux Principles (Barinov, 2002). For example, the Association of Independent Directors (2004) starts its discussion of ethical norms with a detailed elaboration on the Caux Principles, explaining that these principles need to be followed by Russian firms when conducting business in international markets.

The majority of influential normative documents regulating or prescribing the rules of ethical business behavior in Russia were published by either governmental agencies or professional groups and associations in the late 1990s to mid-2000s. Among the most influential of these are the Russian Code of Enterprise Ethics, issued by the Russian Chamber of Commerce and Industry (1998); Charter of Corporate Business Ethics of the Russian Union of Entrepreneurs and Industrialists (2003); Code of Corporate Conduct, created by the Russian Federal Commission on Securities and Stock Markets (2002); Code of Independent Directors (2003); and *Business*

Ethics: Guidelines for Russian Firms (Association of Independent Directors, 2004). More recently, the normative documents started to focus on issues of social responsibility (e.g., the new Social Charter of Russian Business, adopted in 2008). In addition to the organizations listed, norms of business ethical behavior are influenced by the activities of the fund Russian business culture, the nongovernmental organization (NGO) CSR[1] – Russian Centre, and the Center for Business Ethics and Corporate Governance (St. Petersburg).

The Guidelines for Russian Firms, developed by the Association of Independent Directors (2004), contain what seems to be the most comprehensive set of guidelines for business ethics in Russia today. However, the principles listed in the document are largely the same as those found in the codes of conduct of many large corporations or professional associations in the West and include items related to issues such as professionalism, informed consent, confidentiality, reporting of unethical behavior, etc. On the other hand, the Charter of Corporate Business Ethics of the Russian Union of Entrepreneurs and Industrialists includes principles that reflect some conditions and needs unique to Russia. For example, the second principle emphasizes the need to protect and respect private property (an obvious reference to the fact that the institution of private property is still a fairly new phenomenon in post-Communist Russia). The fourth principle points out that businesspeople should avoid actions that may lead to social tensions in society. The fifth principle advises businesspeople to avoid exercising undue influence on the decisions of legislative and law enforcement agencies, and the sixth principle warns against the use of illegal methods in dealing with one's competitors.

Speaking about the informal norms of Russian society, perhaps the most important and influential normative institution that shapes all aspects of business life is that of *blat/svyazi*. As pointed out earlier, *blat* has emerged as the main response to shortages and stifling government bureaucracy during the Soviet times. *Blat* was

---

[1] CSR stands for Corporate Social Responsibility.

defined by Puffer and McCarthy (1995) as "reliance for favors upon personal contacts with people in influential positions" (p. 37). In recent years, this word was replaced by the word *svyazi* (connections). Puffer and McCarthy elaborated in their recent research that a favor can be defined as "an exchange of outcomes between individuals, typically utilizing one's connections, that is based on a commonly understood cultural tradition, with reciprocity by the receiver typically not being immediate, and its value being less than what would constitute bribery within that cultural context" (McCarthy et al., 2012, pp. 27–28).

From the point of view of Western business ethics, *blat* or *svyazi* could be viewed as a form of corruption (McCarthy & Puffer, 2008; McCarthy et al., 2012). However, the exchange of favors under *blat/svyazi* does not necessarily involve bribery and is not perceived by many Russian managers and employees as an unethical or unacceptable way of doing business. Analyzing the literature on other BRIC (Brazil, Russia, India, and China) countries, McCarthy et al. (2012) came to the conclusion that practices similar to *svyazi* exist in all BRIC countries, and these practices are a response to strong and stifling bureaucracies, usually existing as a legacy of either colonialism or Communist regimes. As means of circumventing bureaucracies and finding ways of still achieving the desired economic outcomes, these practices are regarded as completely normal ways of doing business, and the associated informal norms (*svyazi* in Russia, *guanxi* in China, *jeitinho* in Brazil, and *jaan-pehchaan* in India) are "widely accepted informal cultural institutions" (McCarthy et al., 2012, p. 28). As pointed out by McCarthy et al., an important consideration is that under these norms, favors are provided without an expectation of immediate reciprocation by the recipient, especially when the favor grantor is a person of considerable means. This also suggests that the practice is often viewed as a manifestation of selfless kindness to other people. An important observation made by McCarthy et al. is that, while *svyazi* are not necessarily associated with bribery and corruption, there is a strong potential for escalation

Table 2.1. *Comparison of Hofstede's Scores for Russia and the United States*

Dimension	Russia	United States
Power distance	93	40
Individualism	39	91
Masculinity	36	62
Uncertainty avoidance	95	46
Long-term orientation	81	26
Indulgence	20	68

Source: The table was created by the author using data from http://geert-hofstede.com/russia.html

to bribery and corruption. Such an outcome is especially likely in situations where a person needs to obtain a favor from someone located outside their immediate in-group, in another region of the country, etc.

The Cultural Pillar

With regard to cultural influences on business ethics, we need to examine the cultural dimension scores and interpretations provided by Geert Hofstede's research center (Hofstede Centre, n.d.). If we compare scores for the United States with Russia, we note strong differences on three dimensions: power distance (very high for Russia, low for the United States), individualism (very high for the United States, low for Russia), and uncertainty avoidance (very high for Russia, low for the United States) (see Table 2.1).

Hofstede defines power distance (PD) as "the extent to which the less powerful members of institutions and organizations within a country expect and accept that power is distributed unequally" (Hofstede Centre, n.d.). He further explains that Russia, with a score of 93, is one of the most power distant countries. One of the indications of power concentration is the fact that so much wealth and power is concentrated in just two centers: Moscow and St. Petersburg.

Hofstede suggests that organizational management tends to be hierarchical and top-down in high PD countries.

Individualism is defined as "the degree of interdependence a society maintains among its members," or whether "people's self-image is defined in terms of 'I' or 'We.'" Hofstede explains that in collectivist cultures people feel strong affiliation with their "in-groups," are extremely loyal to them, and define themselves through these affiliations. As pointed out by Hofstede, Russians tend to say "we" instead of "I" (e.g., "We with friends" instead of "I and my friends"), may call all their cousins "brothers and sisters," and rely a great deal on informal relationships with their in-group members to obtain information and resources.

Referring to the masculinity/femininity dimension, Hofstede indicates that in societies with high masculinity scores, people are driven by achievement and success, while in more "feminine" societies, "caring for others and quality of life" are more important. Hofstede points out that Russians' low score on this dimension is reflected in their tendency to understate their own achievements, and to be modest in words and in their way of life. He also points out that this often does not apply to top executives or government officials who, in line with high PD, are expected to show off their wealth and power.

Uncertainty avoidance (UA) is defined as "[t]he extent to which the members of a culture feel threatened by ambiguous or unknown situations and have created beliefs and institutions that try to avoid these" (Hofstede Centre, n.d.). Russia's very high score on this dimension corresponds to their tendency to over-prepare for presentations or business negotiations, trying to procure data and background information to cover all contingencies. Hofstede also interprets the Russian tendency to be highly formal in conversations with strangers as a sign of high UA.

Indulgence versus restraint is "the extent to which people try to control their desires and impulses," and this difference is assumed to be "based on the way they were raised." The low score for Russia suggests a restrained culture that does not put much emphasis on leisure and "fun" activities. Such societies also have a tendency toward cynicism and pessimism.

Note that the scores on the sixth dimension, long-term orientation, are not discussed here. This dimension is rather controversial and received a lot of criticism from various researchers. In addition, the Hofstede Centre's interpretations, provided in the case of Russia, do not seem to be as clear and consistent as the explanations of the other five dimensions.

When interpreting Hofstede's scores, we need to be mindful of several caveats. First, the scores tend to change over time. For example, research conducted with large samples of Russian managers and employees in the 1990s showed that at that particular point in time the masculinity score shot up: it was above 90, compared to the score of 36 reported by Hofstede (Ardichvili, 2001). This interesting aberration could be explained by the unique conditions in which managers and employees had to operate at that time (i.e., the abrupt transition to market-based competition and the need to literally fight for survival in the new "Wild East"). In these circumstances, it is not surprising that a focus on surviving the cut-throat competition in the marketplace was of the utmost importance. It is possible that in more recent years, with the stabilization of the economy and a return to more orderly competitive conditions, the score will have returned to its earlier, low levels.

Second, while the Hofstede scores may provide a fairly accurate picture of general tendencies in Russian society, we need to remember that the Russian Federation is a multiethnic state, where multiple nationalities and various religions coexist, which will affect societal perceptions of business cultures and ethics. The Federation includes a number of semi-autonomous republics and administrative units, and the majority of their inhabitants differ from the rest of Russia in ethnic composition and religious affiliation (e.g., the Republic of Tatarstan, or several republics located in the Caucasus). In addition, since Russia was part of a larger multiethnic entity (the Soviet Union), and many nationals of currently independent former Soviet Republics live and work in Russia, it is unreasonable to assume that they will all adhere to the same cultural norms of behavior as the dominant ethnic Russian population. Furthermore, Russia is the largest country on Earth, and those parts of the country that are geographically distant from the center have their own specific local cultural norms. Therefore, the ethnic and religious backgrounds of individuals need to be taken into account on a case-by-case basis.

RESEARCH ON BUSINESS ETHICS IN RUSSIA AND INTERNATIONAL COMPARISONS

Avtonomov (2006) analyzed the business climate and ethics of post-Communist Russia. He argued that universalist, rule-based ethics, central to Western market economies, failed to develop in modern Russia despite the radical economic reforms of the last 15 years. According to Avtonomov, one of the main differences between Western market economies and the new economic arrangements emerging in Russia is the state's dominance over the business sphere and legal institutions. In these conditions, business behavior is based on personal loyalty and in-group allegiances, not on universal considerations of right and wrong, or of potential impact on community and society.

A study by Ahmed et al. (2003) focused on business students' perceptions of ethical business practices in six countries: China, Egypt, Finland, Korea, Russia, and the United States. The study found that in all six countries students shared a common understanding of the basic foundations of ethical behavior in business. However, students from Russia and China differed on one significant dimension: they showed a stronger readiness to behave unethically if these actions could, in their opinion, help increase the profits of their companies. In addition, Russian students were more likely than students from all the other countries in the sample to see less harm when presented with scenarios of potentially unethical behavior.

Jaffe and Tsimerman (2005) compared responses from samples of business students in three leading Russian business and economics programs at higher education institutions. The study results suggested that a high percentage of students believed that in order to be successful in business "it is necessary to compromise one's ethics" (p. 95). In addition, the authors observed a high level of emphasis on self-interest, as opposed to an emphasis on the interests of the organization or society.

Bailey and Spicer (2007) compared the business ethics attitudes of three groups: US managers working in the United States, US expatriates working in Russia, and Russian managers. All three groups of managers agreed on the higher-level ethical norms of business behavior (e.g., management's obligation to inform their employees about the existence of a risk of exposure to hazardous materials). The groups differed in their evaluation of practices that might be needed in order to conform to local norms (e.g., most Russian respondents agreed that it may be necessary to keep a set of double books as a safeguard against extortion by government officials or by racketeers; or, it may be acceptable to offer small personal payments to local officials or clerks to expedite the processing of government permits).

Similarly, Robertson et al. (2003) found that Russian employees were significantly more particularist than universalist when compared to US employees and tended to use a situational approach to ethical decision-making. Beekun et al. (2005) compared the ethical criteria used by US and Russian managers in decision-making. Both Russian and US managers displayed a strong preference for relativism in their decisions. However, while the US managers were driven more by considerations of justice, Russians placed much stronger emphasis on utilitarian considerations.

McCarthy and Puffer (2008) asserted that any interpretation of Russian managers' ethical behavior should take into consideration a combination of two sets of values: traditional Russian cultural values (grounded in collectivism and Orthodox Christian beliefs) and market-oriented values, which have emerged fairly recently as a result of the dissolution of the socialist system. McCarthy and Puffer (2008) argued that "[f]or the foreseeable future, Russian managers and other stakeholders will likely continue to exhibit behaviors that reflect traditional Russian norms and values, and these behaviors might often be seen by Westerners as unethical" (p. 14). Some of the differences between Russian and Western assumptions about acceptable business conduct are Russian reliance on personal networks rather than on legal contracts; lower degree of respect for private property; and higher tolerance of corruption (McCarthy & Puffer, 2008).

While in the first decade of the 21st century most of the research articles published in Russia on business ethics were focused on either ethical behavior of individuals in organizations or on a general discussion of ethical principles and norms, in recent years Russian business ethicists started to make a more explicit connection between business ethics and corporate social responsibility (CSR). For example, Saychenko's article (2013), "The Key Aspects of the Development of Business Ethics in Russia," discusses the CSR projects of Russian companies and utilizes the term "social-ethical business policies." Saychenko pointed out that there are encouraging examples of large-scale social-ethical projects implemented by large Russian businesses like Lukoil and Wimm-Bill-Dunn. However, the majority of such projects still focus on solving local and small-scale problems rather than addressing larger issues of societal development or ecological change. According to a 2010 survey conducted by the Russian Partnership for the Development of Business, 62 percent of Russian firms have some form of a social responsibility program (cited in Saychenko, 2013). Saychenko suggests that progress in expanding socially responsible activities is hampered by the fact that the government is not providing tax incentives for charity work (having recently eliminated the already modest 3% deduction for charitable donations).

IMPLICATIONS FOR WESTERN BUSINESSPEOPLE
WORKING WITH RUSSIAN COMPANIES AND/OR
RUSSIAN EMPLOYEES

The previous overview of the regulative, normative, and cultural factors, and of recent empirical research on business ethics and ethical decision-making in Russia, allows us to formulate a number of implications for Western businesspeople working with Russian companies or Russian employees of local subsidiaries.

When considering the current state of the Russian regulatory "pillar," it is important to compare this framework with those existing in most Western societies. In Western democracies, the regulatory pillar is usually characterized by a combination of clearly articulated and transparent laws and regulations that create favorable conditions for ethical behavior in business organizations by reducing ambiguity and increasing incentives for doing the right thing. In addition, the checks-and-balances systems provided by executive and legislative branches of the government ensure that opportunities for corruption, abuses, and an undue influence of government bureaucracy on businesses are limited. In contrast, in Russia today the regulatory pillar is shaped by two different, but converging, trends. The first is the progressive weakening of legislative structures and weak and ambiguous economic legislation. The second is the fast-growing power of the central government (more precisely, of the presidential administration) and of a handful of super-rich businesspeople aligned with the president and his entourage. Under these conditions, opportunities for corruption and extortion on the part of government officials of all levels abound, and businesspeople are forced to engage in unethical behaviors – ranging from bribes to using connections within the government elite – to obtain contracts and advantage over competitors. Admittedly, foreign businesses may be shielded from some of the abuses that Russian businesspeople are exposed to. However, they still face many of the same problems (e.g., extortion by low-level officials, or complex schemes aimed at squeezing them out of the Russian market, hatched by well-connected local competitors).

An important implication of the current highly centralized, state-corporate, capitalist model is the difficulty that employers face when trying to observe the laws of confidentiality and the protection of privacy of individual consumers or employees. Given that the government not only is actively regulating business activities but also gets directly involved in managing and owning business enterprises, requests for sharing private information can come from various government officials. However, given the level of corruption and pursuit of private interests, it is often hard to distinguish between legitimate requests and illegal attempts to obtain sensitive competitive information (Kantemirova, 2004).

As mentioned earlier, Western businesspeople also need to be mindful of the legacy of the Communist regime's historic ban on private property. Thus, in Russia, attitudes to whether an employee can use company supplies or equipment for personal business are much more liberal compared to the United States and most Western countries. This is rooted in the normative perception that company property belongs to the "collective."

Despite the negative influence of the normative pillar, it must be noted that there are some positive trends. First, consider the role of various ethics-related documents and codes produced by various professional groups and independent think tanks. The emergence over the last 10 years of numerous such documents should be regarded as a positive sign, indicating that the process of self-organizing around strong moral principles has started in the Russian business community. Second, the growing importance of Orthodox religious thinking and principles in the business sphere could lead to the creation of stronger moral foundations for the emergence of an ethical business culture, both at a country and at an industry level, as well as in individual business organizations. On the other hand, there could also be potential for negative effects. For example, with the strengthening of the central state apparatus, many of the previously independent professional groups and think tanks may fall under the direct control and influence of the government, thus promoting through their normative documents the agenda of the authoritarian state.

Cherepanova (2013) observed that in Russia the regulatory (laws) and normative documents (e.g., codes adopted by business associations) do not play such an important role as in the United States and Western Europe. According to her, only the company-level codes and norms have a real influence on individual ethical behavior at this stage. She also pointed out that the general assumption is that these company codes are created for employees, but do not apply to top-level management.

There are numerous practical implications of our earlier analysis of Russian cultural dimensions. High power distance is associated, as a rule, with paternalism (a relationship between managers and their subordinates in which superiors provide protection and various forms of assistance in exchange for loyalty on the part of employees) (Ardichvili, 2001). This leads to the expectation that enterprise management is obligated to provide various additional support structures for their employees (e.g., kindergarten for employees' children, free housing, on-site health-care facilities, benefits for family members, etc.). Ardichvili and Zavyalova (2015) found that the majority of the large Russian firms that they studied had programs providing such benefits to their employees, and also to members of local communities. Such programs and activities are often considered to be part of corporate responsibility programs and are presented as evidence of "ethically responsible" behavior on the part of the companies. A further implication of high collectivism, high power distance, and high paternalism in Russia is that employees are not likely to report or point out any ethical violations committed by their superiors. The assumption is that top management is above reproach and should not be criticized under any circumstances and that such criticism (or reporting of ethical violations) would be perceived not only as disloyal but even as unethical.

A related issue is the significant concentration of power in the hands of top executives. Such power concentration is supported by networks of personal relationships between executives, on the one hand, and executives and their employees, on the other. In hierarchical, high power distance (and highly collectivist) cultures like Russia, the role of a leader in creating conditions for ethical behavior is even stronger than in low power distance cultures like the United States (Cherepanova, 2013). According to Cherepanova, while in more individualistic cultures the individual responsibility of employees for ethical behavior is assumed, in Russia employees not only defer all the important business decisions to the boss but also tend to shift the responsibility for making ethical decisions to the boss.

In addition to exhibiting higher power distance and higher collectivism, Russian managers and employees differ from their Western counterparts in that they are likely to be more particularistic than universalistic when solving ethical dilemmas (Trompenaars & Hampden-Turner, 1998). Trompenaars and Hampden-Turner defined universalism as a strong belief that laws and rules apply to all equally, regardless of specific circumstances, which contrasts with the particularistic assumption that rules can be interpreted more loosely, based on the specifics of a situation and the nature of relationships with the people involved. Thus, Russian managers would be more inclined to apply situational decision rules when solving ethical dilemmas and feel that being loyal to their in-group is a sign of ethical behavior, even if general societal rules are violated.

Our earlier discussion of the *blat/svyazi* phenomenon has a number of implications for Western businesspeople operating in Russia. First, Russians are more likely to consider the exchange of favors with their informal network of business connections (*blat*) as part of standard and ethical business practices. It is important to note that in this respect Russians seem to have much in common with the Chinese (given the similarities between the concepts of *blat* and *guanxi*). Second, the most difficult question for foreign firms is how to break into a market where everything is based on such informal networks. The usual advice provided to foreign firms is to find an experienced local professional who can act as an intermediary, as an entry point into local networks, as an information and resource finder. However, while this advice is generally sound, there are also hidden dangers of overreliance on such local "experts." For example, a sense of loyalty to their in-group may lead these local experts to take an action that would be perceived as perfectly normal in the local business space, but unethical according to the standards of the Western country where the headquarters of the company is located.

In summary, Western businesspeople, and those working with Russian business partners (and, increasingly, with Russian-born employees working in Western countries), need to be mindful of some of the institutional factors unique to Russia that shape individual and organizational behavior. Differences in what is ethical or unethical are due to specific cultural-historical dynamics and may not indicate a lack of ethical awareness or individual moral deficiencies. One of the ways of addressing these gaps in understanding is to provide training and development to both foreign managers and employees working with Russian firms and to Russian employees of foreign corporations. Such training could point out both the nature of these differences and the specific reasons for their existence.

REFERENCES

Ahmed, M., Chung, K. Y., & Eichenseher, J. (2003). Business students' perception of ethics and moral judgment: A cross-cultural study. *Journal of Business Ethics*, 43, 89–102.

Ardichvili, A. (2001). Leadership styles and work-related values of managers and employees of manufacturing enterprises in post-communist countries. *Human Resource Development Quarterly*, 12(4), 363–383.

Ardichvili, A., & Zavyalova, E. (2015). *HRD in the Russian Federation*. New York: Routledge.

Aslund, A. (2007). *How Capitalism was built: The transformation of Central and Eastern Europe, Russia, and Central Asia*. New York: Cambridge University Press.

Association of Independent Directors (2004). *Business ethics: Recommendations for Russian firms* [Ассоциация Независимых Директоров (2004). Деловая этика: Методические рекомендации для российских компаний]. Moscow: AID.

Avtonomov, V. (2006). Balancing state, market and social justice: Russian experiences and lessons to learn. *Journal of Business Ethics, 66*, 3–9.

Bailey, W., & Spicer, A. (2007). When does national identity matter? Convergence and divergence in international business ethics. *Academy of Management Journal, 50*(6), 1462–1480.

Baranova, Y. A. (2013, December 17). Деловая этика старообрядцев – первооснова социально ответственного бизнеса в России [Business ethics of old believers: The foundation for socially responsible business in Russia]. Retrieved from http://opora-sozidanie.ru/?p=4515

Barinov, V. (2002). Корпоративная культура организации в России [Corporate culture of organizations in Russia]. *Management in Russia and abroad, 2*. Retrieved from www.mevriz.ru/articles/2002/2/995.html

Bazunov, P. (2009, April 14). Этика в бизнесе и проблемы деловых отношений в России [Business ethics and problems of business relationships in Russia]. Retrieved from http://ruskline.ru/analitika/2009/04/14/tika_v_biznese_i_problemy_delovyh_otnoshenij_v_rossii/

Beekun, R., Westerman, J., & Barghouti, J. (2005). Utility of ethical frameworks in determining behavioral intention: A comparison of the U.S. and Russia. *Journal of Business Ethics, 61*, 235–247.

Central Intelligence Agency (2016). The CIA World Factbook: Russia. Retrieved from www.cia.gov/library/publications/the-world-factbook/geos/rs.html

Cherepanova, N. V. (2013). Russian business ethics and national cultural traits. *Siberian Scientific Bulletin, 1*(7), 163–167.

Clendenin, D. (2003). *Eastern Orthodox Christianity*. Grand Rapids, MI: Baker Academic.

Feldman-Leibovich, A. (1995). *The Russian concept of work: Suffering, drama, and tradition in pre- and post-revolutionary Russia*. Westport, CT: Praeger.

Fortune (2014). *Fortune Global 500*. Retrieved from http://fortune.com/global500/

Frank, C. (2012). *Unternehmensethik in der russischen Transformationsökonomie und ihr gesellschaftlicher Mehrwert [Business ethics in Russian transforming economy and its societal contribution]*. Frankfurt am Main: Peter Lang.

Hofstede Centre (n.d). Comparisons of culture dimension scores for Russia. Retrieved from http://geert-hofstede.com/russia.html

Hofstede, G., Hofstede, G. J., & Minkov. D. (2010). *Cultures and organizations: Software of the mind*. New York: McGraw Hill.

Jaffe, E., & Tsimerman, A. (2005). Business ethics in a transition economy: Will the next Russian generation be any better? *Journal of Business Ethics*, 62(1), 87–97.

Kantemirova, T. (2004*). Factors determining business ethics of Russian entrepreneurs*. Retrieved from www.unn.ru/pages/vestniki_journals/99990201_West_soc_2004_1%283%29/18.pdf

Kornai, J. (1992). *The socialist system: The political economy of communism.* Princeton, NJ: Princeton University Press.

Lawrence, T., & Suddaby, R. (2013). Institutions and institutional work. In S. Clegg, C. Hardy, T. Lawrence, & W. Nord (eds.), *The Sage handbook of organizational studies* (pp. 215–254). Los Angeles, CA: Sage.

Matolygina, N. V., & Ruglova, L. (2012). Этика предпринимательства в современной России [Enterprise ethics in modern Russia]. *Naukovedenie*, 4, 1–4. Retrieved from http://naukovedenie.ru/PDF/116pvn412.pdf

McCarthy, D., & Puffer, S. (2008). Interpreting the ethicality of corporate governance decisions in Russia: Utilizing integrative social contracts theory to evaluate the relevance of agency theory norms. *Academy of Management Review*, 33(1), 11–31.

McCarthy, D., Puffer, S., Dunlap, D., & Jaeger, A. (2012). A Stakeholder approach to the ethicality of BRIC-firm managers' use of favors. *Journal of Business Ethics*, 109, 27–38.

Newman, K. (2000). Organizational transformation during institutional upheaval. *Academy of Management Review*, 25, 602–619.

North, D. (1990). *Institutions, institutional change, and economic performance.* Cambridge, UK: Cambridge University Press.

Oliver, C. (1991). Strategic responses to institutional processes. *Academy of Management Review*, 16(1), 145–179.

Puffer, S. M., & McCarthy, D. J. (1995). Finding common ground in Russian and American business ethics. *California Management Review*, 37(2), 29–46.

Robertson, C., Gilley, M., & Street, M. (2003). The relationship between ethics and firm practices in Russia and the United States. *Journal of World Business*, 38, 375–384.

Roth, K., & Kostova, T. (2003). Organizational coping with institutional upheaval in transition economies. *Journal of World Business*, 38, 314–330.

Saychenko, O. A. (2013). Основные аспекты развития деловой этики в России [The key aspects of the development of business ethics in Russia]. *Scientific and Technological Bulletin of the St. Petersburg State Polytechnic University*, 1(1), 39–43.

Scott, R. (2014). *Institutions and organizations* (4th ed.). New York: Sage.

Trompenaars, F., & Hampden-Turner, C. (1998). *Understanding cultural diversity in business*. Irwin, CA: McGraw-Hill.

Visokov, K. A. (2013). Культура и этика российского предпринимательства [Culture and ethics of Russian entrepreneurship]. *Contemporary Research and Innovation*, 12. Retrieved from http://web.snauka.ru/issues/2013/12/30352

Zhuravlev, A. (2004). Религиозная Этика и Бизнес [Religious ethics and business]. *Russian Entrepreneur*, 1–2(19). Retrieved from www.ruspred.ru/arh/18/1rr.html

3 Ethical Business Cultures in the Emerging Market of India

Thomas Thakadipuram

ABSTRACT

Ethical business cultures in the emerging markets are shaped by historical, geopolitical, and socioeconomic contextual factors. India, as one of the fastest-growing global economic powers, is not an exception to this phenomenon. Liberated from the British Raj in the year 1947, India adopted a multiparty political system that is democratic in nature. The end of the colonial era saw the disappearance of the recurring famines and economic depression that were endemic to India, and the country began to witness phenomenal growth of its economy. As the world's largest democracy and second most populous country, India emerged as a major world power in the 1990s.

With a population of more than one billion people and one of the largest economies in the world, India's purchasing power GDP was an estimated US$7.277 trillion in 2014 (Central Intelligence Agency, 2014). After adopting the framework of democratic socialism in the post-independence era and, later, policies of liberalization and expansion on global markets, India is moving toward democratic capitalism, integrating both public sector and private sector business perspectives.

In this chapter, we explore the major macroeconomic, sociopolitical, and cultural factors that influence the current business climate in India. We show that religious beliefs and ancient philosophical systems of India have a profound effect on the way business is done and how business behavior is perceived ethically. The changing role of Indian government, regulatory environment, and managerial leadership culture in the emerging economy is discussed. We examine the historical development of Indian business ethics and present a unique indigenous paradigm of ethics that guide business leaders in engaging in successful organizational ethical practices and avoiding the pitfalls of corporate wrongdoing. Practical implications are presented for business professionals and leaders from other countries and/or Indian companies operating globally.

HISTORICAL BACKGROUND OF THE INDIAN ECONOMY

The economic history of India dates back to the Indus Valley Civilization. With the advances made in transportation, the economy at that time depended significantly on trade. Intensive trade, commerce, and urban development were the hallmarks of the era. The Maurya Empire annexed numerous smaller monarchies by 320 BC and united most of the Indian subcontinent. Political stability and military security during this period resulted in an efficient system of finance, trade, and commerce with enhanced agricultural productivity. Indian empires were feudal monarchies with a caste system that oppressed and exploited the lower castes, especially the Shudras.

Khanna (2005) found that tradesmen on the Indian subcontinent utilized an ancient corporate form of business organization called *sreni* from 800 BC, or even earlier. The *sreni* appeared to have had a highly centralized business management system, represented in the king's court by a headman. The headmen were elected by the assembly and had administrative authority to sign contracts and set conditions of work within the *sreni* system.

Until the 17th century AD, India had the world's largest economy (Maddison, 2001). However, throughout its history numerous invasions and colonizers plagued India: the Persians (543 AD), the Greeks (326 AD), the Arabs (10th–15th centuries), and the Portuguese (16th century). Prior to colonization by the British in the 18th century, the country was divided into smaller kingdoms and territories, each territory having its own currency. From the 18th to mid-20th century, the country was united under the system of the British Raj and ruled by a massive bureaucratic apparatus of colonial administration that regulated all aspects of life, including business systems.

Modern Indian business culture and administrative and judicial systems emerged from three centuries of British presence. The legal and normative institutions of the country still bear the significant imprint of British institutions, and the English language is widely used across the population. Currently, India has the largest number of English-speaking people in the world.

After achieving independence from the United Kingdom, India adopted a system of centralized five-year plans of financial and economic planning, based mostly on a socialist model that included some elements of capitalism. This system existed for a large part of India's independent modern history and was characterized by extensive public ownership, government regulation, massive bureaucratic red tape, and trade barriers. After the 1991 economic crisis, the central government led by Prime Minister Manmohan Singh launched economic liberalization policies. Consequently, India emerged as one of the fastest-growing large economies in the world, with liberalized markets and globally oriented economic sectors.

THE CURRENT ECONOMIC ENVIRONMENT

India's economy is now clearly on a growth path. The World Bank (2016) reported that in 2015 India's GDP growth rate was at 7.5 percent, surpassing China's rate of 6.9 percent. Medium-term growth prospects have also improved following recent policy initiatives toward the deregulation of coal and mining industries, the liberalization of foreign direct investment policies, and a renewed emphasis on public investment in infrastructure. According to the International Monetary Fund (IMF), India is currently the fourth largest economy based on its purchasing power parity GDP, after the United States, China, and Japan (Worstall, 2015).

Due to the improved domestic macroeconomic situation and the continued favorable global monetary conditions, India has received large foreign direct investment inflows in the recent period – much higher than the current deficit. This has enabled the Reserve Bank of India to build up its foreign exchange reserves, which in March 2016 reached US$355.95 billion, up from US$14.31 billion in March 2015 (International Monetary Fund, 2016a). As such, India is now better prepared to deal with any future global financial market volatility.

Rapid economic growth has led to the emergence of a large middle class that has an insatiable demand for consumer goods. An example of this runaway demand can be seen in the explosive growth of the phone industry in India. The number of phone subscribers has grown exponentially since the early 1990s: from 0.5 million in 1991 to 960 million by May 2012 (the majority of the new subscribers were cell phone users) (Picardo, 2014). Picardo (2014) identified six long-term growth drivers for India: a demographic dividend, a growing middle class, a sizable untapped consumer market, a vibrant democracy, and thriving companies and financial institutions.

DEMOGRAPHICS

India is expected to overtake China to become the world's most populous country by 2030, reaching 1.6 billion people (compared to China's 1.4 billion) (US Census Bureau, 2015). The population has grown from 357 million in 1950 to 1.1 billion in 2016. The demographic situation of the country is favorable, since the percentage of young people who can participate in the workforce is significantly larger when compared to most countries of the developed and emerging market world (currently, there are 540 million Indians under the age of 25). The labor force is expected to increase by 32 percent in the next 20 years, whereas it will decrease by 4 percent in industrialized countries, and by 5 percent in China (US Census Bureau, 2015). According to Tharoor (2012), "India's favorable demographic profile can add significantly to its economic growth potential in the next three decades provided the young are educated and trained properly" (p. 5). India has one of the largest higher education systems in the world, producing the second highest number of scientists and engineers in the world and ranking second in terms of student enrollment.

The country has a number of world-class higher education institutions, for example, the Indian Institute of Technology, whose graduates have flourished across the globe.

SOCIOCULTURAL CONTEXT

India's sociocultural context is highly diverse with many religions, cultures, and languages. According to the 2011 census (*The Hindu*, 2017), 79.8 percent of the population of India practice Hinduism. Islam (14.2%), Christianity (2.3%), Sikhism (1.7%), Buddhism (0.7%), and Jainism (0.4%) are the other major religions practiced in India. The country has 22 official languages and more than 22,000 dialects, with English being the most widely used language, especially by the urban population.

Social heterogeneity and economic inequality make the social and political environment in India quite complex, and it is difficult (although not impossible) in this dynamic cultural environment to gain support and organize collective action toward long-term reform and overall growth. A diverse cultural heritage and stable family culture creates a hospitable environment for the global exchange of ideas, services, and goods. India's democratic pluralism has provided the means of addressing many ongoing social conflicts and violent confrontations, such as the riots in Gujarat and uprisings in Naxal, as well as those in Kashmir, Khalistan, Jharkand, Nagaland, and Assam. By and large, India is a legislative and deliberative democracy, although popular mobilization and political activism through the election process is often a successful political strategy for change.

The democratic framework has spread to the remote reaches of this far-flung country, and there is increased political awareness and self-assertion by previously marginalized groups. These groups have a growing faith in the efficacy of the political system, which is reflected in their active participation in the electoral process, and in activism that demands changes to improve the socioeconomic conditions of its marginalized people. However, the staggering income disparity in India remains a major problem. Liberalization of India's economy in the 1990s increased the GDP growth rate and benefitted the top 25 percent of its 1.2 billion people; at the same time, it has transferred an enormous amount of wealth to a very small number of families, whereby merely 100 individuals now own a quarter of the GDP (Roy, 2014, p. 7). According to Shirali (2011), the top 5 percent of Indians own 53 percent of the total wealth, in contrast to 90 percent of people possessing only 54 percent of the wealth. The top 16 million is super rich, whereas the bottom 684 million is classified as deprived.

The country is continuing on its path of rapid economic development, but it faces complex and enduring internal problems, such as those in the caste system and religious conflicts. While India has enormous potential for change and growth, this growth is threatened by massive overpopulation, poverty, rising religious intolerance, corruption, and environmental problems. India is now at a stage where it needs to make a strong commitment to continue on the path of growth and transformation: it has the right demographics, its government has the mandate, and its economy is growing. The government needs to install transparent, data-driven processes and programs that deliver measurably superior results. Changing the way government does business – in particular, focusing on civil service productivity without the License Raj (a rigid bureaucratic system of obtaining permits from the government for doing business) – will be essential to co-opt the business community in engaging the world market.

INDIGENOUS INDIAN PARADIGM OF ETHICS

While there are many indigenous ethical beliefs in Indian culture, both theistic and non-theistic, the prominent ethical ideal common to many Indian philosophical systems is the concept of "dharma," understood as moral well-being or ethical responsibility. The concept of dharma is a dominant indigenous ethical perspective shared by Hinduism, Buddhism, and Jainism. The word "dharma" in Sanskrit is derived from the root *dhru* meaning, "to hold," "to bear," "to carry," or "to support." "*Dharma* encompasses all ethical, moral, social and other values or principles, codes of conduct and behavior which contribute to the well-being, sustenance and harmonious functioning of individuals, societies and nations and which prevent their disintegration" (Ramamurthy, 2011). Dharma sustains and supports the whole world. The word "dharma" is used in Indian languages to signify "duty, righteousness, responsibility, virtue, justice, morality, charity, and ethical wholeness" (Ramamurthy, 2011). Sastri (1923) explained that the essential ethical mantra *Satyam vadadarmamchara* from Taitiriyopanishad (1:11), means "Speak the truth and do the duty." Dharma is the determining factor in the greater scheme of *Purusharthas* (Knapp, 2006, p.31), the four human pursuits, which include, in addition to dharma, pursuit of wealth (*artha*), pleasure (*kama*), and freedom (*moksha*). These four principles provided the framework for a classical Hindu society. Moksha is the ultimate aim of human pursuit and it gains priority over *artha* and *kama*, which are legitimate pursuits but need to be guided and regulated by *dharma* (ethics) to ensure the common good and welfare of all (Bhagavatham, 2008).

MORAL RULES AND MORAL IDEALS

Das (2009) highlights a key difference between moral rules and moral ideals, pointing out that "[m]oral rules are minimum demands of behavior that a civilized society expects from members" (p. 272). For example, the Ten Commandments in the Bible are moral rules. Moral ideals are the highest form of behavior demonstrated by persons of ethical excellence. As an example, the Sermon on the Mount offers moral ideals of the highest aspiration. In Mahabharata, one of the two Sanskrit epics of ancient India, the moral ideal of *Youdhisthira-anrishamsya* (the ideal human being subordinating self-interest for the sake of others or the principle of altruism, *nishkamakarma* [action without selfish motive]) is highly admirable, even though it is seemingly difficult to attain. It is inspiring and can stir us to greater heights. When Gandhi turned the other cheek to the British colonial rulers, he was demonstrating an ideal of moral excellence.

John Stuart Mill made a similar distinction between a perfect obligation to obey moral rules and an imperfect obligation to obey moral ideals.

The principle of dharma comprises both moral rules and moral ideals that help people attain the highest stage of personal ethics and collective morality. The ideal of dharma can give significance to a life that might otherwise be adrift. Das (2009) argued that the ethical ideal of dharma has many shades of meaning and applications in different contexts of business decision-making, political strategies, and interpersonal relationships. The theory of dharma advocates that businesses need to function in harmony with nature, human society, and individuals.

INDIAN MYTHOLOGY AND MANAGEMENT

Ethical business cultures in organizations are "based on alignment between formal structures, processes, and policies, consistent ethical behavior of top leadership, and informal recognition of heroes, stories, rituals, and language that inspire organizational members to behave in a manner consistent with high ethical standards that have been set by executive leadership" (Ardichvili & Jondle, 2009, p. 446). In contrast to the Western model of business ethics, Devdutt (2013) proposes a 3B model of Indian business organizational ethics: Belief-Behavior-Business. The beliefs of most Indians can be traced back to mythology, which embodies myths, stories, symbols, and rituals, and is comprised of socially constructed truths in the cultural psyche. Why we do business impacts how we do it and what ultimately gets done. Devdutt (2013) noted: "As is belief, so is behavior, so is business; this is Business Sutra, a very Indian way of doing business" (p. 11). He takes inspiration from the ancient Hindu culture, mythology, stories, and symbols and scriptural texts. The mythological literature of India is highly diverse and prolific and includes, among numerous other sources, puranas (ancient Indian myths and legends), *Itihasas* (epics of Ramayana and Mahabhartha), and mythological stories in the form of art, dances, and literature.

Mythology reveals a diversity of cultural patterns rooted in the traditions, mind-sets, and life contexts of the particular country. For example, *rangol* is the name for the patterns or columns of decoration drawn at the entrance to houses as a sign of hospitality. The Rangoli art form uses dots and a single line to create patterns. When the individual creates unique patterns using dots, which can be likened to data, and a line, representing a different way of thinking, patterns that are intricate and beautiful emerge. In the same way, each cultural pattern embedded in mythology is intricate and fascinating. According to Tharoor (2006), "If America is a melting pot, then to me India is a thali" (p. xiv; as described in the following paragraph). Diversity is honored and celebrated, and not just tolerated. "How can one portray the present, let alone future of an ageless civilization that was the birthplace of four major religions, a dozen different traditions of classical dance, eighty-five major political parties and three hundred ways of cooking the potato?" (Tharoor, 2006, p. 8).

The Indian way of thinking is cyclical, synchronous, and highly contextual. A telling metaphor for this is a comparison between the four-course Western meal, which is linear, sequential, and controlled by the chef, and the Indian *thali* way of serving a meal that is cyclical, simultaneous, and controlled by the one who eats. This is similar to the way in which meetings are conducted by management in Indian companies and corporations. In the West, the CEO comes to the meeting with a pre-planned agenda, adheres to the agenda, conducts the meeting focusing mainly on the tasks, and leaves the room when the meeting time is up, regardless of whether all the goals of the meeting were achieved. In India, a CEO comes to a meeting with one agenda but ends up discussing other items including his or other participants' family matters and leaves the meeting with not only many tasks accomplished but also good relationships established. The meeting is cyclical and spontaneous and respects the emerging energy patterns and the persons in the room. It is more people-oriented than task-oriented. It is not sequential, linear, or systematic.

Studies of mythology help us understand the deep cultural assumptions and values behind such thinking, beliefs, and behavior that determine business outcomes. Without embracing these differing patterns of thinking, doing business in India can be very uncomfortable and ineffective for foreign businesspeople. There is a saying that "nothing is impossible" in India, so long as one knows how to "adjust." The Indian way of doing successful business needs to be context-based, humane, and relationship-oriented. Senge (2009) understood the importance of recognizing the unique cultural contribution of India when he noted that India and China will move somewhat together, but in very distinctive ways, balancing the inner beliefs and the outer behaviors of doing business. In India, the business climate and cultural patterns are highly contextualized, and therefore standardized Western models of business usually don't take deep roots. Overall, the main ethical position inherent in Indian business culture can be called "contextual ethics" or "situational ethics": a system of ethics under which acts are judged within their contexts instead of by categorical principles.

INDIAN BUSINESS CLIMATE AND ETHICAL BUSINESS PRACTICES

Successful ethical business practices may be implemented by respecting the cultural norms and discerning the needs of the local market. Business ventures face tough challenges and will most likely fail if cultural and religious sentiments are not taken into account. There are many examples of successful business practices adopted by major international business corporations operating in India while being mindful of the country's cultural specificity.

The ethical business practices of McDonald's, Kentucky Fried Chicken (KFC), and a number of other multinational corporations operating in India indicate that respecting the cultural norms and social needs of the populace is essential for doing successful business in this country. Entering a new market in India is never easy, but many foreign companies have achieved resounding success in this complex environment.

McDonald's achieved great success in India by localizing the business with new brands and adapting the food according to Indian culture and tastes, for example, 320 million customers in India have purchased Maharaja Veggie Burger meals or other customized items since they were added to the menu. Doing business by respecting the local culture and traditions paved the way for success.

Similarly, Special KFC was established taking into account the social environment and catering to the needs of the disadvantaged. For instance, 10 percent of the population in India is hearing impaired, therefore, to address social equity in its business, 10 percent of employees in all KFC locations in India is hearing impaired. This resulted in a very successful venture that is socially appreciated (American India Foundation, 2014).

THE ROLE OF GOVERNMENT AND THE REGULATORY ENVIRONMENT

Prior to 1991, the Indian economy was highly regulated, governed by the five-year plans, and a large portion of the main industrial sectors was publicly owned. After 1991, the pace of liberalization increased rapidly. By the mid-1990s, the number of sectors reserved for public ownership was slashed dramatically, and private-sector investment was encouraged in areas such as energy, steel, oil refining and exploration, road building, air transportation, and telecommunications (however, the defense industry was still closed to the private sector). At the same time, foreign exchange regulations were liberalized, foreign investment was encouraged, and import regulations were simplified. The average import tariff was sharply reduced from 87 percent in 1991 to 8.6 percent in 2009. Despite these changes, the economy remained highly regulated by international standards, and the deregulation process continues to this day.

In India there are two main laws governing business transactions: the Foreign Exchange Management Act (FEMA) of 1999, which regulates the entry of foreign capital into the country, and the Companies Act of 1956 (amended in 2013), which governs business activity. FEMA was promulgated to consolidate and amend the law relating to foreign exchange with the objectives of facilitating external trade and payments and of promoting the orderly development and maintenance of the foreign exchange market in India (FEMA, 1999).

In recent years, the procedures for authorizing foreign investments have been improved, and, in many cases, bureaucratic barriers removed. Three Indian government bodies are important in regulating the process of entry of a foreign company into Indian markets: the Reserve Bank of India (RBI), the Secretariat for Industrial Assistance (SIA), and the Foreign Investment Promotion Board (FIPB). Any entry into India as a foreign entity will require the approval of the RBI, and if the activity requires an industrial license, the SIA and/or FIPB must be informed or grant approval according to the entry method chosen.

In 2013, the Indian Parliament passed its first amendment to the country's corporate law in more than 50 years. This legislative act included several important provisions that modernized India's corporate governance rules. The Companies Act of 2013 requires that one-third of a company's board should comprise independent directors and that at least one board member be a woman. It also requires companies to disclose executive salaries. This act mandates that the board must ensure that any company that does business in India spends at least 2 percent of the average net profits of the company made during the three immediately preceding financial years on corporate social activities (CSA). The act defines CSA as activities that promote poverty reduction, education, health, environmental sustainability, gender equality, and vocational skills development.

Although India became the first country to mandate CSR for corporations, studies that evaluate the CSR activities of Indian companies indicate poor participation and mostly poor ratings. A recent study of 50 companies in India revealed that these companies spent only US$48.231 million on CSR for the financial year 2013–2014, which was equivalent to only 1.3 percent of their net profits (Chandra & Kaur, 2015, p. 76).

The political business climate has changed in India with the passage of the Companies Act of 2013. In 2011, the Indian Ministry of Corporate Affairs released the predecessor of Companies Act, the National Voluntary Guidelines on Social, Environmental and Economic Responsibilities (NVGs) for India (Ministry of Corporate Affairs, Government of India, 2011), which listed the following nine principles (that are similar to the 10 United Nations Global Compact principles):

- **Principle 1:** Practicing transparency and accountability
- **Principle 2:** Providing goods and services that are sustainable over entire life cycle
- **Principle 3**: Assuring well-being of employees
- **Principle 4**: Being responsive toward stakeholders, especially the disadvantaged
- **Principle 5:** Respecting and promoting human rights
- **Principle 6:** Protecting and restoring the environment
- **Principle 7:** Enhancing public good by responsible policy advocacy
- **Principle 8:** Supporting inclusive growth and development
- **Principle 9:** Providing value to customers responsibly

Furthermore, the Securities and Exchange Board of India (SEBI) mandates the top 100 companies by market capitalization to submit Annual Business Responsibility reports based on the NVGs as part of their annual reports (Thakkar, 2015).

The World Bank survey (2015) ranked India 142 out of 189 countries on the ease of doing business, which suggests that both in registering property and in enforcing contracts, the Indian system is among the most cumbersome and involves an excessive amount of procedures, delays, and higher than average costs. With the current Narendra Modi's government, which has won an absolute majority in the 2014 elections, it is becoming much easier to do business in India, as measures are taken to cut through the bureaucratic red tape. The new government has a great opportunity to move forward on these and other necessary structural changes to deliver on the promise of "minimum government, maximum governance."

Markets and capitalist development in India are often seen as ambiguous terms. On the one hand, they are associated with exponential growth of the economy and the creation of opportunities for millions of people. On the other hand, this growth is perceived as uprooting the livelihoods of the disenfranchised portion of the population and leading to exploitation of the environment. For example, the Indian government is currently focusing on the legislation for a land reform bill to replicate the Chinese-style special economic zones to attract foreign investments. Among all the development projects, the Smart Cities project is one of the most ambitious, with the plan to establish 100 smart cities in the next two decades all over the country. A smart city uses world-class digital technologies or information and communication technologies (ICT) to enhance the quality and performance of urban services, to reduce costs and resource consumption, and to engage more effectively and actively with its citizens ("Smart City," 2015). This project is seen as a game changer for the nation, as the pace of development ramps up to a new, previously unattainable level with the participation of foreign investment, aided by liberalized, pro-business policies. However, while accelerating the incorporation of the Indian economy into the global economy, projects may only benefit a small number of the elites rather than the masses.

MANAGERIAL CULTURE AND THE ROLE OF LEADERSHIP

Managerial culture and the role of leadership play key parts in shaping the culture of the firm. The cultures of Indian firms need to be understood within "the general backdrop of increasing urbanization, gradual breakdown of the traditional rigidities of the caste system particularly in urban areas, increasing literacy and education, and above all rising levels of awareness and expectations" (Chhokar, 2005, p. 2). The situation in India appears to be evolving into "the sharing of environment and collaboration by communities and of their vibrant participation in political and economic processes and ritual roles provide a sense of harmony...in spite of conflicts and contradictions" (Singh, 1992, pp. 100–101).

According to Chakraborty (1997), US managers are more analytical in their ethical decision-making, whereas Indians rely more on intuition and context. Furthermore, US managers rely more on normative ethics, whereas Indians rely more on assessing the situation in which the case occurred (Ardichvili et al., 2012).

Jackson (2011) found that Indian managers consider unconditional loyalty to their organization a highly ethical behavior and that breaching loyalty is considered highly unethical and tantamount to betrayal. Indian business culture prioritizes favors and friendships, since it is relationship-oriented, rather than task-oriented. The Western concept of conflict of interest does not always align with the Indian value of loyalty to one's group (Ardichvili et al., 2012). To get things done, personal connections and influence within high levels of Indian management play a pivotal role, and the laws and regulations are often ignored.

Indian culture in general is predominantly collectivistic, although the caste system, class divisions, and feudal structures in the villages of India create social division, conflicts, and exploitation of the poor. Hence, there should be greater emphasis on corporate social responsibility (Hofstede, 2005). This emphasis should be reflected in the move from focusing on shareholders to focusing on stakeholders and by placing more importance on environmental sustainability. The ancient culture of India, immersed in spirituality and religion, favors intuitive and contextualized ethical decision-making. This sets it apart from the Western approach, which is based on standardized norms. Although India is a liberal democratic country, the business environment is highly hierarchical, bureaucratic, and non-participatory. The government acts as a gatekeeper rather than an enabler, complicating business transactions with slow approval processes, a complex bureaucracy, and corruption.

THE ROLE OF ETHICAL BUSINESS LEADERS

In India, business leaders with high ethical ideals are admired and respected. The founder of the Tata Group, Jamsetji Tata, and later his successor, JRD Tata, have both been highly admired for their community-centered leadership. The Tata Group's stated core purpose is to improve the quality of life of the communities it serves globally in 150 countries through long-term stakeholder value creation based on leadership and trust. Similarly, top executives at Infosys and Wipro are highly respected for their moral leadership and corporate social responsibility programs. These leaders manage by vision, inspiration, influence, empowerment, and expertise (Cappelli et al., 2010). They are known for their sense of leadership wholeness by achieving ends through ethical means. Leaders are expected to be role models who demonstrate high ethical values, dynamism, and innovation. Ethical leadership is considered as not only desirable but also necessary, and even admirable. Business leaders usually have high status and are generally looked up to and respected. Thakadipuram (2010) indicated that as CEOs move to higher levels of self-consciousness, their leadership becomes holistic and effective in situational contexts.

Cappelli et al. (2015) conducted research on how Indian leaders drive their organizations to high performance by interviewing senior executives at 98 of the largest India-based companies. In conversations with leaders at Infosys, Reliance Industries, Tata, Mahindra & Mahindra, Aventis Pharma, and many others, a picture emerged of a distinctive Indian model. Almost without exception, these leaders said that their people were the source of competitive advantage of the company. An earlier study by the same authors revealed an important difference between Indian and Western company leaders in how they focus their energy. Indian leaders identified their top four priorities as follows (Cappelli et al., 2010):

- High input for business strategy
- Keeper of organizational culture

- Guide, teacher, or role model for employees
- Representative of owner and investor interests

NATIONAL CULTURAL CHARACTERISTICS
AND BUSINESS ETHICS

Yognian (2009) noted four main characteristics of Indian culture: religiosity, diversity, inclusiveness, and spirituality. These values have been deeply embedded in the Indian psyche for ages. To understand how a country's cultural values affect its business behavior, it is instrumental to refer to the influential studies of cross-cultural management conducted (Hofstede & Hofstede, 2010; Hofstede et al., 2010; Trompenaars & Hampden-Turner, 1998). These frameworks offer sets of cultural dimensions along which values and norms can be studied, influencing not only individual thinking, feeling, performance, and decision-making but also the behavior of organizations and institutions.

Hofstede's six cultural dimensions are power distance, individualism, masculinity, uncertainty avoidance, long-term orientation, and indulgence (Hofstede et al., 2010). In India, collectivism, humane orientation, and power distance can be expected to be relatively high. In addition, gender differentiation is likely to be high, since India continues to be a male-dominated society in spite of a number of laws and reforms that have been initiated from time to time. A high tolerance for uncertainty can be expected, hence low values on the uncertainty avoidance dimension. On the other hand, one may expect high future orientation. This is in some way influenced by the teachings of what has been called the most famous ethical text of ancient India, the Bhagavad Gita. The essence of the teachings "is summed up in the maxim 'your business is to do the duty without selfish motive,'" or *Nishkamakarma* (Basham, 1967, pp. 344–345), the general philosophy being that in every circumstance there are actions that are intrinsically right and the right course must be chosen according to the circumstances.

As a high-context, hierarchical culture, India demonstrates high power distance and long-term orientation. Although traditional caste systems have been outlawed, the large power distance score indicates that the hierarchical attitudes still remain.

An analysis of more than 30 empirical studies on cross-cultural ethical behavior (Christie et al., 2003) has shown a strong correlation between ethical attitudes of business managers and culture. Two areas of commonality between India and the United States are a democratic culture and the use of English language between businesspeople. Hofstede and Hofstede's (2010) typology indicates two significant differences between the United States and India: high power distance due to the culture of hierarchy and collectivism due to a family-oriented lifestyle. At the same time, prevalent patriarchal family styles in India oppress women's rights. The power distance index and individualism dimensions are considered to be most strongly related to ethical attitudes of power and authority (Christie et al., 2003).

The study by Hofstede et al. (2010) suggests that India and the United States are significantly different on several cultural dimensions, with India having twice as high a score in power distance (77) and the United States having twice as high a score in individualism (91). The high power distance score for India is attributed to the culture of hierarchy. The roots of this hierarchy can be traced to the caste system that dates back 3,000 years (Kumar & Sethi, 2005). The caste system is a hierarchical ordering of society into groups, each having their own set of norms, status, and function, such as priest, warrior, merchant, and worker. The Bhagavad Gita, the most popular religious scripture of Hinduism, is interpreted to say that an individual's ethical choices are based on the situation (caste) to which he or she is born, although originally it was based on the division of labor in society (Sekhar, 1995). The caste system is rigid, and upward mobility is difficult if not impossible. Although the caste system was officially abolished when India declared independence in 1947, the caste system remains a powerful legacy, with a person's status in society playing an important role in business and personal life (Schuster & Copeland, 2006).

This legacy of hierarchy in India creates a business environment in which all authority lies with the boss, and the decision-making model is top-down, with little employee involvement. The hierarchical order is so powerful that employees will rarely challenge orders from their bosses, even when they know that the orders are incorrect (LeFebvre, 2011). Pejoratively, this has come to be known as the "Sir Culture" – a legacy of British colonialism (Kumar & Sethi, 2005). More positively, this creates an atmosphere of high respect for those in a position of authority and seniority.

Organizations in India often find it challenging to develop and articulate standards of ethics because the societal culture makes it difficult for employees to discuss sensitive matters with their management. Expressing disagreement with the boss is perceived as detrimental to an employee's job security. This culture of strict hierarchy is generally not found in US businesses, where the power distance index is smaller. In India, upward mobility is sought by many and upheld as a sign of success.

India is more of a collectivist culture, whereas the United States is strongly individualistic, as can be seen in Hofstede's second cultural dimension of individualism. The family is at the center of Indian society, which is largely patriarchal. Several generations of a family are brought together to live in one household. The hierarchical nature of Indian culture, as previously discussed, extends into the business sphere as well, where 75 percent of businesses are family owned (Kumar & Sethi, 2005). An Indian's primary loyalty usually lies with family rather than work. In the United States, people are more self-reliant and are encouraged to pursue their own personal decisions. Careers and family are often separate aspects of one's life, and balancing the conflicting needs of the two have come to be known as the challenge of "work–life balance."

A final distinction between the two cultures is the level of context they use in communication. The United States is considered to be a low-context culture in which communication is more explicit, leaving little to be implied. India, on the other hand, is a high-context culture in which communications are more implicit and leave some things unsaid and to be understood according to the context. High-context cultures are those in which the rules of communication are primarily transmitted through the use of contextual elements (i.e., body language, a person's status, and tone of voice) and are not explicitly stated (Hall, 1990). As regards the implications of the distinction between high- and low-context cultures, US businesses rely more on explicit language that translates into a high reliance on creating codes of professional and business conduct, whereas Indian businesses tend to rely more on relationships and implicit agreements and are more contextual in their decision-making (Jakubowskiet al., 2002). Furthermore, American managers prefer an analytical approach to ethical decision-making, which helps streamline the decision processes, whereas Indian managers prefer to take a more intuitive approach and attribute more importance to the context of the situation (LeFebvre, 2011).

CURRENT STATE OF ETHICS POLICIES WITHIN COMPANIES

Hussaini (2014) found that up until the 1990s ethics was not on the agenda for many companies in India. Many business schools did not include business ethics as an important topic in their curriculum until recently. In general, Indian corporations are highly sensitive to corporate social responsibility and environmental ethical practices. Research on codes of conduct has indicated a clustering of topics into three broad categories of company, society, and individual (O'Dwyer & Madden, 2006). Today, many large businesses in India display their codes of conduct and policies on their websites.

A comparative study of the codes of conduct of the top 50 public companies in the United States and India showed how cultural differences are manifested in the definition of ethical business practices in corporations (LeFebvre, 2011). The hierarchical and collectivist nature of Indian culture versus the universalist and individualistic nature of US culture are reflected in four main findings from the comparative analysis. First, US companies apply their codes of conduct to all employees, whereas Indian companies believe that their codes of conduct apply only to senior management. Second, US companies require their employees to report on their colleagues or superiors if they see them violating the code, and they provide mechanisms for anonymous reporting in order to encourage this behavior. Very few of the Indian companies have this requirement. Third, Indian firms are not specific about defining what a relative is especially how they can cause conflict of interest. Finally, in both US and Indian cultures, there is a strong expectation to protect the interests of the company and not achieve personal gains at the company's expense.

CULTURE CHANGE EFFORTS

In India, the common mind-set is that standardized ethics are of little benefit, since ethical practices are highly contextualized (Ardichvili et al., 2012). This thinking makes a code of conduct an ineffective document in practice. Therefore, there is an even stronger need than is the case in the United States or other Western countries to embed ethical culture into a firm's organizational strategy to ensure ethical business behavior. Sheth (2008) found several ways in which Indian business practices are unique and different – and these may give rise to ethical practices that may or may not be compatible with Western ethical business practices. For example, Indian business culture puts a high premium on loyalty, favors, friendship, and clanship, as the culture is collectivistic. Unconditional loyalty is highly valued, whether based on multigenerational family affiliations, school friendships, or personal connections. The Western concept of conflict of interest does not always mesh with the Indian value of loyalty to one's group.

IMPLICATIONS FOR PRACTITIONERS

The previous discussion has several important implications for foreign businesspeople doing business in India and with Indian firms. Drucker (2008) noted: "One of the basic challenges managers in a developing country face is to find and identify those parts of their tradition, history and culture that can be used as a management building blocks" (p.11). An important conclusion based on our discussion in this chapter is that Indian ethical values are deeply rooted in the culture of spirituality and religiosity (e.g., the concept of dharma) and that the culture is highly contextualized as opposed to being universalistic. Instead of minimizing wages, maximizing profits, and neglecting the environment, doing business according to the principle of dharma will enhance the common good and sustainability. Furthermore, it is important to keep in mind that in India, a country with a collectivist culture, the networks of relationships based on family, religion, and political affiliations play a significant role in making things happen.

On the other hand, there is a strong foundation of commonality in expectations for ethical business practices across cultures. Companies doing business with India can expect to have their confidential information protected and their company's assets properly used and to experience a respect for the rule of law. The fact that these expectations are equally valued both in India and in other cultures can give businesses more confidence in their dealings across borders.

There are areas for caution as well. Ethical expectations are quite different when it comes to personal accountability at all levels. Businesses from outside the country should not assume that every employee in an India-based company has the same expectation of ethical practices. Businesspeople must be aware of the different levels of management in an organization that they are dealing with and expect senior levels of management to express a stronger motivation for ethical practices than is found at other levels. Junior employees in India are unlikely to challenge ethical decisions made by superiors, given the hierarchical culture, and are generally not expected to intervene in any unethical activity that they observe.

Ardichvili et al. (2012) indicated that the consequences of breakdowns in organizational ethics perpetrated by unethical individuals from diverse backgrounds and cultures are disastrous for business organizations. These include a deficiency in trust, honesty, and integrity; damage to corporate goodwill and reputation; incurrence of financial penalties and fines (at the corporate and individual level); and potential conviction and sentencing of corporate executives and employees.

One size does not fit all, and the information shared in this chapter will hopefully prompt corporations, when doing business globally, to consider the unique cultural and ethical perspectives of Indian businesses on corporate social responsibility. Building ethical practices and behaviors that take into account the variability in cultural perceptions will ensure greater success in global business environments.

REFERENCES

American India Foundation (2014). *Best practices in employment of people with disabilities in the private sector of India.* Retrieved from http://aif.org/wp-content/uploads/2015/03/DisabilityManual_3-2015.pdf

Ardichvili, A., & Jondle, D. (2009). Ethical business cultures: A literature review and implications for HRD. *Human Resource Development Review,* 8(2), 223–244.

Ardichvili, A., Jondle, D., Kowske, R., Cornacchione, E., Li, J., & Thakadipuram, T. (2012). Ethical cultures in large business organizations in Brazil, Russia, India, and China. *Journal of Business Ethics,*105, 415–428.

Basham, A. L. (1967). *The wonder that was India.* Delhi: Rupa/Fontana Books. [First published 1954].

Bhagavatham (2008, October 20). Purusharthas. Retrieved from www .namadwaar.org/articles/bhagavatam/1.2.9-10.html

Cappelli, P., Singh, H., Singh, J., & Useem, M. (2010). The India way: Lessons for the U.S. *Academy of Management Perspectives,* 24(2), 6–24.

Cappelli, P., Singh, H., Singh, J., & Useem, M. (2015). Indian business leadership: Broad mission and creative value. *Leadership Quarterly,*26, 7–12.

Central Intelligence Agency (2014). *The CIA world fact book 2014.* New York: Skyhorse Publishing.

Chakraborty, S. K. (1997). Business ethics in India. *Journal of Business Ethics,*16(14), 1529–1538.

Chandra, R., & Kaur, P. (2015). Corporate social responsibility spending by corporate India and its composition. *IUP Journal of Corporate Governance*, 1(1), 68–79.

Chhokar, J. (2005). *Leadership and culture in India: The GLOBE research project*. Retrieved from https://www2005.hs-fulda.de/fileadmin/Fachbereich_SW/Downloads/Profs/Wolf/Studies/india/india.pdf

Christie, P. M. J., Kwon, I. W. G., Stoeberl, P. A., & Baumhart, R. (2003). A cross-cultural comparison of ethical attitudes of business managers: India, Korea and the United States. *Journal of Business Ethics*, 46(3), 263–287.

Das, G. (2009). *The difficulty of being good: On the subtle art of Dharma*. New Delhi: Penguin Group.

Devdutt, P. (2013). *Business Sutra: A very Indian approach to management*. New Delhi: Alpha Book Company.

Drucker, P. (2008). *The essential Drucker: The best of sixty years of Peter Drucker's essential writings on management*. New York: Harper Collins.

Foreign Exchange Management Act (1999). Parliament of India. Retrieved from https://www.lawctopus.com/academike/foreign-exchange-management-act-1999/

Hall, E. T. (1990). *The silent language*. New York: Anchor Books.

Hofstede, G., & Hofstede, J. (2010, October 21). Comparative cultural dimensions. Retrieved from http://geert-hofstede.com/india.html

Hofstede, G., Hofstede, J., & Minkov, M. (2010). *Cultures and organizations software of the mind: Intercultural cooperation and its importance for survival* (3rd ed.). New York: McGraw-Hill.

Hussaini, N. (2014). Corporate ethics of top IT companies in India, 2–21. TMBU Bihar: India.

International Monetary Fund (2016, April 16). IMFC statement by Arun Jaitley. Retrieved from www.imf.org/External/spring/2016/imfc/statement/eng/ind.pdf.html

Jackson, T. (2011). *International management ethics: A critical, cross-cultural perspective*. New York: Cambridge University Press.

Jakubowski, S. T., Chao, P., Huh, S. K., & Maheshwari, S. (2002). A cross-country comparison of the codes of professional conduct of certified/chartered accountants. *Journal of Business Ethics*, 35(2), 111–129.

Khanna, V. S. (2005, November 1). The economic history of the corporate form in ancient India. University of Michigan Law School. Retrieved from http://ssrn.com/abstract=796464.

Knapp, S. (2006). *The power of dharma: An introduction to Hinduism and vedic culture*. Lincoln, NE: iUniverse.

Kumar, R., & Sethi, A. (2005). *Doing business in India: A guide for western managers.* New York: Palgrave Macmillan.

LeFebvre, R. (2011). A study of business codes of conduct cross-cultural comparison of business ethics in the U.S. and India. *Journal of Emerging Knowledge on Emerging Market,* 3(1), 391–409.

Maddison, A. (2001). *The world economy – A millennial perspective.* Paris: OECD.

Picardo, E. (2014, October 22). India is eclipsing China's economy as brightest BRIC star. Retrieved from www.investopedia.com/articles/investing/102214/india-eclipsing-chinas-economy-brightest-bric-star.asp.

Ramamurthy, P. R. (2011, July 23). Dharma: Its wider meaning and connotations. Retrieved from http://stotram.lalitaalaalitah.com/2011/07/dharma-its-wider-meaning-and.html

Roy, A. (2014). *Capitalism: A ghost story.* Chicago, IL: Haymarket Books.

Sastri, S. (1923). *The Aitareya and Titiriya Upanishads and Sankara's commentary.* Madras: the India Printing Works.

Schuster, C. P., & Copeland, M. J. (2006). *Global business practices: Adapting for success.* Mason, OH: Thomson.

Sekhar, R. C. (1995). Ethics and the Indian manager. *Economic and Political Weekly,* 30(47), 159–164.

Senge, P. (2009). The inner side of leadership: Lessons from the East: An interview with Peter Senge. *Journal of Management, Spirituality and Religion,* 6(3), 183–193.

Sheth, J. (2008). *Chindia rising: How India and China will benefit your business.* New Delhi: Tata McGraw-Hill.

Shirali, A. (2011, March 12). The wealth report. *Open.* Retrieved from www.openthemagazine.com/article/business/the-wealth-report

Singh, K.S. (1992). *People of India: An introduction* (Vol. 1). Calcutta: Anthropological Survey of India.

Smart City (2015, February 20). Wikipedia. Retrieved from: https://en.wikipedia.org/wiki/Smart_city

The Hindu (2017, February 13). *The Hindu* News. Retrieved from www.thehindu.com/news/national/National-population-growth-/article10336665.ece

Thakadipuram, T. (2010). Leadership wholeness: A human resource development model. *Human Resource Development International,* 13(4), 463–475.

Thakkar, L. (2015, October 10). *India's CSR Policy and the NVGs.* Retrieved from www.cutsccier.org/brcc/ppt/Indias_CSR_Policy_and_the_NVGs_IICA.pptx

Tharoor, S. (2006). *India: From midnight to millennium and beyond.* New York: Arcade Publishing.

Tharoor, S. (2012, November 14). The emerging world's education imperative. Retrieved from https://www.weforum.org/agenda/2012/11/the-emerging-worlds-education-imperative/

Trompenaars, F., & Hamden-Turner, C. (1998). *Riding the waves of culture: Understanding diversity in global business* (2nd ed.). New York: McGraw-Hill.

US Census Bureau. (2015). International Data Base. Retrieved from www .census.gov/population/international/data/idb/informationGateway.php

World Bank Survey (2014). Ease of doing business. Retrieved from http://data .worldbank.org/indicator/IC.BUS.EASE.XQ?view=chart

World Bank (2016). GDP growth: Retrieved from http://data.worldbank.org/ indicator/NY.GDP.MKTP.KD.ZG?locations=IN

Worstall, T. (2015, January 21). "IMF: India's growth to be faster than China's by 2016," *IMF Report*, 2015. Retrieved from https://www.forbes.com/sites/ timworstall/2015/01/21/imf-indias-growth-to-be-faster-than-chinas-by-2016/ #a366f6b39ac0

4   Ethical Business Cultures in China

Jessica Li

ABSTRACT

Chinese business ethics emerged as a field of research after the beginning of economic reforms in late 1970s to early 1980s. In the 1990s, China grew to become a manufacturing powerhouse, and Chinese products have been widely exported around the world. Issues associated with defective products, such as toothpaste tainted with antifreeze and pet food containing melamine, also arose and generated negative publicity (Lu, 2009). After China entered the World Trade Organization (WTO) in 2001, concerns were raised about the inappropriate conduct of Chinese businesses (Brand & Slater, 2003). This triggered an interest in examining the ethical conduct of Chinese business organizations.

The first part of this chapter covers the development of Chinese ethical business culture and the impact of historical, cultural, economic, and political factors. It discusses the profound influence on ethical business environment and ethics of Confucian philosophy, Communist ideology, and the government regulatory agencies. Special attention is paid to the role of informal networks and the unique practice of *guanxi*. Next, the chapter discusses the ethics policies and practices at the firm level to investigate the roles of leadership, managerial culture, and ethics training in ethical business practices in China. Implications are discussed from the viewpoints of both foreign and Chinese firms to provide a global perspective.

HISTORICAL EVENTS THAT SHAPED CHINA'S SOCIOECONOMIC SYSTEM

China is one of the largest and the oldest civilizations in human history and was controlled by the imperial system under a bureaucratic government for the longest time. It functioned under a household-based economy model, with no separate parallel legal system, thus bureaucratic decisions were often left unchallenged. Supposedly, citizens were protected by the morals of Confucian virtue that was based on the structure of classical social hierarchy. Prior to the 15th century, this system appeared to have worked, because China was more prosperous when compared with the economic output of European countries at the time. The following three centuries, however, were characterized by Western Europe surpassing China in economic leadership (Maddison, 1998).

Western Europe, propelled by the Renaissance and the Enlightenment movement, gradually established an independent commercial and industrial bourgeoisie and created legal protection for merchants with city charters. As a result, modern capitalism emerged and thrived in Europe. In contrast, the bureaucracy and gentry of the imperial system delayed the development of modern capitalism in China. A hierarchical governing structure favored status and privileged the elite groups. Private ventures could not compete with ventures that were controlled by the elites or the state-licensed monopolies. Coupled with a lack of legal protection for private activities, this had stifled the development of the Chinese economy. While the Western world experienced rapid development, China's GDP declined (Maddison, 1998). What was once a superior system became the root cause of the problem.

A close look at Chinese contemporary history since 1820 suggests a country that was impoverished, war-troubled, and tormented by internal turmoil and foreign invasions. Only in 1949 did a significant shift occur, after the Communist Party seized control of the government. Since then, China has experienced several significant economic transitions.

The first transition was from a largely household-based economy to a centrally planned socialist economy governed by Communist ideology. State-owned enterprises (SOEs) were established and strategically positioned across the country. Resources were allocated on the basis of political ideology rather than economic efficiency. Business organizations were tasked with completing production quotas. The success of SOEs was measured by completing their quotas on schedule, not by their profitability. Coupled with some of the most disastrous policies, such as the Great Leap Forward and the Cultural Revolution, this resulted in a disappointing growth period of nearly three decades. However, some have argued that this period might have contributed to the establishment of China's industrial foundation (Naughton, 2007) and instigated the second economic transition toward a market-driven economy (Nolan & Ash, 1995).

The second transition was from a socialist-planned economy to a market-driven economy. The policy of economic reform powered China's rapid growth for more than three decades and made China one of the most influential economic powers in the world. As a developing country and an emerging economy, China represented enormous business opportunities, with one of the largest consumer markets in the world, while offering considerable savings in labor costs. However, it remained a developing country because of its low income per capita and vast income inequality, with a large portion of the population still living under the poverty line (World Bank, 2015).

There is no doubt that China has charted its own path in developing so-called socialism with Chinese characteristics while under the tight control of the Communist Party. The path China took differed from other old socialist regimes. The lack of change in the political structure has led some to perceive China as an overbearing and corrupt country, but others have credited its stable economic development over a long period of time to the methodical and carefully planned government interventions (Guthrie, 2012).

Researchers concluded that the caution and gradualism of this transitional period was designed to avoid the policy-induced chaos of the first transitional period (see examples in Nolan & Ash, 1995). Table 4.1 captures the gradual introduction of policy changes during the second transition.

Table 4.1. *Reform and Policy Changes in China (1978–2004)*

Year	Policy change
1978	"Open door" policy initiated, allowing foreign trade and investment to begin.
1979	Decision to turn collective farms over to households and townships. Village enterprises (TVEs) given stronger encouragement.
1980	Special economic zones created.
1984	Self-proprietorships, of less than 8 persons, encouraged.
1986	Provisional bankruptcy law passed for state-owned enterprises (SOEs).
1987	Contract responsibility system introduced in SOEs.
1988	Beginning of retrenchment of TVEs.
1990	Stock exchange started in Shenzhen.
1993	Decision to establish a "socialist market economic system."
1994	Company law first introduced. Renminbi begins to be convertible on current account. Multiple exchange rates ended.
1995	Shift to contractual terms for SOE staff.
1996	Full convertibility for current account transactions.
1997	Plan to restructure many SOEs begins.
1999	Constitutional amendment passed that explicitly recognizes private ownership.
2001	China accedes to the World Trade Organization.
2002	Communist Party endorses role of the private sector, inviting entrepreneurs to join.
2003 2004	Decision to "perfect" the socialist market economic systems. Constitution amended to guarantee private property rights.

Source: Adapted from OECD Economic Surveys: China (Organization for Economic Co-operation and Development, 2005).

In 1978, a new economic policy was initiated to open up foreign trade and investment, followed by the decision to turn collective farms over to households and townships. To increase small-scale household businesses, a policy to encourage self-proprietorship of businesses of eight persons or less was issued in 1984. This policy was rooted in the traditional Chinese household economy. Small and privately owned businesses successfully sprang up throughout China to meet the market needs that had been neglected under the central planned economy. In addition, the growth of rural businesses and many other organizational forms of the time fueled China's early economic recovery and development (Naughton, 2007).

During the 1980s, special economic zones (SEZs) were created to experiment with foreign direct investment and market-friendly policies. Laws and policies were trialed to protect private ownership in SEZs, and then gradually introduced to the rest of China in an effort to maintain stability. Today, Shenzhen, one of the most successful SEZs, is home to a large number of successful companies that were founded during that time, for example, Huawei Technologies and Vanke Real Estate Company. One might or might not credit the government for the long sustained growth over the past 30 years (Guthrie, 2012; Naughton, 2007), but no one doubts that China has grown to be a world economic power.

China's economic development, however, was not free of challenges, and the carefully crafted policies were not without limitations. Transformational change – from an isolated socialist state to a leading economic power in such a short time – has created stresses and strains in the country. Problems associated with incomplete market reform, income inequality, rapid urbanization, environmental sustainability, uneven regional development (e.g., urban cities versus rural villages; coastal areas versus interior areas), and corruption were widespread and deep-rooted and presented challenges to the development of an ethical business environment.

The operating environment for Chinese business is complex. First, there are three evolving ideologies that influence the understanding of ethical business conduct in China: Confucian ideology, Communist ideology, and capitalist ideology (Ding et al., 2000; Zhang & Zhang, 2006). This trio of ideologies are different yet coexisting, causing a dilemma that is entrenched in today's Chinese business environment (Li & Madsen, 2009). Second, there are a number of different types of organizations coexisting in China, such as SOEs, joint ventures, private firms, and foreign-owned firms. SOEs were designed to have dual responsibilities, economic and political, and still play an important role in the Chinese economy. Subsequently, dual organizational structures were established to support production and political initiatives (Zhang & Keh, 2010). It is, therefore, essential for foreign companies to understand the meaning of dual responsibilities when working with Chinese SOEs.

CHINESE CULTURAL CHARACTERISTICS AND BUSINESS ETHICS

Understanding culture is relevant to the understanding of ethical business practices because ethical values, attitudes, and behaviors are subject to the influence of culture (Scholtens & Dam, 2007). Cross-cultural studies can enhance the understanding of one culture in relation to other cultures in the world. Such comparisons afford a frame of reference to build awareness of the differences and similarities between cultures, increase cross-cultural sensitivity, and promote effective cross-cultural understanding and communication. Presenting Chinese cultural characteristics using a cross-cultural framework offers an opportunity for one to interpret and understand ethical business culture through a familiar lens of one's own culture as a point of comparison.

Globalization has increased the prominence of cross-cultural comparative studies. There are a number of notable studies in the field of international business that have generated worldwide discussion and applications, such as Hofstede's model and the framework of GLOBE's culture studies. Hofstede's work, first published in 1980, took into consideration geographical location, societal beliefs, and values that shape organizational cultures. The results of the GLOBE study, published in 2004, cover 62 societies. Both studies are considered significant scholarly works for their influence in international business and cross-cultural management studies (Shi & Wang, 2011;

Tung & Verbeke, 2010). In this chapter, Hofstede's model was used to guide the discussion of Chinese cultural characteristics. It is used as a reference for understanding potential tendencies in decision-making and behavior due to cultural influence. However, to truly understand what drives ethical business decision-making, one also needs to take into consideration other factors, such as personal and organizational values and social, legal, political, and institutional environments (Ekici & Onsel, 2013).

Hofstede's Model and Chinese Cultural Characteristics

Hofstede (1980) developed a four-dimensional model to place culture in relation to four comparative dimensions: power distance, individualism, masculinity, and uncertainty avoidance. According to the Hofstede Centre (2015), the power distance dimension of the model relates to the basic problem of human inequality and the attitude of the culture toward inequality among its members. China ranks high in this dimension, meaning that inequalities as the result of differences in authority (power), wealth, or status are accepted. Li and Madsen (2009) also found a common attitude toward reverence for authority and that people were more likely to choose to remain silent when a person in power made an unethical decision or behaved unethically. Uncertainty avoidance measures the level of stress in a society in the face of an unknown future. China scores low and this can be interpreted to mean that Chinese people are rather comfortable with ambiguity; this often makes Western business partners uncomfortable, because they never know how and when decisions are made. The individualism dimension relates to the integration of individuals into primary groups. The opposite of individualism is collectivism. China scores very low, which indicates that China has a highly collectivist culture. However, the collective benefits may only favor the in-group members or *guanxi* network (detailed discussion on guanxi is provided later). The dimension of masculinity versus femininity has to do with whether the society is driven by competition, achievement, and success or driven by values of caring for others and quality of life. China scores relatively high in this dimension, indicating that China has a comparatively masculine society where people are driven by success and are willing to sacrifice leisure, quality of life, and family for professional success. It is important to point out that this study uses the original four dimensions because the later-added values of long-term orientation and indulgence are still being validated and have faced serious criticism from a number of scholars.

Confucius and Business Ethics

Confucian ideology has been the predominant social fabric of Chinese culture for thousands of years. It is impossible to understand Chinese culture without referencing the influence of Confucius. The philosophy of Confucianism, in the abstract, stresses the values of interpersonal harmony, social hierarchy, family integrity, kinship affiliation, and individual responsibility (Lim & Lay, 2003). Under the influence of Confucian ideology, hierarchical relationships of emperor–subject, father–son, husband–wife, elder–younger siblings, and friend–friends must be maintained for a stable and harmonious society. This was similar to other agrarian societies that built on limited resources of land. The Confucian value system consists of a set of moral and ethical codes, such as trustworthiness, propriety, altruism and filial piety, and having a sense of shame, which are believed to be the essential elements of a peaceful and harmonious moral world. The primary responsibility of the individual is first to the family, then to the community, and finally to the state (Guthrie, 2012; Song & Gale, 2007).

Cultural values do not stay static, especially during economic transitions. Chinese cultural virtues, particularly the ethical understanding of business transactions, have gone through significant modifications over the years. While the classical Confucians recognized the benefits of business transactions, there was a time when merchants were considered untrustworthy and immoral for making a profit. Making a profit was equated with taking advantage of others. The usefulness of profitable business transactions was slowly acknowledged, mainly after the Western invasion in the 19th century, when attitudes toward market activity underwent a marked change. Competitive activity in the market was accepted as an important mechanism for economic growth; however, the beneficiaries were still responsible for sharing their wealth with more unfortunate groups (Lam, 2006). During this time, Confucian moral and ethical codes mostly stayed intact.

Communist Ideology and Business Ethics

When the Communist Party took power in 1949, Confucian social hierarchy was replaced by a socialist structure. During this time, the country was not only centralized through its political structure but also centralized through economic institutions. The economic mechanism of the household-based economy was replaced by a centrally planned economic system. Everyone's performance was linked to the plan, and the fate of individuals was tied to the state through party affiliations (Guthrie, 2012). Ethics were discussed in the context of loyalty toward the party and state, first and foremost. An individual's primary responsibility was to the party and the state; the tradition of family as the primary unit of society and business activities was challenged and shattered. Confucian moral and ethical codes were abandoned. Business ethics, as we understand them today, was nonexistent and only emerged as a field of research and practice when the market economy was reinstated and economic reform was initiated (Lu, 1997).

When China initiated economic reform in 1978, foreign investments not only brought new technology, new capital, and new opportunities but also introduced elements of Western culture and free-market values. The principles of a free-market economy guided by capitalist ideology had a significant influence on the newly established business and market operations in China (Ding et al., 2000). Free-market economy brought competition, meritocracy-based reward systems, employment mobility, and new career opportunities (Cao, 2003). Employees now expected to be rewarded for better performance and higher skills. When expectations were not met, they could leave and seek better opportunities elsewhere. Loyalty to the organization that fulfills the needs of the state and the party was no longer a priority for individual employees.

Profiting for personal gain and getting rich are encouraged as part of the national policy to promote market activity; however, the appropriate rules and regulations to govern free-market transactions are either lacking or not well established at this time. While the economy grew, China became a breeding ground for market behaviors that are neither ethical nor socially responsible, for example, cutting corners or using substandard materials. This has resulted in an ethically troubled business environment (Shafer et al., 2007). Many have blamed the traditional Chinese virtues of guanxi and *mianzi* (face) for the decline of Chinese business ethics, even though it most likely is the result of valuing profit-making more than business ethics and social responsibility and a lack of appropriate legal systems to protect businesses and consumers (Ang & Leong, 2000).

Guanxi and Business Ethics

Guanxi, often seen as an outgrowth of Confucian philosophy on personal relationships and responsibilities, is one of the most important Chinese social values. Guanxi can be defined as interpersonal relationships based on a common background or existence of direct particularistic ties (Tsui & Farh, 1997). Guanxi leads to the formation of relation-based network groups and a highly collective culture (Hofstede Centre, 2015). Hence, China often is labeled as having a relation-based society.

Social contacts, such as where one works and whom one knows, often help establish the connections to formulate guanxi. The eminence of the group is often represented by the position power and/or economic power of its members. Having the right guanxi to potentially influence decision-making often shapes an individual's social status (Yang, 1993). Concerns about guanxi and social ethical dilemmas are rooted in the problematic nature of guanxi practices.

On the one hand, guanxi is a very important social concept in the Chinese business context because people see it as an inherent part of the work ethic, and it is critical and "ethical" to act accordingly (Su et al., 2003). On the other hand, guanxi by definition encourages inequality because of its intrinsic elements of reciprocity and obligation (Gold et al., 2002).

Guanxi requires nurture and maintenance. Guanxi requires members to do right by other in-group members. Favoritism and personal gain are often the reasons for people acquiring guanxi, while discrimination against out-group members is commonly accepted. This may present a challenge to those intending to be impartial in decision-making, because guanxi favors in-group members. By examining its influence on ethical business practices, Au and Wong (2000) found that guanxi causes Chinese auditors to loosen auditing standards. In another study, Tan and Snell (2002) found that Chinese people have exhibited tendencies of paying attention to roles, intentions, obligations, and consequences, in addition to following the moral and ethical code.

The influence of guanxi on business ethics has been associated with certain sensitive social phenomena, including corruption, labor rights, and distributive justice (Fan, 2000; Lu, 2009). However, it is important to point out that guanxi itself is not unethical; it is a set of powerful yet implicit rules that govern informal personal and business relationships. It is the people who take unethical actions in the name of guanxi who cause unethical outcomes (Li & Madsen, 2011).

It is conventional wisdom to believe that guanxi is essential to completing virtually any task in China (Gold et al., 2002). Research has also found that there is practically no distinction between an individual's professional and personal network (Li & Madsen, 2009). People often form a personal bond first, and business transactions occur after the personal bond has been carefully maintained and cultivated.

Three streams of guanxi were often examined: the micro-level of individual and interpersonal relationships; the macro-level of organizational, industrial relationships; and the issue of guanxi and the social ethical dilemma (Chen et al., 2013). At the micro-level, guanxi is formed through two particular channels: preexisting ties or professional networks. Preexisting ties include kinships, former classmates, former neighbors, and former colleagues. Professional networks include people met through work and social interactions. In terms of supervisor and subordinate relationships, Chen et al.'s study found that Chinese supervisors might let personal relationships influence their decisions when allocating rewards, and that could result in a loss of trust among other subordinates (Chen et al., 2004; Jiang et al., 2011).

The macro-level of guanxi relates to the interpersonal ties between senior managers from different firms (Chen et al., 2013). Research has shown that when the institutional environment is challenging due to the lack of legal protection and market mechanisms, this level of guanxi is effective (Lovett et al., 1999), especially for small, private, and newly established firms in less developed areas. Large, well-established firms that operate in well-developed Chinese regions rely less on guanxi comparatively (Park & Luo, 2001). Guanxi between firms more consistently leads to beneficial outcomes than to political ties (Sheng et al., 2011). Even though current research at this level remains sporadic, the findings have suggested that guanxi has had positive effects on organizational-level performance (e.g. Chen et al., 2013).

The influence of Confucian social hierarchy still shapes the relationship between manager and subordinate in today's Chinese organizations. Subordinates rarely choose to speak out about their managers' unethical behaviors (Li & Madsen, 2011). Some believe that the true line of defense of ethical business practices depends on the ethical and moral bottom line of the business owners and managers (Ip, 2009a; Lu 2009). Some Chinese corporations have started to focus on establishing a corporate culture that values personal ethics and building a "good person culture" (Lu, 2009). Since 1994, the Chinese government has issued policies and regulations to tackle unethical conduct through institutional means, such as introducing corporate social responsibility (CSR). Though the result is yet to be evaluated, it has raised the profile of business ethics in China (Ip, 2009b; Lu, 2009).

RESEARCH ON CHINESE BUSINESS ETHICS AND COMPARISONS WITH WESTERN COUNTRIES

China's business ethics practices have received increasing attention in both public media and scholarly publications, particularly when problems associated with defective products have been blamed on inappropriate business practices and unethical conduct (Brand & Slater, 2003). However, as observed by Chan et al. (2009), current Chinese business ethics-related studies suffer from the insufficient participation of indigenous researchers and a scarcity of empirical research. A significant portion of current publications focuses on ethical perceptions or is based on comparative studies.

Comparisons with Western Countries

Research studies have reported differences in how business ethics were perceived and practiced in China and Western nations (e.g., Ardichvili et al., 2012; Armstrong, 1993; Ralston et al., 1993; Tsui & Windsor, 2001). In a study of 13 countries across Europe, Asia, and the Americas, Ardichvili et al. (2010) found statistically significant differences between a subset of countries that includes China and the subset of Anglo countries that consists of the United States, the United Kingdom, Australia, and Canada. Businesspeople in Anglo countries place stronger emphasis on the leaders' role in upholding ethical standards and prefer to have clearer policies and procedures to report ethics violations, compared to businesspeople in China.

In a comparative study, Tsui and Windsor (2001) revealed the differences between Australian and Chinese auditors in their ethical reasoning scores. Australian auditors received an average ethical reasoning score that was higher than the Chinese auditors. The difference, however, cannot be simply interpreted as Chinese auditors being less ethical than Australian auditors. Australia has a rule-based society, where people are more individualistic and prefer a less hierarchical relationship between people. Decisions are often made on the basis of rules and procedures. China has a relation-based society (guanxi), often demonstrates a culture of collectivism, and is more comfortable with hierarchy. Decisions are often made by the hierarchy and are influenced by many other factors such as guanxi. Hence, while cross-cultural studies offer insightful observations, explaining the findings requires taking into consideration the right cultural lens (Lovett et al., 1999).

The differences between a rule-based society and a relation-based society often contribute to the misunderstandings between Western and Chinese firms when they try to work together (Langenberg, 2013). Some researchers found that Chinese business-people are less idealistic, less concerned with social justice, and more concerned with personal interest and profit making when compared with their Western counterparts (Redfern & Crawford, 2004). The gap between China and the West in terms of business ethics is believed to be significant, and possibly divergent.

However, the commonalty between the two may be greater than is generally understood (Berger & Herstein, 2014; Lu, 2009). Elements such as loyalty, trust, and justice are considered to be important components of both systems in supporting a healthy business environment. China is in transition; the rapid market development left behind much-needed regulatory support. Practices are improvised without appropriate legal guidance and may have even been manifested in institutionalized corruptive practices (see examples in Donleavy et al., 2008). As China's market matures, new rules and regulations have been created and some practices that were common at one time are deemed unethical now, which suggests that business ethics in China is improving. The ethical ideals of Confucius are not mutually exclusive from those of Western business ethics, rather, they complement each other (Tao, 1996). The return of the Confucian moral code could positively influence Chinese business ethics, and therefore, the divergence between Chinese and Western business ethics may be temporary.

Chinese Business Ethics Studies

A number of authors have examined Chinese business ethics. Lu (1997) first identified three stages of Chinese business ethics development: 1978 to 1984, 1984 to 1994, and 1994 to 1997. In his 2009 article, he discussed the development in terms of two stages: 1978 to 2001 and 2001 to present. A more recent publication by Berger and Herstein (2014) presented a framework of five developmental stages of Chinese business ethics, which appeared to provide a more comprehensive analysis.

In Berger and Herstein's paper, the first stage covered the progress made from 1949 to 1978. This stage was signified by the transition from a largely household-based economy to a socialist economy. Communist ideology was implemented to support a centrally planned economic system. Amidst the most disastrous policies of the time, the traditional business goal of profitability was abolished, and the closest thing to a concept of business ethics was the pledge to the Communist Party. The second stage covered the initial opening up of the country to the outside world, from 1978 to 1982. This period saw two important policy changes (see Table 4.1): opening up to the world and returning collective farms back to households and townships for the purposes of reducing government control and diversifying the economy. Business ethics started to emerge as a field of academic research, and the government started campaigning for public morality. Business ethics was not well defined, but businesses started to establish moral rules and norms for a "good worker" (Lu, 1997).

The third stage was from 1982 to 1994. Not only had economic reform been deepened and expanded to the countryside but also it included economic activities in towns and cities. A series of reform policies was issued with the aim of building a socialist market economic system. The field of business ethics was more extensively examined by Chinese and foreign scholars from multidisciplinary fields in this period, compared to the early stage. The research agenda not only reflected the government campaign on public morality but also included topics provoked by issues related to economic regulations, unfairness in social distributions, etc. (Berger & Herstein, 2014; Lu, 1997).

The next stage was characterized by a new wave of reform policies to privatize and restructure SOEs, the backbone of the socialist economy. From 1994 to 2001, China experienced rapid decentralization and privatization of SOEs and a significant growth of private firms. SOEs and private firms were in direct competition with each other and with foreign firms for the first time. Differences in the understanding of ethical business conduct – or lack thereof – became apparent. Underneath a surge in wealth generation, issues of mistreatment of migrant workers in sectors such as construction, mining, and manufacturing revealed a miserable picture of basic human rights violations (Ip, 2009b). Business ethics-related discussions entered the center stage, and company laws were introduced, one of them being to protect the rights of employees, including migrant workers (Berger & Herstein, 2014; Chan, 2001).

The fifth stage covered the period from 2001 to 2014. During this time, China joined the WTO, and the need became urgent for Chinese organizations not only to understand but also to comply with WTO regulations and requirements. At this time, the negative consequences of economic development on China's environment emerged (Economy, 2005). Product safety issues tarnished China's global image (Li, 2005; Liu, 2007). China introduced corporate social responsibility-related policies to require companies to look beyond profit making and stockholder values (Berger & Herstein, 2014). The Chinese government intensified its campaign against corruption.

A few important observations should be noted. First, the initial transition was primarily profit driven, and a series of socially undesirable consequences have emerged, such as a lack of business integrity, distrust in corporations and government agencies, and social discontent and unrest (Ip, 2009b). Second, China's ethical business culture is rooted in complex historical and current events. China has experienced drastic economic and structural changes, but legal and regulatory systems have lagged behind, leaving fertile ground for unethical behaviors, compounded by feeble and ineffective enforcement from improperly trained and/or corrupt party officials. Third, the early transition was initiated without moral guidance. Old virtues and norms were deemed to be irrelevant and abandoned, and new ones were yet to be established (Ip, 2009b), which created a void in the guiding principles of Chinese business ethics. These are the fundamental reasons for today's institutionalized corruption in China.

THE ROLE OF CHINESE GOVERNMENT AND THE REGULATORY ENVIRONMENT

Business organizations compete not only for resources and customers but also for political influence and legitimacy (DiMaggio & Powell, 1983). Hence, organizations should be concerned about issues such as safety, quality, human rights, and environmental sustainability; but most importantly, they need to comply with governmental regulations. This is especially important because China remains an autocratic country under the leadership of one party. China's economic reform is a government-driven initiative; the government has been, and will continue to play, a significant role in governing and regulating the market.

Establishing an ethical business environment and maintaining social stability are at the top of the Chinese government agenda. For example, in 2001 the central government passed the State Council's Decision Concerning Correcting and Regulating the Order of Market Economy (Ju, 2005) to promote awareness of business ethics and corporate social responsibilities. In 2005, the 18th session of the Standing Committee of the Tenth National People's Congress of the People's Republic of China amended the Company Law of the People's Republic of China. The newly amended law requires businesses to abide by codes of social ethics, business ethics, honesty, and trustworthiness and to fulfill social responsibilities (Ip, 2009b).

Regulatory agencies need to be independent of political influence in order to enforce regulations in a fair and independent manner. It is difficult for China to have regulatory independence because the government still owns the country's strategic assets, such as telecommunications and power companies. Hence, the government can exert influence on the design of policies and regulations in the favor of state companies. The state agencies that control major government investments are designed to uphold the party's strategy and vision through the country's strategic assets. The country's regulatory agencies are part of the governmental structure, hence they are constrained by the country's broader political agenda (Pearson, 2005). Nonetheless, evidence exists that China is working toward a rational legal system that can effectively govern market activities. It is evident by a broad-based institutional reform that will decrease personal decision-making power by following procedural and official processes (Berger & Herstein, 2014). Recently, large firms have begun to comply with the rules and regulations. It is the hope that medium and small firms will follow suit in the not too distant future.

THE DEVELOPMENT OF BUSINESS ETHICS AT THE FIRM LEVEL

Ethics Policies and Practices of Chinese Firms

Research has shown that the organizational work climate affects the behavior of employees. The ethical climate of the organization reflects shared perceptions of how ethical issues should be addressed and dealt with in the organization (Deshpande et al., 2011). An ethical organizational culture supported by a code of ethics can help create a positive influence and enhance employees' ethical behaviors (Stevens, 2008).

The development of ethics policies and practices in China at the firm level is uneven. Haier and Lenovo are examples of large successful Chinese companies that have realized the need to develop a corporate ideology and culture. These companies stress the development of ethical conduct as part of their business and human resource practices. But others, especially the majority of smaller and newly established companies, still think survival is the priority. They still believe it is justifiable to participate in unethical business conduct if it leads to achieving profit targets, while ignoring the importance of ethical business policies (Lu, 2009). Ethical policies in these companies are either weak or nonexistent. For Chinese companies, even when there is a well-designed ethical policy, ethical decision-making is still subject to the influence of guanxi, position power, and government. It is difficult for Chinese people to make business decisions without considering these three factors.

In a study on ethics codes for enterprises in Chinese cultural society, Chang (2012) found that in order to develop effective codes of ethics in China, companies need to consider three components: general moral imperatives, professional responsibilities, and scenarios relevant to ethical dilemmas. General moral imperatives reference Chinese culture and Confucian traditions of moral standards, plus newly developed imperatives of a market economy, such as intellectual property rights and confidentiality. Professional responsibilities include industry-specific and profession-specific skills, abilities, and regulations, and company leadership imperatives. Discussion using hypothetical scenarios, in which employees can have an open discussion on how to navigate the pressures of guanxi, authority, and organization-specific situations, has been found to be an effective strategy to develop ethical behaviors in employees (Tjosvold et al., 2009).

The working culture in many Chinese firms can be characterized as collective, centralized, and risk-avoiding. Employees are accustomed to doing what they are told to do and to avoid taking responsibility (Fan & Zigang, 2005). When there are neither rules nor positive role models, the risk of employees acting unethically or following negative role models is relatively high (Singhapakdi & Vitell, 1991). However, there is a willingness to do the right thing, and China has been moving toward a more ethical business environment (Snell & Tseng, 2003), but the challenges remain significant.

The Role of Leadership and Managerial Culture

Successful managers can often serve as role models for peers and subordinates, thereby influencing the ethical climate of the organization. Organization leadership plays an important role in building and sustaining an ethical culture that supports continual discussion and teaches business ethics. Researchers have shown that ethical managers are often successful managers in the long run (Deshpande et al., 2011).

Traditional Chinese managerial culture can be characterized as people-centered relationship building, morality-centered organizational behavior, and harmony-driven operation (Pun et al., 2000). People-centered relationship building can be explained by guanxi. Managers build relationships with peers, superiors, and followers. These relationships are important in a relation-based society where management needs to model and show benevolence toward employees, who in turn will show loyalty. Morality-centered organizational behavior is supported by the Confucian idea of the individual becoming a righteous person first and then being rewarded with an increasing amount of respect and autonomy (Watt, 1999). Hence, leaders often provide general guidelines and goals to allow followers considerable leeway for task completion, because employees operating according to this morality principle would do more than simply follow the job requirements. The pursuit of harmony is influenced by the desire to maintain guanxi and a concern to save (each other's) face. Essentially, it suggests that managers need to be reasonable and willing to compromise in order to maintain harmony (Pun et al., 2000). However, during the centrally planned economic system, a manager's responsibility was to implement state plans, and they had very little leeway or decision-making power themselves. As a result, senior managers couldn't or would not delegate; middle or lower-level managers had to passively seek approvals from higher authority (Cooke, 2012).

As the next generation of Chinese managers move into key management positions, Chinese managerial culture might evolve, since the younger generation appears to be more independent, individualistic, and risk-taking in pursuit of profit (Cooke, 2012). Though it is difficult to predict what Chinese management culture will become, the influence of the relation-based culture will most likely prevail. As some researchers have suggested, positive supervisor–subordinate relationships generate higher employee job satisfaction and organization engagement (Wang, 2008), and supervisory support can engender trust among managers and subordinates (Zhang et al., 2008). The desire to maintain good guanxi will continue to influence Chinese managerial culture (Hui et al., 2008).

Ethics Training and Culture Change Efforts

When China amended its Company Law to require companies to abide by codes of social ethics, business ethics, honesty, and trustworthiness and to fulfill social responsibilities, a growing number of Chinese companies (mostly large and well established) started to publish CSR reports on their websites. Companies such as Haier Group, Shanghai Yougle, Triangle Group, and Hong Dou Group were promoted as excellent CSR cases (Ip, 2009b). Yet, little detail was given in the publications on how they achieved that status and what practices could be adopted by others.

Efforts to improve business ethics and scientific integrity in China have been reported in the last four years; more than eight million undergraduate and graduate students have attended lectures on scientific integrity. This reflected a growing emphasis on academic integrity in China (Chen & Macfarlane, 2016). However, the training remains mostly an academic exercise. China initiated engineering ethics training as early as the 1980s, and the training was conducted using two courses: a course on Marxist theory and a course on ideology and morality. Codes of engineering ethics and appropriate ethical behaviors were not included (Cao, 2003). Focusing on general moral development and reinforcing ideological preparations alone may not be sufficient in building an ethical business culture; future efforts need to include topics like ethical business conducts, codes of ethics, and professionalism.

IMPLICATIONS FOR CHINESE COMPANIES

Using codes of ethics to guide employees' ethical behavior is a widely accepted practice in rule-based Western cultures. Codes of ethics are used to define with clarity a range of behaviors that are unacceptable and can assist in misconduct prevention and in developing the ethical judgment of employees (McKinney & Moore, 2008). Creating a code of ethics, appointing ethics officers, establishing systematic monitoring, and providing training programs are common strategies to build and sustain ethical organizational cultures in order to develop and manage the ethical behavior of employees.

To make it effective, a code of ethics needs to reflect the social context of a specific time and place (Rhodes, 1986). The ethical components of Confucianism could serve as fundamental guidelines to meet the challenge of current market reform in China (Lu, 2009). However, a newly developed code of business ethics must reflect the significant social changes that China has experienced. It will have to maintain specifically Chinese thought and practice, while being sufficiently clear to be understood by global business partners.

The code of ethics needs to be explicit on ethical issues pertaining to the influence of guanxi and how employees might withstand the pressure of social hierarchy. It should embrace a hierarchical organization structure in a high power distance culture. Procedures or mechanisms must be in place to facilitate open and honest ethical discussion between managers and subordinates and prevent possible repercussions. Additionally, organizations must explicitly communicate what to do when encountering ethical concerns to help save face and maintain harmony in the workplace. These are complicated and difficult issues but are important factors to consider when addressing the design and implementation of business ethics-related processes and procedures.

In addition to developing codes of ethics, appointing ethics officers, and establishing systematic processes and procedures that support ethical business practices, companies also need to develop mandatory training and compliance programs. Mandatory training and compliance programs can help curtail unethical behaviors. These programs are the responsibility of human resource professionals (Buller & McEvoy, 1999). Human resource leaders can initiate a rigorous recruiting and selection process to disqualify candidates who falsify their documents and eliminate them from consideration by using interview techniques to identify potential employees who are willing to cut corners when under stress. Once employees are hired, human resource professionals can provide training programs to develop and sustain ethical capabilities and communicate company ethical policies (Hulpke & Lau, 2008).

IMPLICATIONS FOR FOREIGN COMPANIES

Western companies operating in the international space are often subject to the same ethical standards and regulatory controls as their home-country counterparts. This means that differences in interpretation of ethical and regulatory standards may present challenges for foreign companies when doing business in China. For example, after Google entered the Chinese market, concerns about its inability to protect users' privacy according to US standards forced it to back out of China. It is important for foreign firms to learn about these differences and determine where to draw the line. How to interpret commonly (globally) accepted moral rules and principles in the Chinese context is a challenge many foreign companies have to face when doing business in China. As long as China is under the leadership of the Communist Party, economic development will always be guided by government policies and influenced by regulatory agencies. Working out a China-specific strategy that takes into consideration

Chinese government policies, regulatory control, guanxi networks, and pervasive corruption may be an important first step.

When working with Chinese companies, one also needs to investigate the history of the company in order to decipher its decision-making agenda. Chinese business leaders may be subject to the influence of political pressure and the guanxi network in addition to the interests of the company. They have to balance these influences in making business decisions. Making an effort to understand the dilemmas Chinese managers face in decision-making may improve cross-cultural understanding and develop tolerance for ambiguity and uncertainty.

To have a successful operation in China, one may need to cultivate political connections, to build guanxi networks, and to become an insider in a culture that favors in-group members. Foreign firms also need to develop strategies to counter environmental concerns, discrimination, and human rights issues. It is therefore prudent to ask a Chinese company to clarify company policies and to share ethics policies or code of conduct prior to making important investment decisions.

REFERENCES

Ang, S. H., & Leong, S. M. (2000). Out of the mouths of babes: Business ethics and youths in Asia. *Journal of Business Ethics*, 28, 129–144.

Ardichvili, A., Jondle, D., & Kowske, B. (2010). Dimensions of ethical business cultures: Comparing data from 13 countries of Europe, Asia, and the Americas. *Human Resource Development International*, 13(3), 299–315.

Ardichvili, A., Jondle, D., Kowske, B., Cornachione, E., Li, J., & Thakadipuram, T. (2012). Ethical cultures in large business organizations in Brazil, Russia, India, and China. *Journal of Business Ethics*, 105, 415–428.

Armstrong, R. (1993). A comparison of the perceptions of Hong Kong and Chinese and Australian international marketing managers regarding ethical problems. *Asia-Australia Marketing Journal*, 1, 55–60.

Au, A. K. M., & Wong, D. S. N. (2000). The impact of guanxi on the ethical decision-making process of auditors – an exploratory study on Chinese CPAs in Hong Kong. *Journal of Business Ethics*, 28, 87–93.

Berger, R., & Herstein, R. (2014). The evolution of Chinese business ethics. *Management Research Review*, 37(9), 778–790.

Brand V., & Slater, A. (2003). Using a qualitative approach to gain insights into the business ethics experiences of Australian managers in China. *Journal of Business Ethics*, 45, 167–182.

Buller, P., & McEvoy, G. (1999). Creating and sustaining ethical capability in the multinational corporation. In R. Schuler and S. Jackson (Eds.), *Strategic human resource management* (pp. 326–343). Oxford: Blackwell.

Cao, Y. (2003). Behind the rising meritocracy: Market, politics, and cultural change in urban China. *Social Science Research*, 33, 435–463.

Chan, A. (2001). *China's workers under assault: The exploitation of labor in a globalizing world.* Armonk, NY: M. E. Sharpe.

Chan, A. K. K., Ip, P. K., & Lam, K. C. J. (2009). Business ethics in greater China: An introduction. *Journal of Business Ethics*, 88, 1–9.

Chang, C. L. (2012). How to build an appropriate information ethics code for enterprises in Chinese cultural society. *Computer in Human Behavior*, 28, 420–433.

Chen, C. C., Chen, X. P., & Huang, S. S. (2013). Guanxi and social network research: Review and future directions. *Management and Organization Review*, 9(1), 167–207.

Chen, C. C., Chen, Y, R., & Xin, K. (2004). Guanxi practices and trust in management: A procedural justice perspective. *Organization Science*, 15(2), 200–209.

Chen, S., & Macfarlane, B. (2016). Academic integrity in China. In T. Bretag (Ed.), *Handbook of academic integrity* (pp. 99–105). Singapore: Springer Science+Business Media.

Cooke, F. L. (2012). *Human resource management in China: New trends and practices.* New York: Routledge.

Deshpande, S. P., Joseph, J., & Shu, X. (2011). Ethical climate and managerial success in China. *Journal of Business Ethics*, 99, 527–534.

DiMaggio, P., & Powell, W. (1983). The iron cage revisited: Institutional isomorphism and collective rationality in organizational fields. *American Sociological Review*, 48(2), 147–160.

Ding, D. Z., Goodall, K., & Warner, M. (2000). The end of the "iron rice-bowl": Whither Chinese human resource management? *International Journal of Human Resource Management*, 11(2), 217–236.

Donleavy, D., Lam, J. K. C., & Ho, S. S. M. (2008). Does East meet West in business ethics? *Journal of Business Ethics*, 79(1–2), 1–8.

Economy, E. (2005). *The river runs black: The environmental challenges to China's future.* Ithaca, NY: Cornell University Press.

Ekici, A., & Onsel, S. (2013). How ethical behavior of firms is influenced by the legal and political environments: A Bayesian causal map analysis based on stages of development. *Journal of Business Ethics*, 115(2), 271–290.

Fan, Y. (2000). A classification of Chinese culture. *Cross Cultural Management: An International Journal*, 7(2), 3–10.

Fan, P., & Zigang, Z. (2005). Cross-cultural challenges when doing business in China. *Singapore Management Review*, 26(1), 81–90.

Gold, T., Guthrie, D., & Wank D. (2002). An introduction to the study of guanxi. In T. Gold, D. Guthrie, & D. Wank (Eds.), *Social connections in China: Institutions, culture, and the changing nature of guanxi* (pp. 3–20). New York: Cambridge University Press.

Guthrie, D. (2012). *China and globalization: The social, economic and political transformation of Chinese society*. New York: Routledge.

Hofstede, G. (1980). *Culture's consequences: International differences in work-related values*. Newbury Park, CA: Sage.

Hofstede Centre (2015). What about China? Retrieved from geert-hofstede.com/china.html.

Hui, C., Law, K. S., Chen, Y. F., & Tjosvold, D. (2008). The role of co-operation and competition on leader-member exchange and extra-role performance in China. *Asia Pacific Journal of Human Resource*, 46(2), 133–152.

Hulpke, J., & Lau, D. (2008). Business ethics in China: A human resource management issue? *Chinese Economy*, 41(3), 58–67.

Ip, P. K. (2009a). Is Confucianism good for business ethics in China? *Journal of Business Ethics*, 88, 463–476.

Ip, P. K. (2009b). The challenge of development a business ethics in China. *Journal of Business Ethics*, 88, 211–224.

Jiang, X., Chen, C. C., & Shi, K. (2011). Favor in exchange for trust? The role of subordinates' attribution of supervisory favors. *Asia Pacific Journal of Management*, 30, 513–536.

Ju, J. (2005). *The historical development of corporate ethics in today's China*. Nanking, China: Jiangsu People's Press.

Lam, K. J. (2006). Confucian and Christian ethics about the market economy. In X. Lu & G. Enderle (Eds.), *Development business ethics in China* (pp. 44–51). New York: Palgrave Macmillan.

Langenberg, E. A. (2013). Chinese guanxi and business ethics. In Lutege, C. (Ed.), *Handbook of the philosophical foundations of business ethics* (pp. 955–981). Netherlands: Springer.

Li, Z. (2005). Lack of corporate social responsibility behind recent China accidents. Retrieved from www.worldwatch.org/lack-corporate-social-responsibility- behind-recent-china-accidents

Li, J., & Madsen, J. (2009). Chinese workers' work ethic in reformed state owned enterprises: Implications for HRD. *Human Resource Development International*, 12(2), 171–188.

Li, J., & Madsen, J. (2011). Business ethics and workplace guanxi in Chinese SOEs: A qualitative study. *Journal of Chinese Human Resource Management*, 2(2), 83–99.

Lim, C., & Lay, C. S. (2003). Confucianism and the Protestant work ethic. *Asia Europe Journal*, 1(3), 321–322.

Liu, M. (2007, July 16). Unsafe at any speed: The downside of China's manufacturing boom: Deadly goods wreaking havoc at home and abroad. *Newsweek*. Retrieved from https://www.highbeam.com/doc/1G1-166272929.html

Lovett, S., Simmons, L. C., & Kali, R. (1999). Guanxi versus the market: Ethics and efficiency. *Journal of International Business Studies*, 30(2), 231–247.

Lu, X. (1997). Business ethics in China. *Journal of Business Ethics*, 16, 1509–1518.

Lu, X. (2009). A Chinese perspective: Business ethics in China now and in the future. *Journal of Business Ethics*, 86, 451–461.

Maddison, A. (1998). *Chinese economic performance in the long run*. Paris: OECD.

McKinney, J. A., & Moore, C. W. (2008). International bribery: Does a written code of ethics make a difference in perceptions of business professionals. *Journal of Business Ethics*, 79, 103–111.

Naughton, B. (2007). *The Chinese economy: Transitions and growth*. Cambridge, MA: MIT Press.

Nolan, T., & Ash, R. F. (1995). China's economy on the eve of reform. *China Quarterly*, 144, 980–998.

Organization for Economic Co-operation and Development. (2005). OECD Economic Surveys: China. Retrieved from http://homepage.ntu.edu.tw/~lbh/ref/OECD/42.pdf

Park, S. H., & Luo, Y. (2001). Guanxi and organizational dynamics: Organizational networking in Chinese firms. *Strategic Management Journal*, 22(5), 455–477.

Pearson, M. M. (2005). The business of governing business in China: Institutions and norms of the emerging regulatory state. *World Politics*, 57(2), 296–322.

Pun, K. Chin, K., & Lau, H. (2000). A review of the Chinese culture influences on Chinese enterprise management. *International Journal of Management Review*, 2(4), 325–338.

Ralston, D. A., Gustafson, D. J., Cheung, F. M, and Terpstra, R. H. (1993). Differences in managerial values: A study of U.S., Hong Kong and PRC managers. *Journal of International Business Studies*, 24(2), 249–275.

Redfern, K., & Crawford, J. (2004). An empirical investigation of the ethics position questionnaire in the People's Republic of China. *Journal of Business Ethics*, 50, 199–210.

Rhodes, M. L. (1986). *Ethical dilemmas in social work practice.* Milwaukee, WI: Family Service America.

Scholtens, B., & Dam, L. (2007). Cultural values and international differences in business ethics. *Journal of Business Ethics*, 75(3), 273–284.

Shafer, W. E., Fukukawa, K., & Lee, G. M. (2007). Values and perceived importance of ethics and social responsibility: The U.S. versus China. *Journal of Business Ethics*, 70, 265–284.

Sheng, S., Zhou, K. Z., & Li, J. J. (2011). The effects of business and political ties on firm performance: Evidence from China. *Journal of Marketing*, 75(1), 1–15.

Shi, X., & Wang, J. (2011). Cultural distance between China and US across GLOBE model and Hofstede model. *International Business and Management*, 2(1), 11–17.

Singhapakdi, A., & Vitell, S. J. (1991). Analyzing the ethical decision making of sales professionals. *Journal of Personal Selling and Sales Management*, 11, 1–12.

Snell, R., & Tseng, C. S. (2003). Images of the virtuous employee in China's transitional economy. *Asia Pacific Journal of Management*, 20(3), 307–326.

Song, S. R., & Gale, A. (2007). The work values of Chinese project managers. *Cross Cultural Management: An International Journal*, 14(3), 217–228.

Stevens, B. (2008). Corporate ethical codes: Effective instruments for influencing behavior. *Journal of Business Ethics*, 78, 601–609.

Su, C., Sirgy, M. J., & Littlefield, J. E. (2003). Is guanxi orientation bad, ethically speaking? A study of Chinese enterprises. *Journal of Business Ethics*, 44, 303–312.

Tao, J. (1996). The moral foundation of welfare in Chinese society: Between virtues and rights. In G. K. Becker (Ed.), *Ethics in business and society: Chinese and Western perspectives* (pp. 9–24). Berlin: Springer.

Tjosvold, D., Snell, R., & Su, S. F. (2009). Codes of conduct for open-minded discussion and resolution of ethical issues in China. *Journal of International Business Ethics*, 2(2), 3–20.

Tsui, A. S., & Farh, J. L. (1997). Where guanxi matters: Regional demography and guanxi in the Chinese context. *Work and Occupations*, 24(1), 56–80.

Tsui, J., & Windsor, C. (2001). Some cross-cultural evidence on ethical reasoning. *Journal of Business Ethics*, 31, 143–150.

Tung, R. L., & Verbeke, A. (2010). Beyond Hofstede and GLOBE: Improving the quality of cross-cultural research. *Journal of International Business Studies*, 41(8), 1259–1274.

Wang, Y. (2008). Emotional bonds with supervisor and co-workers: Relationship to organization commitment in China's foreign-invested companies. *International Journal of Human Resource Management*, 19(5), 916–931.

Watt, L. (1999). Managing in the PRC. *Better Management*, 35(December), 24–28.

World Bank (2015). China overview. Retrieved from www.worldbank.org/en/country/china/overview

Yang, K.S. (1993). Chinese social orientation: An integrative analysis. In L. Y. Cheng, F. M. C. Cheung, & C. N. Chen (Eds.), *Psychotherapy for the Chinese: Selected papers from the First International Conference* (pp. 19–56). Hong Kong: The Chinese University of Hong Kong.

Zhang, J., & Keh, H. T. (2010). Interorganizational exchanges in China: Organizational forms and governance mechanisms. *Management and Organization Review*, 6(1), 123–147.

Zhang, A. Y., Tsui, A. S., Song, L. J. Li, C., & Jia, L. (2008). How do I trust thee? The employee-organization relationship, supervisory support, and middle manager trust in the organization. *Human Resource Management*, 47(1), 111–132.

Zhang, Y., & Zhang, Z. (2006). Guanxi and organizational dynamics in China: A link between individual and organizational levels. *Journal of Business Ethics*, 67, 375–392.

5 Business Ethics in South Africa

Deon Rossouw

ABSTRACT

The business ethical culture in South Africa was and is still being shaped by a number of social and political influences that include its colonial history, the legacy of Apartheid, and the election of the first democratic government in 1994, after which President Nelson Mandela's government started the process of redressing the racial imbalances and inequalities that resulted from Apartheid. Since 1994 business ethics has enjoyed considerable corporate attention. One of the main reasons for the prominence of business ethics is the King Reports on Corporate Governance for South Africa that emphasized the importance of an ethical business culture as an essential element of good corporate governance. In this chapter the business ethical culture that was shaped by these influences is unpacked. Research on business ethics in South Africa is highlighted, as well as the ethics management practices that are typically found in South African enterprises. These ethics management practices pose opportunities, but also challenges, to businesspeople and companies who wish to enter the South African market. These opportunities and challenges are unpacked in an attempt to help those who wish to invest in South Africa.

COUNTRY BACKGROUND

South Africa, located at the southern tip of the African continent, has a population of around 52 million people according to the 2011 census. The earliest inhabitants of what is now known as the Republic of South Africa were the San people (also known as the Bushmen). They were followed, and in some cases driven out, by the Khoikhoi people. During the Iron Age, the so-called Bantu people started moving into the northern regions of South Africa and gradually dispersed over the country – ever moving further south (Deegan, 2014, p. 5).

The first Europeans settled in South Africa when the Dutch established a settlement in 1652 in the area that is now known as Cape Town. The purpose of this settlement was to serve as a half-way station for ships from the Dutch East India Company that sailed between Europe and Asia. The strategic position of what was initially called the Cape of Good Hope made it an attractive region for other colonial powers. Consequently, the British later occupied it, only to be reclaimed by the Dutch again, and then taken over by the British again.

The discovery of rich deposits of gold and diamonds in South Africa further heightened the interest of colonial powers in South Africa. The country formally terminated British rule over South Africa when it became the independent Republic of South Africa on 31 May 1961.

As a result of the trade between European colonial powers and Asian countries, a small, but substantial number of Indians and other peoples from Asia were also brought to South Africa, mostly as slaves or indentured labourers. Interracial marriages between local inhabitants, especially the Khoikhoi people with the European settlers, but also with Indians and other Asians, led to the emergence of a new population group still known today as the coloured people.

In more recent history, South Africa became globally infamous for its political dispensation based on the forced segregation of races that was enforced by a white ruling minority. This dispensation, globally known as "Apartheid" (the Afrikaans word for separateness), came to an end when one of the leading anti-Apartheid activists, Nelson Mandela, who was jailed for 27 years for his opposition to the Apartheid regime, was elected as president in the first post-Apartheid election in 1994.

The South African population consists of a variety of ethnic, cultural and language groups. According to the 2011 census, the main population groups are black Africans (79%), whites (9%), coloureds 9% and Indians (2.5%). Amongst the main language groups in the country are Afrikaans, English, Ndebele, Northern Sotho, Sotho, Swazi, Tswana, Tsonga, Venda, Xhoza, and Zulu – and all these 11 main languages enjoy official language status in South Africa.

HISTORICAL FACTORS THAT SHAPED SOCIOECONOMIC SYSTEMS

South Africa's socioeconomic systems were influenced first by colonialism, then by Apartheid, and more recently by the attempts of the post-Apartheid government to redress the imbalances created by Apartheid. Under colonial rule, the economy was deliberately developed in ways that suited the colonial masters. Since the Cape of Good Hope was initially established as a refreshment station for ships that sailed between Europe and Asia, the initial emphasis in economic development was on agriculture. But when rich deposits of copper, gold, diamonds, and other minerals were discovered in South Africa, mining became a major area of economic focus.

When the National Party came into power in the elections of 1948, Apartheid became the official policy and was gradually institutionalized in all spheres of society. The ideal pursued by Apartheid was that the different population groups should co-exist and develop separately. However, since the vast majority of South Africans were disenfranchised under Apartheid, and a minority government consisting only of whites governed the country, Apartheid steered social and economic benefits to the advantage of whites and to the detriment of blacks, coloureds and Indians. This resulted in whites enjoying good public services and easy access to top positions in the economy, whilst the other groups were given poor social services and access to only the lower levels of the economy.

The African National Congress (ANC) came into power in 1994 after South Africa's first democratic elections. The ANC government is a coalition consisting of the ANC as leading party, COSATU (Congress of South African Trade Unions, South Africa's largest trade union), and the SACP (South African Communist Party). Given the legacy of a radically unjust and racially segregated society, the new ANC-led government introduced a wide-ranging set of policy reforms aimed at racial integration, affirmative action and redistribution of wealth via black economic empowerment.

A vast number of laws and regulations have since been introduced by the ANC-led government to give effect to its agenda of socioeconomic reconstruction and development. The corner piece of all these reforms is the Constitution of South Africa that lays the foundation for a democratic, non-racial and equal society. The two most prominent laws aimed at redressing the inequalities of the past are the Employment Equity Act and the Broad-Based Black Economic Empowerment Act – both of which will be discussed in more depth later in this chapter.

BUSINESS CLIMATE

When South Africa is compared with the global community in terms of its dominant cultural values, it appears that the country's value orientation is more closely aligned to that of continental Europe than to the rest of Africa and other parts of the world. West (2012) drew on the cross-cultural studies of business culture conducted previously by Hofstede and also by Trompenaars and Hampden-Turner to compare South African business culture with that of other world regions. Based on these comparisons, he came to the following conclusion:

- South Africa scores low on the *power distance* dimension, which is an indication of low tolerance for social inequality.
- It also scores low on the *masculinity–femininity* scale, which indicates that relationships and care are prioritized over achievement and success.
- South Africans tend to favour individualism over collectivism on the *individualism–collectivism* scale.

The latter finding by West is particularly surprising, as African communities are generally seen as more collectivist than, at least, Western European and North American societies. This more collectivist or communitarian approach is often referred to as the African philosophy of *Ubuntu*.

Ntibagirirwa (2014) contends that despite the obvious and rich variety in African culture, there is a "common metaphysical backbone" that unites African thinking and doing (p. 111). The term *Ubuntu*, which is widely used in South(ern) Africa, captures this notion of an African worldview that is commonly held by Africans across the region.

The core of the Ubuntu worldview revolves around the idea that there is an intimate and reciprocal relationship between the individual person and the community to which that person belongs. A popular way of expressing this belief is through the expression: "a person is a person through persons" (cf. Ramose, 2003). Ramose, a leading thinker on African philosophy, describes the notion of Ubuntu: "[T]o be a human being is to affirm one's humanity by recognizing the humanity of others and, on that basis, establish humane relations with them. *Ubuntu*, understood as being human (humanness); a human, respectful and polite attitude towards others" (p. 231).

There are opposing views as to whether the concept of Ubuntu is compatible with capitalism. West (2012) demonstrated through a literature survey that while some proponents of Ubuntu regard capitalism and Ubuntu as mutually exclusive, others consider the two concepts as compatible. Ubuntu, from the latter perspective, is seen as a corrective to the extreme self-centeredness of rational economic man that is often associated with capitalism.

Whilst the term "Ubuntu" is widely used in South Africa, there is no clear evidence of its impact on business culture in South Africa. There are, however, six aspects of the current socioeconomic dispensation that are widely recognized as having an important bearing on the business climate and opportunities in South Africa, viz.

education, corruption, HIV AIDS, labour unions, unemployment and an inclusive corporate governance approach (cf. Irwin, 2011).

Education

Although South Africa's spending on education is one of the highest government expense items (20% of the 2014/2015 annual budget), primary and secondary education in South Africa is not in good shape. The current situation of education in schools can be blamed on many factors – some going as far back as the Apartheid system and others that have to do with shortfalls in the way that primary and secondary education is currently managed. The World Economic Forum's *Global Competitiveness Report 2014–2015* ranked the quality of the education systems in South Africa in 140th position out of the 144 countries that were surveyed. The position of higher education, however, is very different. South Africa has 25 public universities and about an equal number of private universities. Most of the private universities are satellites of European and North American universities. In the same *Global Competitiveness Report 2014–2015*, the quality of management education was ranked 24th out of the 144 countries.

Corruption

South Africa's ranking on the Transparency International's *Corruption Perception Index* showed a consistent decline over the period 2004–2014. The best ranking that South Africa achieved over the period was when it was ranked in 43rd position (out of 175 countries) on the list of least corrupt countries. The worst ranking achieved over the same period was in 2013 when it was ranked in 72nd position (out of 177). The average ranking over the period 2004–2014 was in 56th position of the least corrupt countries.

The above mentioned perception of a steady increase in corruption is corroborated by the findings of Transparency International's *Global Corruption Barometer 2013*, which indicated that South African citizens believed that corruption in the country is on the increase. The police service is regarded as the most corrupt public service department.

HIV AIDS

South Africa is one of the countries in the world that is worst affected by the HIV pandemic. In a study published in 2014 by the Human Science Research Council (Shisana et al., 2014), it was reported that 12.2 percent of the South African population is infected by the HIV virus, which makes South Africa the country with the highest HIV incidence in the world. South Africa's situation regarding HIV infections and AIDS-related deaths was severely aggravated by a denial of the link between HIV and immune system failure by South Africa's second democratic government under the presidency of Thabo Mbeki. This denialist stance on the link between HIV and AIDS slowed down the provision of anti-retroviral treatment to HIV-positive persons. This situation was, however, turned around under the third democratic government, which led to a substantial improvement in the provision of anti-retroviral treatment to HIV-positive persons.

Labour Unions

South Africa is a highly unionized country. There are two main reasons why labour unions enjoy such high prominence. The first explanation goes back to the Apartheid era, when most political structures that were opposed to Apartheid were banned. Labour unions consequently became a legitimate structure for mobilizing opposition to the Apartheid regime. It is therefore unsurprising that labour unions became highly politicized and that they played a significant role in the liberation struggle in South Africa.

The high visibility and politicized nature of labour unions continued in the post-Apartheid dispensation when COSATU joined the ANC and SACP to form a tripartite alliance that became the first democratic government in 1994 and that has governed South Africa since then. COSATU's role as part of the ANC-led government has given it an extraordinary influence in determining labour standards in the country. Its role as part of the governing alliance has, however, severely politicized labour union activity, as non-COSATU-aligned labour unions almost by default find themselves not only in opposition to COSATU but also in opposition to the governing political alliance.

Unemployment

South Africa's unemployment rate has been hovering around 25 percent for the last decade. The government launched a number of initiatives in recent years to counter this stubbornly high rate of unemployment, but without any significant success. The high unemployment rate is exacerbated by the poorly performing primary and secondary educational system, which produces people who do not always have the skills required, specifically in a sophisticated service economy. Also, South Africa's liberal immigration policy with regard to its African neighbours has led to a significant influx of immigrants from other African countries that has increased the competition in the job market for local job seekers (cf. Irwin, 2011, p. 7).

Inclusive Corporate Governance Approach

South Africa produced a series of corporate governance reports in the post-Apartheid dispensation. In 1992, the private sector and professional associations involved in corporate governance voluntarily formed the King Committee on Corporate Governance for South Africa (chaired by a former judge of the supreme court, Mervyn King). The committee published its first report, King I Report, in 1994. This was followed by the King II Report in 2002, and the King III Report in 2009. These reports, consisting of voluntary best practice corporate governance recommendations, became highly influential in South Africa, especially after the Johannesburg Stock Exchange (JSE) Securities Exchange made adherence to the recommendations of the King Reports a mandatory reporting requirement for listed companies.

The first King Report (1994) adopted an inclusive corporate governance approach that was not only followed but also reinforced in the second (2002) and third (2009) King Reports. According to this inclusive corporate governance approach, companies should be governed in a manner that takes due consideration of the interests of their stakeholders. This approach to the governance and management of companies has triggered extensive stakeholder engagement practices.

RESEARCH ON ORGANIZATIONAL ETHICS

The first comprehensive survey on business ethics in South Africa was conducted in 1996 (Rossouw, 1997). Besides covering business ethics as an academic field, the survey also focused on ethics in the private sector. The survey found that the most important business ethical issues at the time were (a) building an ethical business culture, (b) taking affirmative action, (c) creating a sound work ethic, (d) developing information security and (e) showing responsibility of business to society.

The survey also looked at the prevalence of codes of ethics and reported that an earlier study of listed companies (cf. Young, 1995) revealed that only 9 out of the 100 top companies included in the *Sunday Times Top 100 Survey* had a code of ethics in the strict sense of the word. A further 32 companies had some reference to ethics in governance-related documents. The same survey also reported that codes of ethics were perceived as having very little impact on the actual behaviour of companies (Young, 1995, p. 121).

The single factor that had the biggest impact on the development of organizational ethics in South Africa was the publication of the three King Reports on governance. All three King Reports provided recommendations on the governance of ethics, but increasingly so. Whilst there was only a short chapter on ethics right at the end of the King I Report, the King III Report started with a substantial chapter on ethics. Although the King Reports are not mandatory, but rather recommended principles of good governance, the Johannesburg

Securities Exchange requires listed companies to report against the governance principles of the King Reports on a comply (apply) or explain basis.

In a series of regular surveys on the state of ethics in listed companies conducted by the Ethics Institute of South Africa, it is quite clear that the King Reports on corporate governance had a marked effect on organizational ethics.

The first survey of business ethics was published in 2002 under the title, *Corporate Ethics Indicator: Report on the Business Ethics South Africa Survey* (Landman et al., 2002). It was followed by a second survey titled, *The South African Corporate Ethics Indicator 2009* (Punt et al., 2009). A third survey was titled, *The South African Business Ethics Survey 2013* (Groenewald et al., 2013). For the latter survey, telephonic interviews were conducted with 4,099 participants from a sample of companies listed in the JSE Securities Exchange in Johannesburg. The survey found relatively high levels of awareness of ethics management elements amongst participants, as illustrated by the following findings:

- 96% of participants were aware that their company has a code of ethics.
- 83% of participants were aware that their company has a hotline for reporting malpractices.
- 72% of participants were aware that there was someone (or a functional division) in their company that is responsible for managing ethics in the organization.
- 66% of participants were aware that their company offers ethics training.

The 2013 *South African Business Ethics Survey* also looked at the effectiveness of the same ethics management elements mentioned previously and found that perceptions of effectiveness of these elements were also quite high. For example, 90 percent of participants indicated that they found their companies' code of ethics useful in guiding their decisions and conduct and 82 percent of participants who went through ethics training found it effective. The one exception in this regard is the perception about effectiveness of the hotline.

Whereas 83 percent of participants were aware of the hotline facility, only 68 percent of participants regarded the efforts to raise awareness of the hotline as effective.

The *South African Business Ethics Survey 2013* also made an assessment of the general ethical culture that prevails in the companies that participated in the survey. A significant finding in this regard is that despite generally high levels of awareness and effectiveness of ethics management elements in organizations, the perceptions of the general ethical culture of organizations were reported at significantly lower levels. Furthermore, perceptions regarding the general ethical culture also showed no significant movement when compared to the *South African Corporate Ethics Indicator 2009* survey.

When the three surveys are compared, it is clear that in the period 2002 to 2013 there was a very distinct increase in the awareness of ethics management elements in the private sector, as well as an increase in the perceived effectiveness of these ethics management interventions. The worrying aspect, however, is that these positive elements are not complemented by an increase in perceptions of the general ethical culture in companies. This probably suggests that many South African companies take a strong compliance approach to managing ethics, rather than focusing on efforts to internalize company values and standards in their employees.

The London-based Institute of Business Ethics (IBE) also conducted a study on business ethics in South Africa in 2011 and published it under the title, *Doing Business in South Africa: An Overview of Ethical Aspects* (Irwin, 2011). The report focused both on the business environment in South Africa and on the institutionalization of business ethics. However, for its coverage of the institutionalization of business ethics it relied entirely on the survey that the Ethics Institute of South Africa conducted in 2009, viz. *The South African Corporate Ethics Indicator 2009* (as previously mentioned). The most significant contribution of the IBE report is its identification of the key challenges facing businesses in South Africa. In this regard they identified the following four challenges: (a) the lack of willingness

amongst employees to make use of ethics hotlines; (b) the prevalence of conflicts of interest in both the private and the public sector; (c) the difficulties associated with reaching the affirmative action
and black economic empowerment targets set by the South African
government; and (d) the cost and complexities caused by the high
prevalence of HIV/AIDS in the labour force (Irwin, 2011).

The World Economic Forum's *Global Competitiveness Report
2014–2015* (Schwab, 2015) also provides a useful global comparative
perspective on business ethics in South Africa. While South Africa
is rated as the top country in the world for its (a) strength of auditing and reporting standards, (b) the efficacy of corporate boards, and
(c) regulation of securities exchanges, it is rated in the 37th position
out of 144 countries for the ethical behaviour of firms.

THE ROLE OF GOVERNMENT AND THE REGULATORY ENVIRONMENT

Business, like just about everything else in South Africa, is still
affected by the legacy of Apartheid. Consequently, the South African
government is actively involved in the economy in an attempt to
redress inequalities in income, ownership, job opportunities, and
education caused by the Apartheid system.

Amongst several laws aimed at redressing injustices inflicted
by the Apartheid system, the two laws that stand out are the
Employment Equity Act (Act 55 of 1998) and the Broad-Based Black
Economic Empowerment Act. The purpose of the Employment
Equity Act (Act 55 of 1998) is "to achieve equity in the workplace, by
(a) promoting equal opportunity and fair treatment in employment
through the elimination of unfair discrimination; and (b) implementing affirmative action measures to redress the disadvantages in
employment experienced by designated groups, to ensure their equi-
table representation in all occupational categories and levels in the
workforce" (Employment Equity Act, 1998: chapter 1, section 2).

The Employment Equity Act applies to all organs of the state
and municipalities, as well as to businesses above a certain size or

income. Businesses that fall within the scope of the Employment Equity Act are, amongst others things, required to set numerical goals and timetables for affirmative action and to submit these to government on a regular basis. They are also required to report their progress against the said affirmative action targets. Non-compliance with targets can result in an order of compliance being issued, or in financial penalties against the non-compliant company.

The objectives of the Broad-Based Black Economic Empowerment Act (Act 53 of 2003) include the following: "promoting economic transformation in order to enable meaningful participation of black people in the economy and achieving a substantial change in the racial composition of ownership and management structures and in the skilled occupations of existing and new enterprises" (section 2). The Black Economic Empowerment Act is designed to strengthen black ownership and control in enterprises and to enhance black human resource development and affirmative action in companies. Furthermore, it uses the mechanism of preferential procurement to ensure greater participation of black firms in the economy.

Companies that exceed defined levels of annual income have to complete Black Economic Empowerment (BEE) scorecards on an annual basis. The scores achieved on these BEE scorecards play a role in the awarding of licenses as well as in the evaluation of tenders for government and public entity contracts. BEE scores also affect the supply chain decisions of private enterprises, as the BEE scores of suppliers ultimately have an impact on the BEE scores of the procuring companies.

When it comes to the regulation of ethics in South Africa, there are two important developments that had a very distinct impact on the management of ethics, viz. the King Reports on corporate governance for South Africa and the recently introduced Companies Act.

Although the three King Reports that were released thus far (in 1994, 2002 and 2009) are voluntary reports that merely provide companies with best practice recommendations, they nevertheless had a significant influence on regulation and legislation. Over time, some of the best practice recommendations of the King Reports found their way into various legislative reforms and into regulations. The best example of this development is the JSE Securities Exchange that requires companies to annually report on their adherence to the recommendations of the King Report. Since the latest version of the King Reports (2009) contains principles that relate explicitly to the governance of companies' social and ethics performance, all companies listed on the JSE Securities Exchange have to report annually, amongst other things, on their compliance in this regard. The third King Report, for example, recommends in principle 1.2 that "the board should ensure that the company is seen to be a responsible corporate citizen" and also in principle 1.3 that "the board should ensure that the company's ethics are managed effectively" (pp. 22, 24). As a result of governance principles such as these, JSE-listed companies have to report annually on their social and ethics performance.

The Companies Act (Act 71 of 2008) that became operational in 2011 makes it clear in the purpose of the Companies Act that there are definite social and ethics expectations of companies operating in South Africa when it states that the Companies Act wishes to "reaffirm the concept of the company as a means of achieving economic and social benefits" (Companies Act, 2011, section 7). From an ethics perspective, the most significant aspect of this Act is the introduction of a statutory Social and Ethics Board Sub-committee. All companies listed on the JSE Securities Exchange, all state-owned enterprises and all companies that have a public interest score above a certain level are required by the Companies Act to have a Social and Ethics Committee. The mandate of the committee is to monitor a company's social and ethics performance in a number of prescribed areas and then to report on it to the board and to the shareholders of the company at its annual general meeting.

Were companies to use a corporate responsibility map like the one proposed by Crane et al. (2007) that maps corporate responsibility in the four areas of market place, workplace, social environment and natural environment, the aspects that need to be monitored and reported on by the Social and Ethics Committee are as follows:

a. Market place: impact on economic development; corruption prevention; and black economic empowerment
b. Work place: safety; health; decent work; affirmative action; employee relations; and education of employees
c. Social environment: community development; charitable giving; product safety; community health; advertising; consumer relations; and human rights
d. Natural environment: environmental impact

According to the Companies Act Regulations (2011), the criteria against which a company's impact in the previous areas should be monitored are "relevant legislation, other legal requirements or prevailing codes of best practice." It is thus the statutory duty of the Social and Ethics Committees to monitor companies' social performance against the prevailing legal and best-practice standards and then to report deviations from the said standards as risks to the board and shareholders.

An analysis of the Social and Ethics Committee statutory mandate reveals that although the committee has a quite extensive mandate to monitor and report on the social performance of the company, there is not a distinct mandate to monitor and report on the company's ethics management. The fact that the third King Report has a clear principle on the governance of ethics (principle 1.3 states: "The board should ensure that the company's ethics are managed effectively") leaves companies, especially those listed on the JSE Securities Exchange, with the conundrum that the governance of ethics is excluded from the mandate of the said committee. The way in which companies have resolved this conundrum is by voluntarily extending the mandate of the Social and Ethics Committee by adding a specific governance of ethics mandate to the existing statutory mandate of the committee. This extended ethics mandate of the Social and Ethics Committee typically gives the committee the responsibility to exercise governance oversight of the ethics management programme of a company.

MANAGERIAL CULTURE AND THE ROLE OF LEADERSHIP

The managerial culture of enterprises in South Africa has been strongly influenced by the inclusive corporate governance approach that was introduced in the first King Report on Corporate Governance in 1994 and that was further strengthened and reinforced by the second and third King Reports. The inclusive corporate governance approach distances itself from the exclusive corporate governance approach that sees the role of management as serving exclusively shareholder interests. The inclusive approach emphasizes the responsibility of management to consider the best interest of all stakeholders when deciding and acting in the best interest of the company.

This inclusive character of the South African approach to the governance and management of enterprises is clearly reflected in the following statement in the third King Report: "[T]he legitimate interests and expectations of stakeholders are considered when deciding in the best interest of the company. [...] The shareholder, on the premise of this approach, does not have a predetermined place of precedence over other stakeholders" (King Committee, 2009, p. 13). This inclusive approach thus represents a strong stakeholder orientation in companies given that, by its very nature, it implies stakeholder engagement. Since there are a number of principles in the third King Report that deal explicitly with the importance of and need for stakeholder engagement, all companies listed on the JSE Securities Exchange have to report annually on their stakeholder engagement practices. The stakeholder-inclusive approach has been further strengthened by a strong uptake of sustainability and integrated reporting. The London-based IBE found in its survey of business ethics in South Africa that "South African companies publish the fifth highest number of global reporting initiative (GRI)-based sustainability reports in the world and are leading in comparison to other emerging economies" (Irwin 2011, p. 13).

The inclusive approach dovetails well with the African philosophy of Ubuntu. In fact, the second King Report established a direct link between the inclusive approach and Ubuntu. The said report describes the Ubuntu worldview as follows: "The essence of *ubuntu* (humanity) that cuts across Africa is based on the premise that you can be respected only because of your cordial co-existence with others" (King Committee, 2002, p. 18). It further reiterates that Ubuntu puts a greater emphasis on the collective, rather than on the individual, and that it promotes inclusive consultation that seeks consensus.

The situation in state-owned enterprises is, in general, very different. Key state-owned enterprises like Eskom (electricity), the South African Post Office, South African Airways, the South African Broadcasting Corporation and PetroSA (petroleum) have a history of poor performance and economic woes. There are, however, notable exceptions, such as Transnet (transport including railways and harbours).

STATE OF ETHICS POLICIES

A survey conducted by Young (1995) in listed companies in 1995 found that only 9 out of the 100 top companies included in the *Sunday Times Top 100 Survey* had a formal code of ethics. A further 32 companies made some reference to ethics in governance-related documents. The same survey also reported that codes of ethics were perceived as having very little impact on the actual behaviour of companies (p. 121). The survey on business ethics that was conducted some 15 years later by the London-based IBE in 2011 painted a very different picture. The latter study reported: "Every company listed on the Johannesburg Stock Exchange (JSE) has a code of ethics and has some form of ethics management programme in place as a result of the requirement to adhere to *King III*" (Irwin, 2011, p. 13). Considerable momentum was gained in the development of corporate codes of ethics, with the publication of the second King Report on Corporate Governance, which not only recommended that companies should develop their own codes of ethics but also provided companies with guidance on how to go about developing a code of ethics that is relevant and useful to the company.

The high prevalence of codes of ethics, at least among companies listed on the JSE Securities Exchange, was also confirmed in the *South Africa Business Ethics Survey 2013*, conducted by the Ethics Institute of South Africa. This study looked at both the awareness that employees have of their companies' code of ethics, as well as to employee perceptions of the usefulness of codes of ethics. A total of 96 percent of employees of JSE-listed companies that participated in the survey reported that they were aware of their companies' code of ethics. From those who indicated awareness of their companies' code of ethics, a total of 90 percent of participants indicated that they found their companies' code of ethics useful in guiding their decisions and conduct (Groenewald & Geerts, 2013).

It seems that the wide prevalence of codes of ethics in South Africa does have some impact on the ethical behaviour of companies, as the *Global Competitiveness Report 2014–2015* (published by the World Economic Forum) ranked South Africa in the 35th position overall for the "ethical behaviour of firms," out of the 144 countries included in the report.

Besides codes of ethics or codes of conduct (the terms are often used interchangeably in the South African context), it is also common for companies to have supporting ethics-related policies on matters such as gifts and entertainment, conflict of interests and whistle blowing. The introduction of the United Kingdom Bribery Act in 2010 also had some impact on South African companies that either have a secondary listing on the London Stock Exchange or are business partners of companies incorporated in the United Kingdom. The UK Bribery Act introduced a new offence, namely the failure to prevent bribery in a company or amongst its business partners. As part of the guidance issued to companies by the UK government on this new offence, companies are encouraged to have clear standards of conduct, particularly in relation to bribery, and to ensure that companies and their business associates are familiar with and adhere to these standards.

ETHICS TRAINING AND CULTURE CHANGE EFFORTS

The high awareness of ethics reported previously is an indication that ethics communication and training are fairly prevalent and effective in South African companies. The *2013 South Africa Business Ethics Survey* found that 66 percent of participants were aware that their companies offer some form of ethics training. A total of 82 percent of participants who went through ethics training reported that they found the training to be effective (Groenewald & Geerts, 2013).

Arguably the most prominent ethics training programme in South Africa is the Ethics Officer Certification Programme. The programme was first introduced in 2004 by the Ethics Institute of South Africa, and by the end of the 2015 it has been presented more than 70 times. The programme is formally certified by the University of Stellenbosch Business School Executive Development (USB-ED).

The Ethics Officer Certification Programme consists of both a training component and a practical component. Participants in the programme first have to complete a five-day intensive training programme, after which they are given a 90-day period to compile a portfolio of evidence of prescribed ethics interventions that they have to conduct in their companies. The portfolio of evidence is then submitted for formal assessment. When candidates are found to be competent in implementing the said ethics interventions, they are formally certified as ethics officers. By the end of 2015, more than 1,100 persons have completed the training part of the programme, and more than 500 of those who completed the training were certified as ethics officers. Companies who are recruiting for ethics officers often require that candidates are certified as ethics officers.

In 2015, the first steps were taken towards professionalizing the occupation of ethics officers in South Africa. It is likely that ethics management will become a fully fledged profession over the next decade.

IMPLICATIONS FOR PRACTITIONERS

The situation regarding business ethics in South Africa described in this chapter has a number of important implications for business practitioners wishing to enter the South African market. The good news for foreign companies with a strong ethical orientation is that business ethics is mainstreamed in corporate South Africa. The three King Reports on corporate governance, which all emphasized that corporations should actively manage their ethics, combined with the Companies Act that requires boards of companies to have social and ethics committees, have embedded ethics in the corporate discourse both at board and management levels of companies. Many of the leading companies in South Africa have either a full-time ethics officer or an office with the sole responsibility of managing corporate ethics.

All companies doing business in South Africa are required to play their part in redressing Apartheid's legacy of inequality. Affirmative action and black economic empowerment is a reality that all companies need to deal with when operating in South Africa. Companies' contributions in this regard are regulated through legislation such as the Employment Equity Act and the Broad-Based Black Economic Empowerment Act. Whilst both these acts place a substantial administrative burden on companies, they also enable companies to unlock vast resources of talent and opportunity that are yet untapped.

The King Reports and the Companies Act regard companies as corporate citizens that are expected not to harm their social and natural environment but rather make a constructive contribution to their social and natural environment. Companies are expected to engage actively with their stakeholders and find ways of creating value for them.

The perceived steady increase in corruption poses ethics pitfalls for companies. It is important that foreign companies are fully aware of the risks of being drawn into corrupt practices that can cause companies substantial reputational and financial harm. Companies need to do proper due diligence on potential business partners and should be proactive in promoting and maintaining high ethical standards in their supplier and business partner relationships.

When it comes to the management of ethics, US and European companies in particular wishing to do business in South Africa should be aware that legal compliance and ethics management are regarded as two separate management fields in South Africa. Unlike in the United States and Europe, where ethics and compliance are often combined, South African companies generally split these roles. Ethics management thus focuses on more than compliance with legal and ethical standards; it plays a proactive role in creating ethics awareness and promoting an ethical culture in organizations.

REFERENCES

Broad-Based Black Economic Empowerment Act 53 of 2003 (2003). Retrieved from https://www.environment.gov.za/sites/default/files/legislations/bbbee_act.pdf

Companies Act 71 of 2008 (2008). Retrieved from www.justice.gov.za/legislation/acts/2008-071amended.pdf

Companies Act Regulations (2011). Retrieved from www.justice.gov.za/legislation/acts/2008-071-reg.pdf

Crane, A., Matten, D., & Spence, L. J. (2007). *Corporate social responsibility: Readings and cases in global context.* London: Routledge.

Deegan, H. (2014). *Politics South Africa* (2nd ed.). New York: Routledge.

Employment Equity Act 55 of 1998 (1998). Retrieved from www.labour.gov.za/DOL/downloads/legislation/acts/employment-equity/eegazette2015.pdf

Groenewald, L., & Geerts, S. (2013). *The South African business ethics survey 2013.* Retrieved from www.tei.org.za/index.php/resources/research-reports

Irwin, J. (2011). *Doing business in South Africa: An overview of ethical aspects.* London: Institute of Business Ethics.

King Committee on Corporate Governance (1994). *The King Report on Corporate Governance for South Africa 1994.* Johannesburg: Institute of Directors in Southern Africa.

King Committee on Corporate Governance (2002). *The King Report on Corporate Governance for South Africa 2002.* Johannesburg: Institute of Directors in Southern Africa.

King Committee on Corporate Governance (2009). *King Report on Corporate Governance for South Africa 2009*. Johannesburg: Institute of Directors in Southern Africa.

Landman, W. A., Punt, W. J., & Painter-Morland, M. (2002). *Corporate ethics indicator: Report on the business ethics South Africa Survey*. Pretoria: Ethics Institute of South Africa.

Ntibagirirwa, S. (2014). *Philosophical premises for African economic development: Sen's capability approach* (Doctoral dissertation). Geneva: Globethics. net.

Punt, W. J., Groenewald, L., & Geerts, S. (2009). *The South African corporate ethics indicator 2009*. Retrieved from www.tei.org.za/index.php/resources/research-reports

Ramose, M. B. (2003). The philosophy of ubuntu and ubuntu as a philosophy. In P. H. Coetzee & A. P. J. Roux (Eds.), *The African Philosophy Reader* (2nd ed., pp. 230–238). London: Routledge.

Rossouw, G. J. (1997). Business ethics in South Africa. *Journal of Business Ethics*, 16(14): 1539–1547.

Schwab, K. (2015). *Global competitiveness report 2014–2015*. Geneva: World Economic Forum.

Shisana, O., Rehle, T., Simbayi, L. C., Jooste, S., Zungu, N., Labadarios, D., & Onoya, D. (2014). *South African national HIV prevalence, incidence and behaviour survey, 2012*. Pretoria: Human Science Research Council.

Statistics South Africa (2011). *Census 2011*. Pretoria: Statistics South Africa.

West, A. (2012). *Moral relativism and corporate governance convergence* (PhD dissertation). Pretoria: University of Pretoria.

Young, G. R. (1995). *Corporate Ethical Codes in South African Companies* (MBL research report). Pretoria: University of South Africa.

6   Ethical Business Culture in Turkey: Implications for Leadership in a Global Economy

Ahmet Coskun and Mesut Akdere

ABSTRACT

In a rapidly changing global market, it has become increasingly important and vital for the survival of the organization to be competitive and adaptive. In order to achieve this, organizational leadership needs a better understanding of the business cultures in which their companies are operating. One of the challenges is the lack of literature on ethical business cultures in emerging markets. This is also the case for Turkey, a fast growing emerging market. In this chapter, we use Donaldson and Dunfee's Integrative Social Contracts Theory (ISCT) to explore the ethical business culture of Turkey as an emerging market. Hofstede's cultural dimensions are used to analyze the role of Turkish national culture in shaping business behavior. The role of religion and of the political and administrative institutional structures is also discussed in detail. The development of ethical business cultures in Turkish business organizations is also discussed, with special emphasis on challenges presented by globalization and rapid economic development. Implications for leadership are also discussed.

INTRODUCTION

Because of the rapid developments in information and transportation technologies, the world economy is increasingly becoming global. Global investment is becoming even more crucial for societies as well as countries as governments develop and adopt national policies to attract and retain investors and businesses. In this environment, emerging markets are becoming increasingly attractive locations to do business. However, along with their promising attributes, these markets often present significant ethical challenges as a result of being emerging markets in which institutionalization and business practice is still in the process of maturation (Akdere, 2015). In addition, the norms and values of particular national cultures of the emerging markets can prove to be a significant barrier. Among some of these challenges are ethical perceptions and philosophies; decision-making styles; business attitudes, intentions, assumptions, and behaviors; and the cultural, legal, and institutional infrastructure of emerging markets.

According to various economic and financial classifications (such as the World Bank, International Monetary Fund [IMF], Organisation for Economic Co-operation and Development [OECD], Goldman Sachs, HSBC Bank, Bloomberg, Forbes, Morgan Stanley Capital International [MSCI], and Financial Times Stock Exchange [FTSE], among others), Turkey is one of the most attractive emerging markets for investors. An understanding of the ethical business culture of Turkey is, however, an essential foundation for understanding the Turkish economy. Understanding differences between corresponding parties in business affairs and transactions is likely to result in a better business.

In this chapter, we use Donaldson and Dunfee's (1994) integrative social contracts theory (ISCT) to explore the ethical business culture of Turkey as an emerging market. Donaldson and Dunfee (1994) combine two approaches toward business ethics, i.e., normative and empirical. The normative approach to business ethics deals with rational and universal prescriptions by defining "ought" propositions. On the other hand, the empirical approach involves defining the real situation, or "what ought" and "what is" conditions, of business life as far as ethical problems are concerned. Adopting the ISCT framework, we presuppose that both approaches are relevant and necessary for the understanding of ethical business cultures in emerging markets. While being tied to universal ethical values as a result of globalization, Turkey has some local specificity because of its own realities.

According to ISCT, the ethical sphere of global business is mainly comprised of two components: hypernorms and authentic norms. Hypernorms connote fundamental ethical standards, which all societies abide by, e.g., being just and honest or avoiding deceit. Authentic norms, while not violating hypernorms, reveal the shared values of a particular community, e.g., societies, industries, or even companies. As Donaldson and Dunfee (1994) argue, "the existence of authentic ethical norms can be determined by empirical tests of ethical attitudes and behaviors in particular communities" (p. 264). Thus, we will also refer to the findings of recent empirical studies in order to further discuss authentic ethical norms in Turkish business culture.

HISTORICAL BACKGROUND

Geographically, historically, and culturally, Turkey has been a bridge between Asia and Europe. With a population of more than 75 million, which is predominantly (99%) Muslim, Turkey is also a democratic and a secular country. It has endured more than a century of transformation, which most probably had a profound impact on its ethical culture. In order to create a brand new nation, the founders of the new Republic attempted to radically transform the culture of its people through a process of secularization, affecting all governmental, military, and civic institutions in which all remnants of the Ottoman culture and way of life were to be erased to make way for the new ideology and mentality of the new state and its principles.

In addition to these radical transformations in cultural and institutional areas, Turkey has, since the establishment of the new Republic in 1923, continually attempted to implement different governmental policies for the purpose of economic development and societal growth. Creating a national bourgeoisie has been the core motivator for developmentalist efforts in this regard (Aydın, 2005). This policy and its method of implementation not only failed to address the problem of underdevelopment but also brought with it some chronic ethical problems and practices, including tax evasion, a shadow economy, exploitation of labor, nepotism, partial incentives and protections, low quality goods, products, and services (Kepenek & Yentürk, 2004). Moreover, Turkey has experienced a total of five military coups (1960, 1971, 1980, 1997, and 2007) and 11 economic crises (1929–1931; 1947; 1969; 1958–1961; 1978–1981; 1982; 1988–1989; 1991; 1994; 1998–2002; and 2008) over the last nine decades. Research by Ernst and Young (2009) shows that during times of political and economic crises, the ethical culture of business life is adversely impacted. Inevitably, the turmoil and uncertainty in the national economy and in Turkish politics in the last 50 years has had a considerable negative impact on Turkish business in terms of a failure to develop a vibrant national economy or to establish an ethical business environment.

INTERNATIONAL FACTORS

According to ISCT, international factors surrounding the ecosystem of the Turkish business environment set the hypernorms of ethical business culture in concordance with the global integration level of the Turkish economy.

Since becoming an open market economy in 1980, Turkey has focused on strengthening its economic ties with other countries. While the total share of exports in the GDP of Turkey was at 5.2 percent in 1980, it has grown to 25.6 percent in 2013. Similarly, while the total share of imports in the GDP of Turkey was at 11.9 percent in 2003, it has grown to 32.2 percent in 2013 (World Bank, 2014). In 1995, Turkey signed a customs union agreement with the European Union (EU) to enhance their mutual trading relationships. As a result, the EU countries have been the largest market for Turkish products and services, and their share of Turkey's total exports is nearly 45 percent. This strong trade relationship obliges Turkish companies to pay closer attention to ethical concerns and abide by the product and service quality standards and policies of the EU (World Bank, 2014).

Furthermore, Turkey has acquired $14.6 billion of foreign direct investment (FDI) on a yearly average, and the number of companies with international capital has tripled from 11,700 to 36,500 within the last 10 years. In fact, this may be considered a good indicator for business ethics, at least from a corporate social responsibility (CSR) perspective, as there is a robust relationship between CSR development level and the global openness of an economy (Robertson, 2009). In addition, multinational companies (MNCs) are generally reported to have a more developed CSR culture, and they may play a change agent role for the Turkish economy. But, Turkey is ranked 69th in terms of the ease of doing business, and this ranking does not present an attractive prospect for MNCs (World Bank, 2014).

Turkey has been trying to enter the EU since 1987, and it was officially recognized as a candidate country for full accession to membership in 1999. Since then, 14 assessment chapters have opened to align Turkey's laws and institutions to EU standards. Most of these chapters relate to business ethics, such as company law, intellectual property law, taxation, environment and climate change, consumer and health protection, and human rights. Moreover, Turkey has accepted some crucial conventions and protocols in recent years. It ratified the United Nations Framework Convention on Climate Change in 2004, accepted the Kyoto Protocol in 2009, and signed the United Nations (UN) Convention Against Corruption in 2006. However, despite being a member of the International Labor Organization (ILO) since 1932, Turkey has ratified only 57 of 189 ILO conventions (54th among 190 countries), and 53 of these are mandatory (International Labour Organization, 2015). Turkey is considered to have "a global perspective on economic and management development" (Akdere & Dirani, 2014), and it is "generally more accustomed to dealing with other cultures in both business and social contexts"

(p. 464). It is obvious that an export-led growth strategy, economic integration with the global economy, and the EU membership process are allowing Turkish businesses to internalize ethical hypernorms; however, these businesses and the Turkish economy are still a long way from adopting and functioning within the international norms and standards associated with business ethics.

COUNTRY INDICATORS

After a severe financial crisis at the beginning of the century, which was a result of long-term political instability, there have been significant improvements in several key areas during the considerably more stable administration of the Justice and Development Party (JDP, AK Parti). During this time, particularly as a result of structural transformations in the financial sector, fiscal discipline in the public sector and export-led growth strategy, the inflation rate has gradually fallen from 53 percent to 10 percent, the stock market BIST-100 (formerly İMKB-100) index has risen from around 7,000 to more than 81,000 points, and GDP growth has been 5.2 percent on an average. As a result, with a population of nearly 75 million and more than $820 billion GDP, Turkey is one of the larger countries in the world (18th for population and 17th for GDP). Yet, when it comes to gross national income (GNI) per capita, the country is ranked 50th with $10,950 per capita and finds a place among upper middle-income countries. In addition, more than 20 percent of the population is still employed in the agriculture sector, and the unemployment rate is above 10 percent (Turkstat, 2014).

As illustrated in Table 6.1, Turkey has been dealing with some crucial issues that are essential for the development of an ethical business culture. Although there has been some improvement in recent years, its global rankings associated with an ethical business environment and culture are rather low. Among these rankings are corruption, ranked 64th (Transparency International, 2014); human development, ranked 69th; gender inequality, ranked 69th (United Nations Development Program, 2013); responsible competitiveness,

Table 6.1. *Economic Indicators of Turkey*

Economic Indicators	Amount/Score	Ranking
Population (2013)[a]	74.93 million	18/213
GDP (2013)[a]	$820.2 billion	17/183
GNI per capita (2013)[a]	$10,950	50/172
Foreign direct investment (net, 2013)[a]	$12.9 billion	20/196
Market capitalization (2012)[a]	$308.8	29/109
Human Development Index (2013)[b]	0.759	69/187
Gender Inequality Index (2013)[b]	0.360	69/187
Ease of doing business		69/189
Transparency and Socially Responsible Competitiveness Indicators		
Corruption Perceptions Index (2014)[c]	45	64/175
Global Competitiveness Rankings (2014)[d]	4.5	45/144
Index of Economic Freedom (2014)[e]	64.9	64/178
Responsible Competitiveness Index (2007)[f]	55.6	51/108
World Governance Index (2011)[g]	0.599	94/179
Worldwide Governance Indicators	(score, –2.5 to 2.5)	(percentile rank, 0–100)
Political stability and absence of violence/terrorism	–1.19	11.85
Regulatory quality	0.42	65.07
Rule of law	0.08	55.92
Government effectiveness	0.37	65.55
Control of corruption	0.11	61.72
Voice and accountability	–0.26	40.76

[a]The World Bank; [b]United Nations Development Program; [c]Transparency International; [d]World Economic Forum; [e]Heritage Foundation Program (UNDP); [f]Accountability; [g]Forum for a New World Governance.

ranked 51st (AccountAbility, 2007); and governance, ranked 94th (Forum for a New World Governance, 2011). In these various global indicators of business, Turkey still ranks between 50th and 90th. Moreover, even though it is falling against some measures, Turkey still has one of the highest GINI coefficient (which reflects income inequality) among the OECD countries with its 0.41 ratio versus 0.32 for the OECD average. Also, the relative poverty rate is 14.5 percent in Turkey, while the OECD average is 11.2 percent (Organisation for Economic Co-operation and Development, 2014), and the child labor rate is still 2.6 percent (Turkstat, 2012). The Turkish economy was ranked at 14th among 23 countries in the *Economist* crony-capitalism index in 2014 (1st ranking means the worst condition), whereas its ranking was 8th in 2007 (Economist, 2014).

According to a report published by the Turkish National Revenue Administration (2015), Turkey has high levels of shadow economy – unregistered trade and business (26.5% of the national GDP) and unregistered employment (22% of national employment). High tax rates and repeating tax amnesties encourage the shadow economy problem. Regardless of their firm size, Turkish companies typically perceive tax rates and the informal sector as the biggest obstacles for growth (World Bank, 2013), while they do not perceive tax evasion as a serious crime (Benk et al., 2015). Additionally, there has been a slight increase in both numbers and quantity of bounced checks, contested bills, and nonperforming consumer loans since 2009 (Turkish Risk Center, 2015).

LAWS AND INSTITUTIONS

Following the 2002 financial crisis in Turkey, which occurred partly because of unethical administration and fraudulent practices of commercial banks, the Banking Regulation and Supervision Agency (BRSA) was created to ensure financial and organizational restructuring. One of the main goals of the BRSA is to prevent malpractices of administrators and employees of banking organizations. Thus, in 2005, the agency announced corporate governance regulations, which are legally binding procedures for Turkish financial institutions. Similarly, the Capital Markets Board of Turkey (CMBT) announced corporate governance principles in 2003 and obliged publicly traded companies to abide by these principles, which are based on the OECD Principles of Corporate Governance.

Additionally, in order to address deep-rooted ethical problems in the public sector, such as bribery, favoritism, corruption, etc., the Public Procurement Agency (PPA) was established in 2002, which was followed by the establishment of the Council of Ethics for Public Service (CEPS) in 2005. Yet, due to the lack of legal and organizational capabilities, the CEPS has had a minimal impact on ethical issues in the public sector. In fact, the area of influence of the CEPS comprises little more than didactic educational activities and ineffective recommendations (Arslan & Berkman, 2009).

There are various laws in the Turkish legal system concerning ethical issues in business, such as preventing bribery (Declaration of Wealth Law), corruption (Public Procurement Law), and money laundering (Banking Law); protecting the rights of workers (Union Law), the environment (Environment Law and Renewable Energy Law), and consumer rights (Protection of the Consumer Law); and supporting CSR activities (Income Tax Law). Most of the recent laws have come into effect in accordance with OECD, EU, and UN conventions to align the Turkish legal system with global standards. However, there is still a serious gap in terms of how these laws are implemented and practiced, which mostly arises from cultural factors and prevalent business practices (Omurgonulsen & Doig, 2012).

There are only a handful of nongovernmental organizations (NGOs), which are dedicated to enhancing the ethical practice and culture of business and trade in Turkey. One of the most influential NGOs is the Turkish Entrepreneurship and Business Ethics Association (İGİAD), which organizes training and educational programs, publishes books and research reports, and advocates ethical business in various platforms. The İGİAD also publishes the leading and the only national scholarly and academic journal related to business ethics – the *Turkish Journal of Business Ethics*, established in 2008. The Ethics and Reputation Society (TEİD) and the Turkish Ethical Values Center Foundation (TEDMER) are some other examples of NGOs that are trying to deal with issues around business ethics and to contribute to the efforts of enhancing ethical business culture in Turkey. The Corporate Governance Association of Turkey (TKYD), the Corporate Social Responsibility Association of Turkey (KSSD), the Private Sector Volunteers Foundation (ÖSGD), the Turkish Society for Quality (Kal-Der), the Turkish Industrialists and Businessmen's Association (TÜSİAD), and the Union of Chambers and Commodity Exchanges of Turkey (TOBB) are some other NGOs that support ethical business culture and practices in Turkey.

Business ethics as an academic and popular subject has tended to receive more attention in Turkey in recent years. In 2013, the social responsibility concept was mentioned in the news 30 times more than it was mentioned in 2000 (Turker, 2015). While only 13 percent of academic programs in Turkish universities offered a business ethics class in 2005 (Bayraktaroglu et al., 2005), this ratio has now increased to 32 percent in 2009 (Gölbaşı, 2009). However, there is still a lack of research interest in business ethics. Although there are nearly 200 universities in Turkey, the Management Ethics Research and Application Center (HÜEM) of the Hacettepe University and the Business Ethics Research and Application Center of the Bilgi University are the only academic centers focusing on business ethics in Turkey. Additionally, there are only two CSR awards programs held in Turkey annually (i.e., the TİSK CSR Awards and the European CSR Awards), and there is no business ethics awards program to date.

CSR CULTURE

There is a strong philanthropic tradition in Turkey. Charitable behavior and the widespread prevalence of religious foundations (*waqf* is the Ottoman name for charitable organization) have been essential parts of the Muslim Turkish culture throughout history.

In fact, apart from their benefits, philanthropic activities have satisfied the visible needs of society and diminished the possibility of a broader understanding of CSR. But, in recent years, Turkish business organizations began to pay attention to the triple Ps (people, planet, and profit) and support social projects in different areas such as education, environmental protection, and disadvantaged groups (United Nations Development Programme, 2008).

There are some structural reasons for the lack of CSR awareness in Turkey. For instance, 95 percent of Turkish companies, and almost half of the publicly traded ones, are family-owned or family-managed businesses. According to Robertson (2009), the predominantly family-ownership structure of Turkish economy is one of the reasons that led the Turkish CSR model to become mostly comprised of philanthropic activities. She argues that with a more intensive market capitalization, companies would pay more attention to the expectations of stakeholders as a result of increasing pressures to be a socially responsible organization. Supporting this argument, there are two indices operating on the Istanbul Stock Exchange Market (BIST) to promote ethical business culture in publicly traded companies. One is the corporate governance index (XKURY), which has been available since 2007, and the other is the sustainability index (XUSRD), which was launched in November 2014.

NATIONAL CULTURE

Among different antecedents, national culture is "one of the most important factors" (Singhapakdi et al., 1994, p. 65) that affects ethical culture in business, especially in terms of authentic norms. National culture has an underlying impact on the ethical decision-making process through recognizing potential ethical issues, assessing them, and taking action to address them. In any particular business situation, the perceptions of individuals about what is right and wrong, acceptable and unacceptable, ethical or unethical are significantly affected by their culture (Lu et al., 1999). Specifically, when doing business in emerging countries, as Ferrell (1999, p. 226) states, "cultural diversity and different perceptions of right and wrong create ethical conflicts." Furthermore, Askun et al. (2010) listed three main approaches to the relationship between culture and ethics in an international context:

1. According to the *convergence approach*, by the agency of industrialization and globalization processes, different business cultures would converge and have similar characteristics. This approach stresses hypernorms.
2. Being on the opposite side of the convergence idea, the *divergence approach* places stress on the dissimilarities of individuals, or authentic norms, from different cultures.
3. Finally, offering a hybrid model, the *crossvergence approach* proponents claim that cultures and individuals do not stay on the extremes of convergence and divergence; instead, they are scattered on a continuum in between.

The most suitable approach for ethical business culture in Turkey might be the crossvergence approach. Indeed, there is an interaction between convergence and divergence facets of cultures, and this interaction produces a "unique values system that differs from both the convergence and divergence positions" (Ralston et al., 2006, p. 70).

In order to explain Turkish ethical business culture, we should also take into account the cultural characteristics of the Turkish people. One of the most frequently used approaches for the classification of national culture is Hofstede's model. According to this model, Turkey is categorized as follows (Hofstede Centre, 2014):

1. Power distance (66): This high power distance score means that the Turkish people attach importance to hierarchy, and they usually expect superiors to tell them what to do. Moreover, the empowerment level is quite low, and indirect communication and feedback style is pervasive in this culture.

2. Individualism (37): With a relatively low score on this dimension, Turkish people have the characteristics of collectivist cultures. This implies that group membership and loyalty are the key issues in a Turkish business context. Rather than task performance, relationship management and contextual performance are considered superior goals. People pay attention to harmony and consensus in groups and dislike open conflict.
3. Masculinity (45): In comparison with other cultures, Turkish people sit on the feminine side of this scale. This connotes that conflicts are unwelcome, but mediatory efforts in disagreements and showing sympathy are appreciated in business life in Turkey.
4. Uncertainty avoidance (85): Turkey has quite a high score on this dimension. Turkish people do not feel comfortable with uncertainty and try to reduce their anxiety by following rituals and norms.

Taking these characteristics into consideration, scholars who have undertaken comparative studies of the ethical culture of Turkish business life have presented different, sometimes even conflicting, conclusions. Some of them disclosed that different features of national cultures do not significantly differentiate between ethical predispositions. For instance, in their study, Srnka et al. (2007) compared the ethical reasoning of Turkish and Austrian people. They revealed that, although these people have very different cultural characteristics, they mostly share the same sensitivities toward unethical behaviors. On the other hand, a majority of the studies indicate that cultural features do have an impact on ethical issues. For example, in comparison with people from relatively individualistic cultures, such as the United States or Australia, collectivist Turkish people are found to be more ethically sensitive on issues that involve relationships with others (Park et al., 2008). Similarly, in their study, Burnaz et al. (2009) found Turkish people tend to have varying scores when compared to American and Thai people on ethical business subjects. For instance, Turkish people have lower levels of perceived moral intensity than Americans. Also, the perceived importance of ethics behaviors of Turkish people is lower than American and Thai people.

On the other hand, Turkish people were found to have significantly higher corporate ethical values than Thai people. Additionally, Schneider et al. (2011) asserted that seeking harmony between relevant business parties helps Turkish society to internalize a stakeholder approach. They also avoid harming their loyal personal and professional relationships with their colleagues, customers, or organizations; and they do not attempt to gain short-term personal benefits by engaging in petty theft or cheating (Sims & Gegez, 2004). As a result of high collectivism and power distance, instances of whistleblowing and criticizing the unethical behavior of peers/supervisors are expected to be rare in Turkish business culture, while instances of nepotism are relatively common (Park et al., 2008).

Strong uncertainty avoidance leads Turkish people to follow the prescribed rules and shared values when they face ethical dilemmas. In addition to this, when compared to Americans, Turks tend to display low levels of masculinity and possess a greater degree of ethical idealism in which "highly idealistic individuals feel that harming others is always avoidable" (Forsyth, 1992, p. 462). And, because of its collectivist culture (having a tendency to care about relationships), Turkish society has a lower degree of Machiavellianism – "high machs tended to be less ethical in their decision-making than less machs" (O'Fallon & Butterfield, 2005, p. 932) – compared to more individualistic societies such as the United States, United Kingdom, or Australia (Rawwas et al., 2005). However, Ararat (2008) argued that high power distance and high in-group collectivism result in a negative influence on the CSR awareness of Turkish people.

Customers are an essential part of business life as they orient firm behavior by their choices. Thus, when thinking about the ethical culture of the business environment in Turkey, in order to have a holistic view, customer behaviors should also be taken into account. Although there is criticism that the Turkish economy lacks pressure for a sustainable business environment on the demand side (Ararat et al., 2010), it is argued that Turkish consumers, as members of a relatively collectivistic and high power distance society, are more eager to follow the ethical rules and have a greater degree of idealism than many other cultures (Rawwas et al., 2005; Srnka et al., 2007).

As mentioned previously, there are conflicting findings about the ethical business culture of Turkish society. Aygün et al. (2008) claimed that Turkey is experiencing a cultural transition in which Turkish society may at times demonstrate conflicting cultural characteristics at the same time. For instance, as a result of globalization, it may be argued that the wider Turkish culture may be becoming more individualistic and masculine. For example, as well as embracing group cohesiveness and a strong cooperation culture, Turkish people are also pursuing materialistic individual goals and competition (Rawwas et al., 2005; Sims & Gegez, 2004). Since Turkey scores very low on the corruption perception index (CPI) – which implies a high level of corruption – it might be argued that there is an epidemic of corruption within Turkish business culture (Transparency International, 2014). Yet, this score is most likely affected by malpractices in the public sector. In fact, Turkish business owners have higher levels of public confidence, trust, and reputation awareness when compared to business owners in Western societies (Sims & Gegez, 2004).

RELIGION AND ITS IMPACT ON TURKISH SOCIETY

Turkey has a 99 percent Muslim population, and most Muslim citizens are diligent about their religious practices. For example, more than 42 percent of Turkish society is reported to regularly perform their five daily prayers, while more than 83 percent indicated that they fast during the entire month of Ramadan, the holy month of Islam (Diyanet, 2014). Although Turkish society has long been subject to a harsh and, at times brutal, secularization process, religion – Islam – has still a powerful impact on people's values, both personal and societal. As Uygur (2009) notes, even "most secular people ... consider themselves Muslim, and religion is not completely excluded from their lives" (p. 212). However, the relationship between religion, especially values that are derived from a religious belief, and ethical culture in business life is a larger subject of debate. Some scholars assert that there is no significant relationship; on the other hand, others claim that religiosity does affect ethical values in business life (Vitell et al., 2005).

In fact, the value system that Islam offers has a comprehensive scope, which encompasses every aspect of social life, including business activities. There are several verses from the Qur'an (the holy book of Islam) and the hadith (the sayings) of the Prophet Muhammad (Peace Be Upon Him – PBUH) that mention the virtue and importance of doing ethical business (Akdere & Salem, 2012). The Qur'an has several verses that prohibit conducting unjust, unfair, and unethical business and clearly state the ramifications for doing so.

In Chapter (Surah) An-Nisa (Women) Verse (Ayah) 58, the Holy Qur'an says, "God commands you (people) to return things entrusted to you to their rightful owners, and, if you judge between people, to do so with justice: God's instructions to you are excellent, for He hears and sees everything." Similarly, in Chapter Al-Rahman (The Lord of Mercy) Verses 7 and 8, Allah (God) says, "He has set the balance so that you may not exceed in the balance: weigh with justice and do not fall short in the balance." In another verse, Muslims are warned about improperly and deceitfully conducting business: "Woe to those who give short measure, who demand of other people full measure for themselves, but when it is they who weigh or measure for others give less than they should." (Chapter Al-Mutaffifin [Those Who Give Short Measure], Verses 1–3). And, in a different verse Allah reminds the believers: "You who believe, do not wrongfully consume each other's wealth but trade by mutual consent. Do not kill each other, for God is merciful to you" (Chapter An-Nisa [Women] Verse 29).

In a similar vein, the Prophet Muhammad (PBUH) was regarded as being a highly trustworthy merchant even prior to becoming the Prophet – thus, considered a role model for Muslim businessmen. It is narrated on the authority of Abu Huraira that the Messenger of Allah (PBUH) happened to pass by a heap of grain. He thrust his hand in that (heap) and his fingers were moistened. He said to the owner of that heap of eatables (corn): "What is this?" He replied: "Messenger of Allah, these have been drenched by rainfall." He (the Holy Prophet) remarked: "Why did you not place this (the drenched part of the heap) over other eatables so that the people could see it? He who deceives is not of me (is not my follower)" (The Hadiths, Muslim: The Book of Faith-43). In another hadith, the Prophet (PBUH) stated, "The truthful, trustworthy merchant is with the Prophets, the truthful, and the martyrs" (The Hadiths, Tirmidhi: The Book of Business-4). The Prophet Muhammad (PBUH) also warns Muslim businesspeople about the importance of fully paying employees their dues as soon as they complete the work: "Give the worker his wages before his sweat dries" (The Hadiths, Ibn Majah: The Chapters on Pawning-4).

As evident from the strong emphasis on ethical business conduct in Islam, which has been the most dominant factor in Turkish culture since the Turks became Muslims, one might easily argue that there would be a strong relationship between religion and ethical business culture in Turkey. Nevertheless, there is another view in the literature that Turkish people tend to separate religious and business values. According to this view, along with the impact of secularization and globalization, Turkish businessmen, even highly devout ones, discriminate between religious values and business practice in a pragmatic way (Uygur, 2009). The belief that the "business world has its own rules" is more solid and strong in the Turkish business mindset in comparison to other countries, even the United States (Sims & Gegez, 2004). Kocel and Tekarslan asserted that "religion seems to have no effect on behavior in the work place" of Turkish business life (as cited in Srnka et al., 2007, p. 105).

However, respondents' explicit statements about the lack of relationship between their religious beliefs and ethical business culture do not necessarily mean that we can in any way dismiss the influence of religion on their mindset and inherent culture that determines much of their behavior. Thus, at a subconscious level, they may very well behave and act as businesspeople under the Islamic framework, as it is dominant in their culture and very much mixed with cultural norms. The Islamic moral system praises many important ethical values in business life, such as being honest, trustworthy, ethical, fair, and hardworking, and condemns unethical behaviors, including deceiving, lying, cheating, manipulating, bribing, being corrupting, stealing, and being unjust. Studies disclose that these very same values are shared in Turkish business culture as well (Hisrich et al., 2003; Srnka et al., 2007). So, even if people do not recognize it, there might still be an implicit "moral filter" of Islamic values embedded within Turkish business life (Rice, 1999). For example, Menguç (1998) revealed that when making ethical decisions, Turkish businesspeople use a deontological ethical approach more than they use teleological evaluations. This might well be a reflection of an Islamic rule that the ethical values of intention are much more important than deeds. In addition, it is important to note that Islam encourages its followers not to reveal and make known their charitable deeds or acts, which is a unique characteristic of CSR in emerging countries (Robertson, 2009). Thus, Turkish businesses and companies are expected to be less prone to advertise their CSR activities as compared to their Western counterparts. Indeed, public disclosure and reporting is considered to be one of the weakest sides of CSR engagement in Turkey (United Nations Development Programme, 2008).

Based on non-indigenous models, some authors argue that Turkish people have a significantly greater degree of Protestant work ethic than Protestant people in Britain and the United States (Arslan, 2001; Zulfikar, 2012). In these studies, Turkish people were found to more strongly believe that "hard work brings success"; they have a higher level of internal locus of control; and the endorsement tendency of Turkish people toward money and time saving is more salient in comparison to Catholics and Protestants. Actually,

Turkish businesspeople, especially pious ones, possess these values (e.g., hardworking, honest, frugal), attributing them to Islamic ethics, although, rather than being merely Islamic, they are globally accepted values (Uygur, 2009).

ETHICAL CULTURE IN ORGANIZATIONS

Ethical culture in organizations is comprised of formal and informal cultural systems. Formal cultural systems include factors such as "policies (e.g., codes of ethics), leadership, authority structures, reward systems, and training programs," while informal cultural systems refer to "peer behavior and ethical norms" (Trevino et al., 1998, 451–452). There have been developments in the ethical culture of Turkish business organizations to both formal and informal systems, mostly due to the change of expectations in local and global markets. "Societal expectations about what a corporation can and cannot do as well as should and should not do play a role in shaping CSR culture and framework in organizations" (Robertson, 2009, p. 627). Based on this approach, the stakeholder perspective is becoming more prevalent in the business culture of Turkey, and companies are paying closer attention to their interactions with their stakeholders. Turkish business organizations are now dealing with the rising pressure of civil society on their activities, particularly in relation to human rights, child labor, and working conditions (Auger et al., 2007).

Another influential factor is trust. According to the World Values Survey (2014), Turkish people have one of the lowest trust levels (reported as 11.6%) when compared to people of other countries. Public trust levels in business organizations is also very low in Turkey (GfK, 2013). In the last three years in particular, Turkish citizens have indicated that "being just and transparent" has been the most important feature of business organizations for trust and reputation (Reputation Management Institute, 2013). Hence, companies have begun to recognize "trust" and "reputation" as a crucial value in their assets and are paying attention to business ethics in order to increase their reputation level. As a result, the number of Turkish business organizations having codes of ethics has been increasing. For instance, while 53.3 percent of publicly traded companies had reported having a code of ethics in 2007 (Köseoğlu, 2007), only 23.3 percent of the 500 largest companies in Turkey had a code of ethics (Aydınlık & Dönmez, 2007), but this ratio increased to 36.4 percent in 2012 (Yılmaz, 2012). Although longitudinal studies showed that ethics training has a positive influence on organizational ethical culture (Warren et al., 2014), according to field research, only 25 percent of business organizations in Turkey had ethics training programs (IGIAD, 2013).

One of the most important ethical challenges of business culture in Turkey is the perceived notion of ethics and law, which are regarded as interchangeable by Turkish businesses and organizations (Ararat, 2008). Yet, there are so many grey areas in business life, which are not codified in law, and this lack of clarification makes ethical abuses more possible, especially against less powerful or effective parties. For example, while Turkish companies consider customer satisfaction and high-quality products as the most important values, supplier satisfaction and union relationships have the least importance (Halici & Kucukaslan, 2005). In an empirical study of Ekin and Tezölmez (1999), while Turkish managers declared that ignoring environmental issues, conducting insider trading, and accepting bribery/inconvenient gifts are the most serious unethical behaviors, they view taking longer work breaks, abusing company expense accounts, and obtaining strategic and organizational information about rival companies and competitors in an unethical manner as less serious violations of business behavior.

IMPLICATIONS FOR LEADERSHIP IN A GLOBAL ECONOMY

Research studies indicate that an accurate holistic picture of ethical business cultures cannot be obtained by ignoring global ethical standards or neglecting diverse local features of the countries concerned.

Rather, international investors, firm owners, and managers should keep in mind the unique characteristics of the ethical business culture of the particular country while stressing the need for observing global ethical standards. Furthermore, to establish a strong infrastructure of trust among local and international business actors, governments should effectively identify legal requirements and strengthen associated governmental and public institutions, ensure they work properly, and eliminate unnecessary red tape and cost deterrents such as high taxes in order to encourage business actors to abide by both the ethical guidelines and legal procedures.

It is important to note that Turkish business culture is still developing and needs more time to mature as it aims to transition from a shadow economy to an established and globally integrated system. Some of the specific challenges associated with a shadow economy are total compensation discrepancies, corporate tax evasions, and a predominant way of doing business that influences the entire business, trade processes, and overall culture. Many Turkish employees, particularly those working in entry-level positions, receive higher salaries than what is reported on their official paychecks by receiving undocumented payments in cash. Such practice presents many challenges both to employees and the government. For example, employees receive lower benefits and pensions and are often at risk of not getting paid the difference on time, and they have no legal grounds to claim that they were not fully compensated when any legal issues arise. From the government's perspective, lower wages mean lower taxes and payments to government's national health and retirement programs by employers. In recent years, government officials have been making attempts to identify such illegal practices using technology and social media such as LinkedIn. They compare the official job titles, duties, and responsibilities of employees (mostly white-collar employees) with what is indicated on their professional accounts on social media. It is not uncommon to find tax evasion practices committed by multinational corporations, as is the case in many parts of the world (even in Europe and the United States). In addition, the larger community within the Turkish business ecosystem considers tax evasion as an "accepted practice" by organizations. When a well-known Turkish bank, Türkiye İmar Bankası, went bankrupt in 2001, Turkish authorities found that bank executives had engaged in the manipulation of tax and financial records. Turkish legal and institutional systems are not powerful in preventing, deterring, or identifying such tax evasion practices. Thus, when companies follow ethical business practices, they not only may be disadvantaged financially but also may be subject to pressure from the business community to engage in tax evasion.

There is an obvious and vital need to broaden business ethics education and research capacities in Turkish universities. Based on the low level of research output and scarce academic programs, there is clearly a need for Turkish higher educational institutions to increase their focus on ethical business practices through sound and indigenous research approaches by establishing both academic programs and research centers. Equally important is the need for more Turkish NGOs to inform the public as consumers about the ethical aspects of business life and to advocate an ethical business culture by putting positive pressure on and proactively influencing companies.

Growth in international trade and investment opportunities may help Turkish businesses and companies improve and strengthen their ethical business cultures, both through cooperation and competition. Thus, the integration of the Turkish economy with global markets as well as the capacity and capability of Turkish businesses should be not only maintained and supported but also expanded and enhanced. Turkish businesses may consider shifting their culture toward more ethical business culture and practices while promoting ethical leadership. Furthermore, instead of fostering a rigid value-based culture (solely focused on financial indicators), they should recognize values-based culture (focused on ethical indicators) in which ethical behavior as a performance indicator should take place in performance management systems and CSR should be seen as an essential means to reach organizational goals.

Turkish cultural characteristics imply that employees would rather obey the orders of their supervisors or conform to the group norms than violate harmony in the workplace. Thus, in Turkish business life, ethical leadership can be one of the most powerful determining factors of ethical business culture at any organization. Therefore, organizational leaders should deliberately attempt to build an ethical culture, and to do so, they should "walk the talk." Undoubtedly, their stakeholders, including customers and employees, will not only appreciate their ethical leadership practices but also lead the way in establishing best practices in ethical business culture for long-term sustainability and prosperity.

REFERENCES

AccountAbility (2007). Responsible competitiveness index. Retrieved from www.zadek.net/wp-content/uploads/2011/04/The-State-of-Responsible-Competitiveness_July2007.pdf

Akdere, M. (2015). Human resource development in CIVETS countries. *Refereed Proceedings of the 2015 Academy of Human Resource Development International Research Conference in the Americas*. St. Paul, MN: Academy of Human Resource Development.

Akdere, M., & Dirani, K. (2014). Human resource development in the Middle East. In Rob Poell, Tonette S. Rocco, & Gene Roth (Eds.), *Routledge companion to human resource development* (pp. 457–466). New York: Routledge.

Akdere, M., & Salem, J. M. (2012). Islamic perspectives on work-based learning. In P. Gibbs (Ed.), *Learning, work and practice: New understandings* (pp. 207–217). New York: Springer.

Ararat, M. (2008). A development perspective for "corporate social responsibility": Case of Turkey. *Corporate Governance*, 8(3), 271–285.

Ararat, M., Yurtoğlu, B. B., & Suel, E. (2010). Sustainable investment in Turkey. Retrieved from www.ifc.org/wps/wcm/connect/790c26804885550fb574f76a6515bb18/IFC_Brief_Turkey.pdf?MOD=AJPERES&CACHEID=790c26804885550fb574f76a6515bb18

Arslan, M. (2001). The work ethic values of Protestant British, Catholic Irish and Muslim Turkish managers. *Journal of Business Ethics*, 31(4), 321–339.

Arslan, M., & Berkman, A. U. (2009). *Business ethics and ethical management in the world and in Turkey (Dünyada ve Türkiye'de İş Etiği ve Etik Yönetimi)*. Istanbul: TUSIAD.

Askun, D., Oz, E. U., & Askun, O. B. (2010). Understanding managerial work values in Turkey. *Journal of Business Ethics*, 93(1), 103–114.

Auger, P., Devinney, T. M., & Louviere, J. J. (2007). Using best-worst scaling methodology to investigate consumer ethical beliefs across countries. *Journal of Business Ethics*, 70(3), 299–326.

Aydın, Z. (2005). *The political economy of Turkey*. London: Pluto Press.

Aydınlık, A. U., & Dönmez, D. (2007). Codes of ethics survey in top 500 firms in Turkey (Türkiye'de faaliyet gösteren en büyük 500 işletmede etik kodları araştırması). *Öneri*, 28(7), 151–158.

Aygün, Z. K., Arslan, M., & Guney, S. (2008). Work values of Turkish and American university students. *Journal of Business Ethics*, 80(2), 205–223.

Bayraktaroglu, S., Ozen Kutanis, R., & Ozdemir, Y. (2005). Where are we in ethics training? Example of faculty of economic and administrative sciences (Etik eğitiminde neredeyiz? İktisadi ve idari bilimler fakülteleri örneği). In M. Sen et al. (Eds.), 2nd *Symposium on Ethics in Politics and Management (2. Siyasette ve Yönetimde Etik Sempozyum)* (pp. 377–384). Sakarya: Sakarya University Press.

Benk, S., Budak, T., Puren, S., & Erdem, M. (2015). Perception of tax evasion as a crime in Turkey. *Journal of Money Laundering Control*, 18(1), 99–111.

Burnaz, S., Atakan, M. G. S., Topcu, Y. I., & Singhapakdi, A. (2009). An exploratory cross-cultural analysis of marketing ethics: The case of Turkish, Thai, and American businesspeople. *Journal of Business Ethics*, 90(3), 371–382.

Diyanet (2014). *Religious life in Turkey*. Retrieved from www2.diyanet.gov.tr/StratejiGelistirme/Afisalanlari/dinihayat.pdf

Donaldson, T., & Dunfee, T. W. (1994). Integrative social contracts theory. *Economics and Philosophy*, 11(1), 85–112.

Economist (2014). Our crony-capitalism index: Planet plutocrat. Retrieved from www.economist.com/news/international/21599041-countries-where-politically-connected-businessmen-are-most-likely-prosper-planet

Ekin, M. G. S., & Tezölmez, S. H. (1999). Business ethics in Turkey: An empirical investigation with special emphasis on gender. *Journal of Business Ethics*, 18(1), 17–34.

Ernst & Young (2009). *European fraud survey 2009: Is integrity a causality of the turndown?* Retrieved from www.ey.com/publication/vwluassetsdld/fraudsurvey_au0268_may2009/$file/fraudsurvey_au0268_may2009.pdf?OpenElement

Ferrell, O. C. (1999). An assessment of the proposed academy of marketing science code of ethics for marketing educators. *Journal of Business Ethics*, 19(2), 225-228.

Forsyth, D. R. (1992). Judging the morality of business practices: The influence of personal moral philosophies. *Journal of Business Ethics*, 11(5/6), 461–470.

Forum for a New World Governance (2011). *World governance index*. Retrieved from www.world-governance.org/article754.html?lang=en

GfK (2013). Global trust report. Retrieved from www.gfk-verein.org/en/research/studies/gfk-global-trust-report

Gölbaşi, S. (2009). Role of the business schools in institutionalization of the ethical behaviors. *Turkish Journal of Business Ethics*, 2(4), 21–41.

Halici, A., & Kucukaslan, A. (2005). Turkish companies' ethical statements: Content analysis with comparisons. *Management Research News*, 28(1), 45–61.

Hisrich, R. D., Bucar, B., & Oztark, S. (2003). A cross-cultural comparison of business ethics: Cases of Russia, Slovenia, Turkey, and United States. *Cross Cultural Management*, 10(1), 3–28.

Hofstede Centre (2014). Cultural dimensions: Turkey. Retrieved from http://geert-hofstede.com/turkey.html

IGIAD (2013). *Business ethics report: Turkey (İş Ahlakı Raporu: Türkiye)*. Retrieved from https://www.researchgate.net/profile/Erkan_Erdemir/publication/273629788_IGIAD_2013_Is_Ahlaki_Raporu_IGIAD_2013_Turkey_Business_Ethics_Report/links/5506d9aa0cf27e990e041781/IGIAD-2013-Is-Ahlaki-Raporu-IGIAD-2013-Turkey-Business-Ethics-Report.pdf

International Labour Organization (2015). Normlex. Information system on international labour standards. Retrieved from www.ilo.org/dyn/normlex/en/f?p=1000:1:0::NO:

Kepenek, Y., & Yentürk, N. (2004). *Turkish economy*. İstanbul: Remzi Yayınevi.

Köseoğlu, M. A. (2007). Effects of ethics codes in competitive strategies and a field investigation (unpublished doctoral dissertation). Afyon, Turkey: Afyon Kocatepe University.

Lu, L., Rose, G. M., & Blodgett, J. G. (1999). The effects of cultural dimensions on ethical decision making in marketing: An exploratory study. *Journal of Business Ethics*, 18(1), 91–105.

Menguç, B. (1998). Organizational consequences, marketing ethics and salesforce supervision: Further empirical evidence. *Journal of Business Ethics*, 17(4), 333–352.

O'Fallon, M. J., & Butterfield, K. D. (2005). A review of the empirical ethical decision-making literature: 1996–2003. *Journal of Business Ethics*, 59(4), 375–413.

Omurgonulsen, U., & Doig, A. (2012). Why the gap? Turkey, EU accession, corruption and culture. *Turkish Studies*, 13(1), 7–25.

Organisation for Economic Co-operation and Development (2014). *Society at a glance 2014 highlights: Turkey*. Retrieved from https://www.oecd.org/turkey/OECD-SocietyAtaGlance20142014-Highlights-Turkey.pdf

Park, H., Blenkinsopp, J., Oktem, M. K., & Omurgonulsen, U. (2008). Cultural orientation and attitudes toward different forms of whistleblowing: A comparison of South Korea, Turkey, and the U.K. *Journal of Business Ethics*, 82(4), 929–939.

Ralston, D. A., Pounder, J., Lo, C. W. H., Wong, Y., Egri, C. P., & Stauffer, J. (2006). Stability and change in managerial work values: A longitudinal study of China, Hong Kong, and the U.S. *Management and Organization Review*, 2(1), 67–94.

Rawwas, M. Y. A., Swaidan, Z., & Oyman, M. (2005). Consumer ethics: A cross-cultural study of the ethical beliefs of Turkish and American consumers. *Journal of Business Ethics*, 57(2), 183–195.

Reputation Management Institute (2013). *Corporate reputation research in companies*. Retrieved from www.iye.org.tr/wpcontent/uploads/2013/02/Isletmelerde_Kurumsal_Itibar-Arastirmasi_Raporu_2013.pdf

Rice, G. (1999). Islamic ethics and the implications for business. *Journal of Business Ethics*, 18(4), 345–358.

Robertson, D. C. (2009). Corporate social responsibility and different stages of economic development: Singapore, Turkey, and Ethiopia. *Journal of Business Ethics*, 88(4), 617–633.

Schneider, H., Krieger, J., & Bayraktar, A. (2011). The impact of intrinsic religiosity on consumers' ethical beliefs: Does it depend on the type of religion? A comparison of Christian and Moslem consumers in Germany and Turkey. *Journal of Business Ethics*, 102(2), 319–332.

Sims, R. L., & Gegez, A. E. (2004). Attitudes towards business ethics: A five nation comparative study. *Journal of Business Ethics*, 50(3), 253–265.

Singhapakdi, A., Vitell, S. J., & Leelakulthanit, O. (1994). A cross-cultural study of moral philosophies, ethical perceptions and judgements: A comparison of American and Thai marketers. *International Marketing Review*, 11(6), 65–78.

Srnka, K. J., Gegez, A. E., & Arzova, S. B. (2007). Why is it (un-)ethical? Comparing potential European partners: A western Christian and an eastern Islamic country – on arguments used in explaining ethical judgments. *Journal of Business Ethics*, 74(2), 101–118.

Transparency International (2014). Corruption perceptions index. Retrieved from www.transparency.org/cpi2014

Trevino, L. K., Butterfield, K. D., & McCabe, D. L. (1998). The ethical context in organizations: Influences on employee attitudes and behaviors. *Business Ethics Quarterly*, 8(3), 447–476.

Turker, D. (2015). An analysis of corporate social responsibility in the Turkish business context. In S. O. Idowu, R. Schmidpeter, & M. S. Fifka (Eds.), *Corporate social responsibility in Europe United in sustainable diversity* (pp. 435–468). Switzerland: Springer International Publishing.

Turkish National Revenue Administration (2015). Action plan of the program for decreasing shadow economy. Retrieved from www.gib.gov.tr/sites/default/files/fileadmin/beyannamerehberi/2015kayitdisi.pdf

Turkish Risk Center (2015) Statistical reports. Retrieved from https://www.riskmerkezi.org/en/statistics/23

Turkstat (2012). Child labour force survey. Retrieved from www.turkstat.gov.tr/PreHaberBultenleri.do?id=13659

Turkstat (2014) Main statistics. Retrieved from www.turkstat.gov.tr/UstMenu.do?metod=temelist

United Nations Development Programme (2008). *Turkey corporate social responsibility: Baseline report.* Retrieved from www.tr.undp.org/content/dam/turkey/docs/Publications/PovRed/CSR_Report_en.pdf

United Nations Development Programme (2013). *Human Development Report 2013.* Retrieved from http://hdr.undp.org/sites/default/files/reports/14/hdr2013_en_complete.pdf

Uygur, S. (2009). The Islamic work ethic and the emergence of Turkish SME owner-managers. *Journal of Business Ethics*, 88(1), 211–225.

Vitell, S. J., Paolillo, J. G. P., & Singh, J. J. (2005). Religiosity and consumer ethics. *Journal of Business Ethics*, 57(2), 175–181.

Warren, D. E., Gaspar, J. P., & Laufer, W. S. (2014). Is formal ethics training merely cosmetic? A study of ethics training and ethical organizational culture. *Business Ethics Quarterly*, 24(1), 85–117.

World Bank (2013). Turkey: Enterprise survey of 2013. Retrieved from http://microdata.worldbank.org/index.php/catalog/2182

World Bank (2014). *Evaluation of the EU-Turkey customs union.* Retrieved from http://ec.europa.eu/enlargement/pdf/financial_assistance/phare/evaluation/2014/20140403-evaluation-of-the-eu-turkey-customs-union.pdf

World Values Survey (2014). Welcome page. Retrieved from www.worldvaluessurvey.org

Yılmaz, S. E. (2012). The relationship between organization performance and business ethics applications at human resources management (HRM): A sample of Fortune Turkey's largest 500 corporations (unpublished doctoral dissertation). Sakarya University, Sakarya, Turkey.

Zulfikar, Y. F. (2012). Do Muslims believe more in protestant work ethic than Christians? Comparison of people with different religious background living in the US. *Journal of Business Ethics*, 105(4), 489–502.

7 Business Ethics in Mexico: The Seeds of Justice

Martha Sañudo

ABSTRACT

Business ethics, as the philosophical enquiry into the moral features present in economic activity, ought to be a tool for building a fairer society. To examine how business ethics in Mexico can be such a tool, we first present some economic and cultural consequences of Mexico's privileged geographical position (bordering the United States) and of its joining the North American Free Trade Agreement (NAFTA) in 1994. By adding a political and historical account to the analysis, we explain why the post-NAFTA boost in the economy has divided the country in what we have labeled *Main-Road Mexico* (those who are or seek to be part of the modern economy of Mexico) and *Off-Road Mexico* (those who are unaware of or distant from any "modern" options, or rather, wish to maintain and even strengthen their pre-NAFTA and even pre-Hispanic cultural identity). We then use Hofstede's findings of the cultural dimensions of Mexico to provide the backdrop against which we discuss recent and relevant research done on business in Mexico. We do this to highlight the implications for business practitioners dealing with Mexican companies in Mexico and Mexican companies abroad and to suggest that indeed business ethics can be the seed of social justice.

MEXICO REVEALED

Mexico is geographically North American and culturally Latin American, and the tension created by this juxtaposition has led Mexico to be commercially highly connected and simultaneously a culturally complex country. The World Bank ranks Mexico as a relatively easy place to do business, while Transparency International placed Mexico at the higher end of its corruption index in 2016 (Mexico ranked 123 of 170 countries, where 1 is the least corrupt and 170 the most corrupt) (Corruption Perception Index, https://www.transparency.org/news/feature/corruption_perceptions_index_2016).

Mexico has 12 free trade agreements with more than 40 countries including, notoriously, the North American Free Trade Agreement (NAFTA) with the United States and Canada (1994) and the European Union (2000). However, despite this trans-world, free trade, commercial hyper-connectivity, it is across Mexico's 3,145 km (1,954 mile-long) northern border with the United States that 80 percent of all Mexican exports flow ("México en cifras," 2015).

That Mexico shares this border with the country that is the world's most powerful nation has been the strongest outside influence on the Mexican psyche for more than 100 years. A famous saying, "Poor Mexico, so far from God and so close to the United States!", attributed to Porfirio Díaz, president of Mexico from 1877 to 1911, captures a most salient characteristic when thinking of Mexico in terms of business and ethics. To Mexicans this influential neighbor, the United States, has been a constant reminder of what Mexico could become, if only its people could emulate the American "can do" spirit, blending discipline and efficiency to create economic success. On the other hand, this giant English-speaking and sober neighbor inspires Mexico to defiantly assert the appeal of its differentiation: Latin laxity ("fiesta" and "siesta") and pride in both its pre-Columbian history and the post-Mexican Revolution promotion and celebration of the "Mestizo" culture (the mixing of races) as a means of nation-building that includes both indigenous and Spanish peoples in the new Mexican culture.

GAINS AND LOSSES OF MEXICO'S CHOSEN NAFTA PATH

Today Mexico's present and future is irrevocably stitched to that of its powerful neighbor. This is most obvious in terms of economics, where in 2013 a daily total of $1 billion worth of Mexican exports crossed the NAFTA frontier to the United States ("US Relations with Mexico," 2016). Mexicans know that this increasingly transparent political border and trade connection with the United States and Canada constitutes the main attraction for foreign direct investment in Mexico, since it means easy access to the massive US market.

The presence of the United States looms large in Mexican minds in many other ways. If people in countries around the world believe they know of the American way of life from popular music and Hollywood movies, in Mexico the American presence is felt and increasingly consumed in many other ways than just through the movies: Walmart is the largest Mexican private sector employer and supplies Mexicans with blue jeans, hamburgers, cornflakes, and every imaginable American consumable. So fast and able is the Mexican consumer to adopt new consumption patterns that their traditional diet and lifestyle have been radically altered, causing serious public health concerns. Mexicans are now the second most obese people in the world and have among the highest levels of type 2 diabetes, being the leading cause of death among adults in 2015, Mexico's National Death Registry. Returning Mexican migrants, both documented agricultural and undocumented workers, constitute another cultural influence, spreading the word about opportunities and experiences in the neighboring country. There are approximately 12 million first-generation Mexican migrants living in the United States, and almost every youngster in Mexico entertains the possibility of spending some time in the United States. The "American Dream" has proven to be true for many Mexicans, and the socioeconomic trend of second-generation Mexican-Americans is more positive than ever (Morando, 2013). And yet, in spite of this constant stream of influences from the United States, Mexico retains its differentiated identity.

There is no doubt, however, that the United States determines to a great extent Mexico's economic perspective, and the slow but steady adoption of the United States' entrepreneurial mentality and language of progress and success makes Mexico's political and business class confident in understanding the pattern of development they are to follow (Kras, 2000). This explains why the signing in 1992 of a risky economic treaty, NAFTA, that came into effect the 1st of January 1994, with the United States and Canada was considered a flagship moment for President Carlos Salinas' government.

Even though NAFTA has received a great deal of criticism since its conception, and in-depth studies show that the promise NAFTA embodied in 1994 has been unfulfilled (no genuine decrease in the poverty rate, no rise in wages or the employment rate) (Weisbrot et al., 2014), the liberalization of Mexican industry (based until then on import substitution, which protected Mexican industries from foreign competition and which restricted foreign ownership and investment in Mexican companies) meant that certain goods, like clothing and consumer electronics, would become more affordable for Mexican families. More importantly, it made governmental institutions gear their efforts toward reducing deficits and stopping currency crises, allowing long-term domestic investment and attracting record foreign direct investment.

Figure 7.1 shows the stark difference between the sixfold increase in exports, the nearly fivefold increase in foreign direct investment (FDI), a doubling of the gross domestic product (GDP), and the continuing flat line of the GINI coefficient, which represents income distribution in a nation. Poverty has also flat lined throughout the same period. In 2012, Mexico reported 52 percent of its population living in poverty, the same as in 2010 and in 1994 (Weisbrot et al., 2014). Though the percentage remains unchanged, the population has increased and therefore the actual number of people living in poverty has increased.

It is impossible to know what would have happened to Mexico without NAFTA, but the 2017 trajectory of the Mexican economy is clearly dictated by NAFTA; in a scenario of projected growth, PricewaterhouseCoopers (PwC) predicts that Mexico will be the 9th

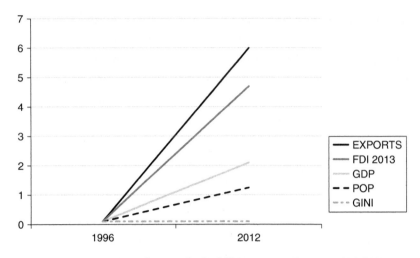

FIGURE 7.I. Significance of a Sixfold Increase in Exports, 1996–2012.

Compiled from the following sources:
GINI: 1996 = 48.5; 2012 = 48.1 http://data.worldbank.org/indicator/
SI.POV.GINI?page=3
Population (POP): 1996 = 95 million; 2012 = 117 million http://stats
.oecd.org/Index.aspx?DatasetCode=SNA_TABLE1#
GDP per head US$, current price, current purchasing power parities
(PPP): 1996 = 7,820; 2012 = 16,80 http://stats.oecd.org/Index
.aspx?DatasetCode=SNA_TABLE1#
Foreign Direct Investment (FDI) Net inflows current US$ 1996 = US$9
billion; 2013 = US$ 42 billion
http://data.worldbank.org/indicator/BX.KLT.DINV.CD.WD/
countries?page=3
Exports gross figures current dollars: 1996 = US$50 billion;
2012 = US$300 billion
http://atlas.cid.harvard.edu/explore/stacked/export/mex/all/show/
1995.2012.2/

largest economy by 2030 (ahead of the United Kingdom and France)
and the 6th by 2050 ("The World in 2050," 2015).

POLITICS AND GEOGRAPHY SHAPING MEXICO'S
SOCIOECONOMIC SYSTEM

Along with NAFTA, many other components of Mexican society
have added to the economic push, mainly the ending in December
2000 of 71 years of the so-called Perfect Dictatorship, a single-party
democracy in which the PRI (Partido Revolucionario Institucional)
won every presidential election (ruling similarly to other Latin-
American dictatorships but with a façade of democracy). Following

the first orderly and democratic change of power, which lasted 12 years (2 x 6-year terms) of the PAN (Partido Acción Nacional), the PRI was returned to power in 2012. These clean elections and the seamless change of the governing party have boosted Mexico's self-confidence, as well as encouraged and reassured record numbers of foreign investors who have helped Mexico catch up with technologically complex industrialized economies (Dussel Peters, 2007). Harvard University's Atlas of Economic Complexity ranks Mexico at 22 in its table of economic complexity, between Belgium at 21 and Israel at 23 (Atlas of Economic Complexity, 2014).

A whole generation of young professionals and entrepreneurs has grown in confidence to compete globally, experiencing as natural the democratic process involved in the change of the ruling party and viewing the NAFTA environment as business as usual. It is also these people, "Generation NAFTA," who are the driving force behind the implementation of an ethical business outlook learnt on the job and at business schools that are changing social consciousness and values. By benchmarking and adopting best business practices from around the world to make Mexican-owned and foreign-owned Mexican-based businesses globally competitive, a new generation of Mexican businesspeople have learned the value of transparent competition. Using their practiced business skills and new technologies to analyze relevant social and political data and finding out that through civil organizations they can lobby for their interests and political demands, this new class is speeding social change and enhancing the nascent Mexican democracy. The modernizing and "cleaning up" of Mexico appears to be taking place in the fast internationalizing business sector rather than in the domestic public and political sector. It is in this context that business ethics can be regarded as a promising seed for social justice in Mexico.

This means, also, that the younger segment of the business class understands that future economic prosperity – their own, their families', and their friends' – is more closely tied to commerce with the United States and beyond than to the vagaries of their own government. This situation may result, unintentionally, in structural changes that will be less profound than Mexico really needs (Shefner, 2007).

DIVERSE MEXICO

Mexico, with almost 2 million square km (more than 760,000 square miles), is the size of Germany, Spain, France, Italy, and the United Kingdom combined (and more than one-fifth the size of the United States). According to the United Nations Environment Program, it is one of the six most biodiverse countries on earth ("Geo-Mexico," n.d.). This biodiversity may well be reflected in the traditional socio-cultural and linguistic diversity of its many peoples that leaves Mexicans who live outside of the political and industrial centers with a sense of being part of a smaller, unique nation. There are 6 million indigenous people whose first language is not Spanish but one of the 67 languages recognized by the Mexican government, and only as recently as 2003 has a law been passed (Ley general de dere-chos lingüísticos de los pueblos indígenas) to protect and promote indigenous languages and to offer bilingual education in the schools that need it.

While cities have grown and apparently prospered, rural and once active agricultural areas have become increasingly isolated, impoverished, and populated mainly by the elderly, with young Mexicans moving to the cities and to the United States looking for economic opportunity. The movement of people from rural to urban areas has long been evident in Mexico, as in much of the industrializing world. But the most recent major negative impact of NAFTA on the vitality of rural and agricultural communities in Mexico resulted from export-oriented industrialization ("Mexico and NAFTA," 2008). This wave has created a pull for men and young women toward NAFTA-oriented industries in Mexico and for men toward the low-pay sector of the US rural and other labor markets. This manpower pull, combined with the push away from the land caused by the collapse of Mexico's domestic agricultural sector, has left Mexico's rural areas further abandoned. Hence, the undoubtedly positive economic picture, though very real and attractive to investors, has yet to noticeably benefit all of Mexico's 119 million citizens ("México en cifras," 2015).

Main-Road and Off-Road Mexico: The Complexity of a National Identity and Development

The Spanish Conquistadores of the 15th century (like most colonial powers) laid a new map of "Mexico" over the pre-Columbian societies and nations of the New World. This map developed according to the ambitions of Spanish soldiers and the Catholic Church, with little cooperative interaction with the prevailing (though decimated) indigenous peoples; afterward the tracks followed an economic, extractive industry design. None of this infrastructure and investment was purposefully built to unite the Mexican nation. Rather, the peoples within the territory of the United States of Mexico have always had to make a conscious effort to go to these towns and decide whether or not to use these routes.

Five hundred years after the Spanish invasion, the development of the NAFTA Super Highway system (promoted by the North American Superhighway Coalition) began, with a south to north trajectory, clustering many of the newly created NAFTA industries, particularly the burgeoning automotive industry. It is within these industrial centers and along these export corridors that most of modern Mexico's wealth and opportunities are created.

Leading on from this, we can theoretically split Mexico into two groups: those who seek to be part of the modernization of Mexico (Main-Road Mexico) and those who are unaware of any options, or wish to maintain and even strengthen their own cultural identity (Off-Road Mexico). It is Main-Road Mexico that most multinational companies encounter and encourage, and it is where we find what appears to be a progressive, scientific, open, liberal, and democratic society (Galindo, 2013).

Off-Road Mexico is less homogenous and much more complex and explains to an extent the entrenchment and efficient operation of the drug cartels. These cartels, living out an alternate Mexican dream of bravado and desperados, have proven very capable of fusing their absolute dominance of their massive off-road fiefdoms with their knowledge of the nation's transport logistics to ship their product through every land, air, and maritime port in Mexico.

CULTURAL CHARACTERISTICS AND IMPLICATIONS FOR BUSINESS ETHICS

The colonial past, which has left Mexico with Spanish as a unifying language and the Catholic religion as its founding culture, can account for certain Latino traits that are well identified in the "chicanos" (residents of the United States of Mexican ancestry), such as the dominant role that family plays on their choices (Steidel & Contreras, 2003). However, there are still cultural studies to be developed that could account for today's divide between Main-Road and Off-Road Mexico. Nonetheless, comparative cultural studies can be used since these have the advantage of openly recognizing that culture and values are theoretical constructs and that modeling dimensions of how different cultures deal with certain basic issues of social life may help better understand the unwritten codes, the implicit norms, and subtle expectations of a country as a whole, independently or in spite of the radical differences they may show internally (Hofstede, 2009).

Many cross-cultural studies refer to the pioneering work of Hofstede in the late 1960s, based on the results of a simple questionnaire given to workers from different countries, where he discovered that their scores would cluster around four "dimensions of cultures." By dimensions of cultures Hofstede means "an aspect of a culture that can be measured relative to other cultures" (Hofstede et al., 2010, p. 31). The publication of his findings in 1980 (Hofstede, 1980) coincided with a wider interest in intercultural studies in sociology and social psychology, as well as with a growing internationalization of business leading to a demand for a better grasp of how to improve intercultural interactions. Research on cross-cultural comparisons has increased notably since the 1980s, and since then it has become common in the literature on international business, international management, international marketing, and so forth to find cross cultural comparisons. The Hofstede Centre has incorporated other researchers' input and expanded their dimensions of culture from four to six dimensions. The results are sufficiently similar to the more recent GLOBE study (Javidan et al., 2006), conducted in the period 1994–1997, to justify using Hofstede's results. (The Hofstede Centre offers online access to the scores of each country for which they have acquired data, which can be found at https://geert-hofstede .com/mexico.html.)

Comparing the scores of these dimensions of culture sheds light on important characteristics of a country's organizations and institutions and its peoples' motivations and interpretations of actions – all issues that help us appreciate, differentiate, and approach a given country's culture. These scores reflect the perceived prevalence of cultural traits. Cultural studies scholars stress that culture is learned, not innate, and therefore changeable; the values of a culture serve as mental programming, a sort of "software of the mind" (Hofstede et al., 2010), which is "installed" through socializing in childhood or cultural assimilation (Bailey & Spicer, 2007) and makes reactions and ways of behaving understandable. Even though individual responses may vary depending on the specific context, the cultural background offers enough similarities to the responses that it serves to identify traits that, when identified, may ease intercultural understanding.

Now, we will examine the interpretations given by the Hofstede Centre of the scores for Mexico (http://geert-hofstede.com/mexico .html) and then expand on each of these dimensions in relation to other relevant research. The interpretation of the results coincides to a great extent with all the studies researched for this chapter and expresses in a nutshell what a foreigner visiting Mexico and doing business in Mexico would notice and experience. The discussion offered here, however, expands on Hofstede's interpretation in order to bring to light newer or more detailed implications for business ethics of the cultural characterization presented, or points at possible departures from such characterizations while examining possible causes for such departure.

Power Distance in Mexico (81 = a high score)

> Interpretation provided by the Hofstede Centre: Mexico has a high power distance score and is thus a hierarchical society. This means that Mexicans accept a hierarchical structure, quickly understand their place in it, centralization is expected, and where "subordinates expect to be told what to do and the ideal boss is a benevolent autocrat." (http://geert-hofstede.com/mexico.html)

When findings point at Mexican managerial and leadership styles being hierarchical, researchers typically recall the Latin-American history of conquistadores, servitude, and religious imposition (Howell et al., 2007). When Mexico entered NAFTA in 1994, the available studies showed that Mexican management and leadership were indeed authoritarian due to the tendency of Mexican firms to reflect the traditional structure of Mexican society: "a paternalistic, hierarchical structure also shown in government, church and family" (De Forest 1994, p. 34; Morris & Pavett, 1992). However, more recent studies show that management style in Mexico has shifted radically from an authoritarian style to a more "consultative style" (that is, in Likert's 4 system), thus asking employees for input and conducting participative-style meetings are increasingly common in Mexican companies (Blanco et al., 2009; Howell et al., 2007; Ruiz et al., 2013). Also, the implementation of various international standards in Mexican companies is transforming management practices. This is particularly apparent in the transfer of manufacturing operations from the United States to Mexico, resulting in Mexican managers having "similar assessments, agreements, perceptions, or opinions on quality" as those of the United States (Schniederjans et al., 2006, p. 16). A paternalist style of management is giving way to a broader, hybrid, more inclusive leadership style, which engages with various organizational stakeholders, such as the company's surrounding community (Elvira & Davila, 2005).

However, research on managerial culture and leadership in Mexico is scarce and often contradictory. Varieties of outcomes found in several studies relate to whether writers want to demonstrate the transferability of managerial practices – and thus the plausibility of American companies doing successful business in Mexico, or ways for Mexican companies to increase productivity – or whether writers want to highlight how management practices are culturally bounded – for example, regarding recruitment practices in Mexico (Howell et al., 2007; Rao, 2009). There is also a major limitation to the studies available in that the data is gathered almost exclusively by questionnaires and focus groups with managers or CEOs who are most often educated in private business schools influenced by American styles of management and leadership and whose worldview is radically different from blue-collar employees who might have deep roots in Off-Road Mexico.

In Hofstede's analysis, a hierarchical society "correlates with income inequality" (Hofstede et al., 2010, p. 39), and as we have mentioned, inequality in Mexico is its greatest challenge. It is economic inequality that pushes many Mexicans to recur to violence (Knight, 2013), and inequality makes it easier for people to rationalize their own corrupt behavior so that corruption becomes endemic, and endemic corruption undermines any country's prosperity and stability (Anechiarico, 2010; Cockcroft, 2014).

In terms of what kind of ethics policies ensue from the power distance situation in Mexico, it is relevant to consider that in countries with high inequality, companies gear their ethical efforts toward "corporate social investment," that is, philanthropic and community work is included as corporate social responsibility (CSR) (Puppim de Oliveira, 2006). Philanthropic work and social commitment in Latin

America have their roots in a long tradition of Catholic Church charity. In this sense, CSR-type activities, which after NAFTA were introduced by multinational companies, are not new to Mexico; there is a long-standing tradition of Catholic patronage and community commitment (Logsdon et al., 2006). In countries where poverty is pervasive (as it is in most emerging countries), companies understand that acting as responsible corporate citizens means responding to their community's needs; that is, companies maintain their social "license to operate" by palliating the effects of weak or bad governments by, for instance, investing in procuring better education and healthcare for their employees and families, as well as other stakeholders, such as people who live close to the company's factory, plant, or offices (Baskin, 2006).

One concern is that even though companies are doing a social good through these social projects, the general population of Mexico does not know or recognize what the term "corporate social responsibility" means or might imply (Velázquez et al., 2009). Thus the incentive for promoting a company's reputation, or the fear of receiving sanctions, does not seem to play a role in companies' ethical practices. Although corporate philanthropy in Mexico has increased considerably since 2000, it is often concentrated in a corporate foundation, which on average employs only three workers and is geared to tangible, short-term outcomes, rather than well-researched projects for social development (Carrillo et al., 2009). Many efforts to promote CSR in Mexico stem from the Centro Mexicano para la Filantropía (CEMEFI; www.cemefi.org/), a non-governmental organization (NGO) that, since 1990, has promoted a logo that companies and organizations can use on their correspondence and websites to distinguish themselves as companies and organizations who voluntarily fulfill certain criteria in terms of social responsibility. Although CEMEFI has similar objectives to the United Nations Global Compact (UNGC) and the Global Reporting Initiative (GRI), it is less rigorous and less efficient in guaranteeing long-term implementation of ethical policies in a company. Nevertheless, it is CEMEFI, together with the Unión

Social de Empresarios de México (USEM; http://www.usem.org.mx), a Catholic organization of Mexican businesspeople, that have positioned CSR within Mexican organizations. Thus, international standards for reporting ethical concerns (GRI, ISO 14001, Dow Jones Sustainability Index) are being adopted by Mexican subsidiaries of multinational companies, or by Mexican companies that have become multinationals or want to become transnational players. An unresolved task is to sustain existent ethical initiatives and take them to deeper levels of social transformation. As the comparative study of Baskin suggests,

> there is not a vast difference in the approach to reported corporate responsibility between leading companies in high income OECD [Organization for Economic Co-operation and Development] countries and their emerging-market peers. Nonetheless, corporate responsibility in emerging markets, while more extensive than commonly believed, is less embedded in corporate strategies, less pervasive and less politically rooted than in most high-income OECD countries. (2006, p. 46)

Hence, work in CSR in Mexico, to be comparable to what CSR implies in more developed countries, would need to include the lobbying of companies for real social transformation. Also, companies would have to acknowledge a possible cost to them when implementing CSR practices as core to their in country corporate policy in less equal societies.

Implications for Practitioners

The managerial style of companies in Mexico has changed, but the latent power distance means that even when an interaction appears to be warm and inclusive, respect and formality is often expected (Chávez-Reyes, 2010). For instance, Mexicans' deference to senior people (either in hierarchy or age) is signaled by the use of the formal word for "you" (that is *usted* in Spanish), in place of the usual and less formal *tú*. A more senior manager may address others as *tú* and expect them to address him (usually a him) as *usted*.

While it is prudent for companies to meet their community's needs and assist with basic development projects, companies could align their ethics policies to more long-term social justice, bringing about needed and long-lasting social transformation.

Individualism in Mexico (30, a very low score = collectivist culture)

> Interpretation provided by the Hofstede Centre: Mexicans have a collectivist mentality, which means they create long-term commitment to the member "group," and loyalty to this group may over-ride other societal rules and regulations. Thus, "employer/ employee relationships are perceived in moral terms (like a family link), hiring and promotion decisions take account of the employee's in-group, management is the management of groups." (http:// geert-hofstede.com/mexico.html)

Cross-cultural studies emphasize that individuals' beliefs and judgments relate to broader cultural constructions of the self and expected ways of relating to others. The classification of cultures into "individualist" or "collectivist" cultures suggests that people judge situations differently according to whether they see themselves as detached from a group or as attached to a group dynamic in which they pursue group goals that reinforce the group's harmony. Thus, researchers have attempted to align individualistic cultures with an ethics of duty, where autonomy and equality are emphasized, and collectivist cultures with a moral reasoning attuned with caring for others and taking heed of specific contexts and situations in which relationships can be protected (Husted & Allen, 2008).

However, experimental social psychologists have suggested that the distinction between individualist and collectivist cultures might be too simplistic. Whether a certain group has power and access to valued resources might explain better an individual's behavior than the attributes associated with "individual or "collective" cultures.

This means for Oyserman (2006) that "both individualistic and collectivistic cultural frames are universally available but differentially likely to be brought online into working memory. This recent development assumes that cultures differ in the number of situations in which individualism or collectivism are cued, but that both individualism and collectivism are universally cue-able and, once cued, produce the same effects across societies" (p. 353). This means that the settings for interaction, which can be the values of a given organizational culture, have more influence on individualist or collectivist traits than the national cultures do (Schein, 2010). For instance, in Mexico, companies' recruiting practices are a highly personal affair (Rao, 2009), but this does not mean that e-recruiting might be easily adopted (Elvira & Davila, 2005).

In Mexico, low individualism and high collectivist traits within companies might be reinforced by companies being mostly family businesses. Of the Mexican companies that were listed on the Mexican stock exchange (Bolsa Mexicana de Valores) in 2012, 70 percent were family owned (Belausteguigoitia, 2012), including Carlos Slim's empire (richest man in the world on the Forbes list in 2010–2012, and 2nd after Bill Gates in 2014–2015, 6th in 2017). Family businesses demonstrate in Mexico, like elsewhere, the advantage of resilience (Espinoza & Espinoza, 2012), and since trust and loyalty are considered important in Mexico, hiring is often made through social connections, which has the advantage of predictability and harmony (Elvira & Davila, 2005). But these family businesses also carry the disadvantage of having family members monopolizing managerial positions, impeding access to the best qualified people for a job, and creating cronyism (La Porta et al., 1999). For the Mexican Stock Market, this has meant equity dynamics problems ("S&P Dow Jones Indices for Mexico," n.d.), since possible investors in family companies fear that family decisions may run against the interests of minority of shareholders. Moreover, larger Mexican companies are often part of a conglomerate, or business group, with interlocking directorates that concentrate power and social capital in a few men (Husted & Serrano, 2002). This has created problems on at least two fronts. First, monopolizing managerial positions goes against the Corporate Governance Code for Mexico (a code suggested for adoption by the OECD) and the New Stock Market Law, passed in 2001 (*Ley del Mercado de Valores*, LMV), where the obligation is to appoint independent members to the board of directors to avoid agency problems. Second, problems could arise due to the lack of transparency and the opportunity for fraud when there are no independent board members and there is little communication to minority shareholders; in this respect, three recent cases of publicly held companies that are being investigated by the Mexican Banking and Securities Commission are Azteca Holding in 2005, Comercial Mexicana in 2008, and Walmart Mexico in 2012.

The dynamics of family business, which are strong in Latin-America and Asia, may create conditions for institutional corporate corruption, but it is not evident that following a Western-imposed pattern of corporate governance is the solution (Rocha González, 2011). Since 2004, the Mexican NGO, Centro de Excelencia en Gobierno Corporativo (CEGC), has helped Mexican companies to implement international financial standards. The CEGC came about as a result of many similar initiatives. In 2000, the OECD and World Bank helped establish the Latin American Corporate Governance Roundtable in order to enhance institutional investor impact on corporate governance, develop corporate governance codes, and promote the study and implementation of best practices of good corporate governance in the region. Several international organizations support this initiative, such as the International Finance Corporation (IFC), the Global Corporate Governance Forum (GCGF), the Commission for Latin American and the Caribbean (ECLAC), the Inter-American Development Bank (IADB), the Andean Development Corporation (CAF), and the Center for International Private Enterprise (CIPE). With yearly meetings, country offices, task forces, toolkits, and the use of "company circles," together with the support of so many international organizations, there has been major advancement in financial transparency and corporate governance in Latin America. ("Latin American Roundtable", n.d.).

While compliance is important, there is a broad area of opportunity in Mexico for combating corruption in such a way that compliance is accompanied by a larger commitment to the subsuming of private and company interests to the overall economic common good. A reduction in corruption in Mexico may require a few "nudges" rather than root-and-branch changes, according to the latest findings of organizational psychology (Thaler & Sunstein, 2009). Also, deep-seated habits can be changed by learning about the cognitive biases that lead to moral and epistemological "blind spots" (Bazerman & Tenbrunsel, 2011). This means that vast institutional changes may happen by changing structures and incentives instead of focusing on rigid regulation and punishment (Thompson, 2013). Business ethics training can be the means to bring companies into contact with new methodologies deriving from the findings of these social sciences, thereby deploying their knowledge to aid other civic organizations promoting anti-corruption agendas.

Implications for Practitioners
If effective leadership is achieved by congruence with cultural expectations, leadership in Mexico must take into consideration the collective frame of mind of employees. Mexican culture is "collectivist"; therefore, this might mean caring about employees' families, for example, by providing space for social interaction and festivities where employees and their families are invited.

In Mexico, familial-type relationships are central. An ethos of reciprocity, that is, an understanding that human bonding happens through giving and receiving favors, allows the possibility of long-term friendships and the sharing of common goals. Recognizing this ancient form of commerce (Mauss, 1990) makes it easier to identify when such reciprocity might devolve into corrupt practices. One of the implications of the previous discussion is that designing an organizational culture based on a proper understanding of motivations and social expectations before corrupt practices appear and are cemented into place might be the most efficacious method of prevention of corruption.

Masculinity in Mexico (69 = a more masculine than feminine culture)

> Interpretation provided by the Hofstede Centre: A high score in masculinity in Mexico denotes certain cultural stereotypes. The macho stereotype appears here. What this means in terms of business is that "managers are expected to be decisive and assertive, the emphasis is on equity, competition and performance and conflicts are resolved by fighting them out." (http://geert-hofstede.com/mexico.html)

One of the markers for masculine societies is their keenness on maximum social differentiation between the sexes. And indeed, the greatest contrast between Main-Road and Off-Road Mexico is in terms of gender equality; this means that the poorest of the poor, in terms of income and opportunities, are girls and women in the indigenous off-road areas of the states of Chiapas, Oaxaca, and Guerrero (United Nations Development Programme, 2011, p. 113).

In major Mexican cities, women are gaining public presence and recognition, but gender equality in rural and small towns is almost nonexistent. Since gender inequality is a major barrier for human development, the United Nations Development Program has produced a Gender Inequality Index (GII) measuring reproductive health, empowerment, and labor market participation. The GII of 2013, which helped produce the Human Development Index of 2014, places Mexico at 71st out of 187 countries (lower than other Latin-American countries such as Cuba, 44; Argentina, 49; Uruguay, 50; Panama, 65; Venezuela, 67; and Costa Rica, 68). To improve gender equality, in 2001 Mexico created a national (federal) governmental institution, the Instituto de las Mujeres (INMUJERES;

www.inmujeres.gob.mx), promoting the need for a gender vision and gender analysis in every governmental public policy decision.

The INMUJERES, and many Mexican NGOs working for women, work amidst pervasive violence against females. The infamous case, which made international news in the mid-1990s, of young women working in *maquiladoras* being murdered in Ciudad Juárez Chihuahua is indicative of the high incidence of violence against women in Mexico (Pick et al., 2006). In a 2011 report, it is stated that 46 percent of Mexican women over the age of 15 years who live with a partner suffer from some form of domestic violence (Eternod Arámburu, 2013). INMUJERES lobbied the law to typify "femicide," the killing of females by males because they are females, in Mexican Law (passed in 2011).

With this cultural backdrop, it is not surprising to find widespread discriminatory practices against women in Mexican companies (Muller & Rowell, 1997; Stevenson, 2004), from pregnancy tests before signing an employment contract to other internationally recognized forms of "vertical" segregation (hierarchically wise) and "horizontal" segregation (ghettoized in certain fields and occupations) (Charles, 2003). According to Zabludovsky (2001), up to the year 2000, companies in Mexico did not have specific programs or plans to advance women in their companies, which meant that practically all women considered that motherhood jeopardized their job opportunities (Zabludovsky, 2001). Today things are changing, particularly in companies where women are involved in CSR policies, and there is an awareness of the advantages of promoting diversity programs and flexible work hours (Arredondo et al., 2013). A public policy since 2011 of securing free childcare for every worker has furthered the participation of women in the labor force, who now number 43 percent (a major rise since 1970, 17%, and 1997, 35%) ("Estadísticas a propósito," 2016).

Since 2006, INMUJERES has offered companies and organizations a model for managing gender equality in companies (Modelo de Gestión de Equidad de Género [MEG], 2003–2015), aiming at institutionalizing programs of gender equality within the organization. By obtaining the certificate attesting that an organization has a MEG in place, the company gains access to several governmental incentives (including reduced taxes, grants, and training). INMUJERES also offers specific programs for women CEOs, women entrepreneurs, and other women in business.

Another characteristic of masculine cultures is that they value achievement, whereas feminine cultures value affiliation. In the United States, another masculine culture according to Hofstede's findings, management by objectives, merit-based reward practices, and clear patterns of job promotion are linked to better productivity (Newman & Nollen, 1996). Although no studies were found testing the link of this dimension with management in Mexico, it would be reasonable to assume that such management practices also work for Mexico.

Implications for Practitioners

In Mexico, good business ethics practice may lead to gender equality in the corporate culture. Setting easily and clearly measured "ethical goals" alongside the usual bottom-line demands may result in positive reforms. In hiring, this would mean setting gender targets for specific job roles; more men in support roles and more women in management. In community and stakeholder relations, this would mean creating measures of those groups' satisfaction and involvement.

Uncertainty Avoidance in Mexico (82, a high score = feeling threatened by ambiguous or unknown situations)

> *Interpretation provided by the Hofstede Centre: A high score here means that people prefer rigidity since it gives predictability rather than experimenting with new and unpredictable ideas. "In these cultures there is an emotional need for rules (even if the rules never seem to work), time is money, people have an inner urge to be busy and work hard, precision and punctuality are the norm,*

innovation may be resisted, security is an important element in individual motivation." (http://geert-hofstede.com/mexico.html)

The rapid change in the economic scene that Mexico has enjoyed has not been accompanied by economic stability. From high volatility in the 1980s, Mexico passed into dependency on international markets, which are vulnerable to externalities, such as crime reports by mass media that unnerve investors. This economic instability, coupled with constantly unpredictable political outcomes, means that many Mexican entrepreneurs cope with uncertainty by embracing stability, whenever this is possible. Systems of control in companies are an expression of this desire to reduce unpredictability. For instance, hiring in Mexico is done through an excessive inquiry into the personal life and habits of the potential employee and by conducting multiple checks on the information provided (Rao, 2009).

Moreover, since Mexican institutions are bureaucratic, and authoritative decision makers are few and far between, making changes in an organization appears to be slow and difficult. A study by Murphy (2006) on Mexican leadership shows that top leaders of the largest Mexican companies, who are seeking to maintain organizational stability, take promotion decisions and make performance evaluations based on the administrative skills of employees, and value insufficiently the employees' leadership potential or international experience. To avoid conflict, employers "tend to seek workers who are agreeable, respectful, and obedient rather than innovative and independent" (De Forest, 1994, p. 34). To counter this Mexican tendency of avoiding ambiguous or unknown situations and personal conflict, the 10 best business schools in Mexico (Eduniversal, 2016) have introduced programs that allow students to have international experience to counteract parochialism and ethnocentrism.

In a culture with high uncertainty avoidance, every change is perceived as a threat, which in turn produces anxiety and intolerance to ambiguity. It also means that innovation is met with distrust. Such cultural settings have had negative implications for

CSR programs in Mexico, where the general public tends to suspect rather than support an organization's investment in new philanthropic programs. Lack of information regarding basic business ethics concepts, such as stakeholders, social contract, CSR, etc., and knowledge of the scandalously corrupt practices of some politicians and entrepreneurs results in confusion about which corporate actions citizens should spurn or applaud. Velazquez et al. (2009) researched the perception of Mexican people toward three nationally well-known efforts of philanthropic CSR and found that "citizens distrusted the intentions of the companies and wondered if those efforts hid tax evasion or fraudulent activities" (Velázquez et al., 2009, p. 281). Yet, Arredondo et al. (2011) show that CSR programs do have a positive impact, but mainly on the workers who volunteer for CSR programs themselves, raising civic awareness and brand loyalty.

We are likely to see a lower score of uncertainty avoidance in Mexico as the democratic governing institutions are strengthened by an increasingly efficient and demanding civil society. These government and civil society institutions will lobby laws to punish illegality and enable economic development. Such changes will cultivate a socioeconomic atmosphere that will permit a more flexible and innovative culture to flourish. Companies will be able to see the benefits of promoting, supporting, and publicly encouraging the efforts made by civil society.

Implications for Practitioners
To induce change and bring about innovation, training provided to employees should be geared toward developing leadership and soft skills. Effort must be made to discuss/introduce international best practices, rather than to maintain what is most commonly practiced locally, regionally, or nationally. Companies that want support for their CSR programs must invest efforts in educating the wider public as to the positive social impact of their initiatives.

Long-Term Orientation in Mexico (24, a very low score = Short-Term Orientation)

> *Interpretation provided by the Hofstede Centre: A low score means "Mexicans have a strong concern with establishing the absolute truth; they are normative in their thinking. They exhibit great respect for traditions, a relatively small propensity to save for the future, and a focus on achieving quick results." (http:// geert-hofstede.com/mexico.html)*

Of Hofstede's six dimensions, long-term orientation (LTO) is the most controversial and difficult to interpret. This dimension was added after Chinese researchers argued that without adding this dimension several core Chinese values would not find a place in the survey. A high score in LTO can be related to four principal teachings of Confucian philosophy: (a) persistence/perseverance, (b) thrift, (c) the ordering relationships by status and observation of their order, and (d) a sense of shame. In opposition, scoring low, as Mexico does, would mean caring for (a) reciprocation of greetings, favors, and gifts; (b) respect for tradition; (c) face-saving; and (d) personal steadiness and stability. According to Hofstede, those societies scoring high are rather straightforward in their desires and tenacity; "Chinese family business," with its willing compliance to authority figures and its diligence in working to achieve a set objective, exemplifies this long-term orientation. But with low-LTO cultures, the outcome of the values involved gives a more complex picture:

> [C]hildren growing up in a *low*-LTO culture experience two sets of norms. One is toward respecting "musts": traditions, face-saving, being seen as a stable individual, respecting the social codes of marriage even if love has gone, and reciprocation of greetings, favors, and gifts as a social ritual. The other is toward immediate need gratification, spending, and sensitivity to social trends in consumption ("keeping up with the Joneses"). There is potential

tension between these two sets of norms that leads to a wide variety of individual behaviors." (Hofstede et al., 2010 p. 242)

It is as if children, and later on adults, in low-LTO cultures have, on the one hand, to maintain appearances and traditions, and on the other hand, feel pressed by the here and now. The interpretation Hofstede gives is that high-LTO citizens go through life searching for skills and good habits (virtue) and are flexible in adapting to circumstances; in contrast, the low-LTO citizens are concerned with following the accepted norms considered wise, feeling pride in personal and national achievements, and doing service for those around them. In terms of business, low-LTO cultures focus on "the bottom line, this year's profits, and think of managers and workers as being in two different camps" (Hofstede et al., 2010, p. 251).

Hofstede's interpretation of this dimension was clearly influenced by the economic expansion of some Asian countries after World War II. Accordingly, the five Asian Dragons (Taiwan, South Korea, Singapore, Hong Kong, and Japan) grew by pursuing the values of high LTO, and their economic growth continues. In contrast, Hofstede explains the economic stagnation of many African countries by their very low LTO. What are the challenges of operating in Mexico given Mexico's cultural short-term vision?

There are several challenges that might come from having a low score in LTO; for instance, because Mexican businesses set little aside for re-investment and hold tight to their own idiosyncrasies, Mexicans would be reticent to learn from others. But, as Hofstede et al. (2010, pp. 274–276) point out, it is the environment that is becoming the most pressing long-term issue. The entire economic system needs to reconcile its tenets with the understanding that our planet has finite resources. This also means that the economic growth of one state cannot be attained at the cost of natural depletion, or at the cost of environmental catastrophe for another state (Stiglitz, 2009, 2012). An enormous challenge is to find ways of aligning business goals with respect for the environment, contribution to public goods, and foresight for future generations. In this respect, Mexico, by following closely North American business models and practices (Petrick et al., 2011), has adopted a more typically North American short-sighted economic vision that leaves little space for exploring new paradigms of responsible, long-term, sustainable business or corporate activity (Brown, 2010).

A promising avenue for new business models, in contrast with Main-Road Mexico, might be found within the indigenous people, whose ancestral values of respect for nature, mutual cooperation, and democratic decision-making was the foundation of a Fairtrade brand, a business model that today involves millions of producers and consumers. The first Fairtrade labelled coffee was sold in 1988 from Mexico into Dutch supermarkets. It was branded Max Havelaar after a fictional Dutch character who opposed the exploitation of coffee pickers in Dutch colonies ("History of Fairtrade", n.d.). Audebrand and Pauchant describe how coffee producers in the state of Oaxaca, Mexico, organized themselves to avoid middlemen (known in Mexico as "coyotes") and negotiated directly with international markets to sell their product. The values of the Oaxacan indigenous farmers held that

> the economic argument is not primordial. The important thing is to leave their children and grandchildren intact, beautiful Earth. They reject the ethos of perpetual growth and market domination. In their view, growth is less important than improvement. In the culture of the indigenous producer, there is an original, prior situation to the one they experience, that of a fair world, which allows satisfaction of primordial needs: working the soil to feed themselves and their family, clothe themselves and maintain good health. The right to the earth is as important as the right to eat. (Audebrand & Pauchant, 2009, pp. 345–346)

Economic theory might learn from such values, encountered almost everywhere among Mexican indigenous groups, and reconsider business practice in a way that offers real freedom to those involved in the exchange of goods, that is, consider a transformation of the existing models of exchange and consumption (King et al., 2013; Nicholls, 2010). The experience of Freetrade and other cooperative experiences in Mexico and elsewhere show that a free market does work when *free* means upholding an ethics of dialogue, interdependence, cooperation, and consensus-based decision-making and when "*trade* not aid" promotes a sustainable lifestyle for everyone (Leunens et al., 2014).

Implications for Practitioners
In order to overcome the effect of low LTO in Mexico, which is the major cause of senior-level employee indifference to companies' sustainability strategies, education about the nature, meaning, and corporate centrality of sustainability must be linked to, and concretely expressed in, measurable targets and goals. Linking modern corporate sustainability with an ancestral Mexican indigenous world view might turn indifference into proactive pride.

Indulgence in Mexico (97 = a very high score indeed)

> *Interpretation provided by the Hofstede Centre: This has to do with how children are socialized, and particularly how they are taught to control their desires and impulses. That Mexico scores so high in this dimension means that Mexicans "exhibit a willingness to realize their impulses and desires with regard to enjoying life and having fun. They possess a positive attitude and have a tendency towards optimism. In addition, they place a higher degree of importance on leisure time, act as they please and spend money as they wish." (http://geert-hofstede.com/mexico.html)*

It is worth noting that this dimension was not added to Hofstede's study until 2008, after the researcher Misho Minkov attempted to compare the results of the World Values Survey conducted in 1998 with Hofstede's dimensions and concluded that this dimension was lacking in Hofstede's survey. And indeed this dimension brings to the fore a clear Mexican trait.

Viva la vida! Mexicans celebrate being alive and have a deep conviction that a good life has more to do with family and friends than with money and success. The ethical outlook of Aristotle, the understanding of ethics as the search for a good life and a happy life, seems very much more at home in Mexico than the practice of ethics as the obedience to norms and duties as the pietist Kantian understood it. And happiness, which at first sight might be taken to be a subjective, unquantifiable concern, has turned out to be an interesting sub-branch of economic theory (a part of welfare economics that studies ways of maximizing happiness-related measures, rather than wealth, income, or profit) (Graham, 2011).

Nowadays, measuring happiness by *The World Happiness Report* (WHR) has become a practically and theoretically useful way for gearing public policies to enhancing the quality of life of citizens ("World Happiness Report," 2015). In the 2015 WHR, Mexico was placed 14th (out of 158 countries), which is consistent with Hofstede's findings of Mexico's high score in "indulgence." The OECD, whose mission statement is "better policies for better lives," has also recommended that member countries, of which Mexico is one, collect data in order to precisely understand what "better lives" mean for the citizens of OECD countries. The guidelines issued for that purpose ("OECD Guidelines on Measuring Subjective Well-being," 2013), resulted from the *Report of the Commission on the Measurement of Economic Performance and Social Progress* led by Stiglitz et al. in 2009, asserted that "[s]ubjective well-being encompasses three different aspects: cognitive evaluations of one's life, positive emotions (joy, pride), and negative ones (pain, anger, worry). While these aspects of subjective well-being have different determinants, in all cases these determinants go well beyond people's income and material conditions" (Stiglitz et al., 2009, p. 216).

This tendency toward indulgence in Mexican culture has immediate consequences for ethics policies within companies and management. For instance, if Mexicans highly value family time and leisure, the incentives for working on weekends or night shifts might need to be more creative than offering extra pay. Blanco Jiménez quotes Kras' *Management in Two Cultures* in which she compares Mexican and American managers and asserts that "the majority of Mexicans consider work necessary to live but they have the attitude that life requires a balance between work and pleasure, and try to incorporate a modest amount of pleasure into their workday, thereby creating a more convivial atmosphere in the workplace. [...] For the Americans in the study, work is seen as intrinsically worthwhile and enjoyable and leisure as a reward for work completed" (Blanco Jiménez et al., 2009, p. 254).

These might be more than subtle differences. If work and personal life are not so clearly divided, then it is understandable that Mexicans see colleagues and company life as extensions of family and align their expectations accordingly. An aim of business ethics is to safeguard the notion that economic activity should be at the service of people and that maximizing profits is not sought at the expense of human well-being. Mexican's high score in indulgence harmonize with these objectives.

Typically, social life, including celebrations of personal and family life with friends and colleagues, involves the Mexican social phenomenon of *compadrazgo* (Gómez & Rodríguez, 2006). Within Mexican practice of Catholicism, a "compadre" and "comadre" are the parents of one's godchild (one is thus the godfather-*padrino* or godmother-*madrina* of that child). Tradition in Mexico and other Latin-American countries is that if the parents of the infant godchild died or are incapable of taking care of the infant, these godparents would adopt or care for the child (Gómez & Rodríguez, 2006). So the bond of *compadrazgo* is a profound one, of solidarity and expected reciprocity. The term *compadrazgo* is now applied, independently of the Catholic ritual, to friends or colleagues that share a sufficient keenness of mind to constitute a social network of camaraderie and exchange of favors, particularly when the understanding is that there are limited amounts of goods (Ginzberg, 2014). Similar to the recent recognition given to the Brazilian term *jeitinho* and the Chinese *guanxi* as social mechanisms of solidarity, networks of influence and mutual favors (Smith et al., 2012), *compadrazgo* serves by securing a personal and friendly recommendation, or favor, helping address practical issues, and thus "softening rigid impersonal bureaucracies through maintaining personal and social relationships, as well as establishing the foundations for the social contract in which employment is embedded" (Davila & Elvira, 2012, p. 550).

Implications for Practitioners

Low impulse control, a key part of indulgence, results in senior managers in Mexico feeling the need to strictly monitor and control more junior staff to prevent the possibility of negative outcomes from hasty, impulsive decision-making. Efforts must be made to strike a good balance between controlling impulses and not frustrating innovation.

CONCLUSIONS

By illustrating the historical factors that produced the divided realities of Mexico, being Main-Road and Off-Road Mexico, this chapter reveals a novel and sharper understanding of the role that business ethics plays in modernizing Mexico. Emerging economies, with an intense drive to connect with international trends, tending to conform to international ethics standards and become active players of a globalized economy, are fertile ground for social transformation. If businesses apply the core objectives of business ethics, namely, to displace the belief that profit maximization is the sole business principle, and choose to analyze the multiple objectives that human exchanges imply (Sen, 1999), then business could contribute to a greater transparency and to the democratizing of Mexico. This will in turn create a fairer playing field for new business to emerge.

Business, like any other social practice, is culturally bounded. Highlighting some of the cultural values of Mexico makes it easier to effectively align business leadership and ethics policies. However, the six dimensions of Hofstede's work are rooted in an anthropological understanding of how different cultures engage with basic human problems, and not directly with ethics. The closest that Hofstede gets to moral judgment or normative language is when speaking of the need to enlarge our moral circle, that is, the size of the circle that includes others whom we consider to be morally significant (Hofstede et al., 2010, p. 13). Business ethics, however, compels us to describe and particularly to confront Mexico's high incidence of corruption, discrimination, and injustice. Business practitioners can be part of the ongoing discussions within Mexico regarding which changes, goals, and processes, and so forth should be applied to enable the country to achieve more equality and justice.

Globalization poses challenges – environmental challenges and equal opportunities challenges – that involve different cultures, and thus learning to work and tackle human basic problems together, by developing skills of intercultural communication, is a promising avenue. Mexico offers a dynamic, accessible, and attractive business environment that adds to the variety of cultural landscapes. A challenge remains: how to make this world not only more varied and plural but also more just and free. What this chapter has attempted to show is that business ethics is a good tool for creating a fairer and freer world.

REFERENCES

Anechiarico, F. (2010). La corrupción y el control de la corrupción como impedimentos para la competitividad económica. *Gestión y política pública*, 19(2), 239–261.

Arredondo Trapero, F. G., Rosas Ferrer, J. A., & Villa Castaño, L. E. (2011). Comportamiento ciudadano organizacional y RSE. *Cuadernos de Administración*, 24(43), 221–239.

Arredondo Trapero, F., Velázquez Sánchez, L. M., & de la Garza García, J. (2013). Políticas de diversidad y flexibilidad laboral en el marco de la responsabilidad social empresarial. Un análisis desde la perspectiva de género. *Estudios Gerenciales*, 29(127), 161–166.

Atlas of Economic Complexity of Harvard University (2014). Retrieved from http://atlas.cid.harvard.edu/rankings/

Audebrand, L. K., & Pauchant, T. C. (2009). Can the Fair Trade movement enrich traditional business ethics? An historical study of its founders in Mexico. *Journal of Business Ethics*, 87(3), 343–353.

Bailey, W., & Spicer, A. (2007). When does national identity matter? Convergence and divergence in international business ethics. *Academy of Management Journal*, 50(6), 1462–1480.

Baskin, J. (2006). Corporate responsibility in emerging markets. *Journal of Corporate Citizenship*, 24, 29–47.

Bazerman, M. H., & Tenbrunsel A. (2011). *Blind spots: Why we fail to do what's right and what to do about it*. Princeton, NJ: Princeton University Press.

Belausteguigoitia, I. (2012). *Empresas Familiares: dinámica, equilibrio y consolidación*. México City, México: McGraw-Hill.

Blanco Jiménez, M., Fasci, M. A., & Valdez, J. (2009). A comparison of management style for Mexican firms in Mexico and the United States. *International Journal of Business*, 14(3), 251–263.

Brown, M. T. (2010). *Civilizing the economy*. Cambridge: Cambridge University Press.

Carrillo, P., Vargas, S. M., & Tapia, M. (2009). *Diagnóstico sobre filantropía corporativa en México*. México: Alternativas y Capacidades A.C.

Charles, M. (2003). Deciphering sex segregation: Vertical and horizontal inequalities in ten national labor markets. *Acta Sociologica*, 46(4), 267–287.

Chávez-Reyes, C. (2010). Racial and ethnic socialization in later generations of a Mexican American family. *Hispanic Journal of Behavioral Sciences*, 32(4), 495–518.

Cockcroft, L. (2014). *Global corruption: Money, power, and ethics in the modern world*. Philadelphia, PA: University of Pennsylvania Press.

Davila, A., & Elvira, M. (2012). Humanistic leadership: Lessons from Latin America. *Journal of World Business*, 47, 548–554.

De Forest, M. E. (1994). Thinking of a plant in México? *Academy of Management Executive*, 8(1), 33–40.

Dussel Peters, E. (2007). *La inversión extranjera directa en México: desempeño y potencial: una perspectiva macro, meso, micro y territorial*. México: Siglo XXI-UNAM, México.

Eduniversal (n.d.). Retrieved from: www.eduniversal-ranking.com/business-school-university-ranking-in-mexico.html

Elvira, M. M., & Davila, A. (2005). Emergent directions for human resource management research in Latin America. *International Journal of Human Resource Management*, 16(12), 2265–2282.

Espinoza Aguiló, T. I., & Espinoza Aguiló, N. F. (2012). Family business performance: Evidence from Mexico. *Cuadernos de Administración*, 25(44), 39–61.

Estadísticas a propósito del...Día internacional de la mujer (8 de marzo) Datos económicos (2016, March). Retrieved from www.inegi.org.mx/saladeprensa/aproposito/2016/mujer2016_0.pdf

Eternod Arámburu, M. (2013, April). Encuesta Nacional sobre la Dinámica de las Relaciones en los Hogares ENDIREH 2011. Retrieved from www.inegi.org.mx/est/contenidos/Proyectos/encuestas/hogares/especiales/endireh/

Galindo, J. (2013). Some considerations regarding the persistence of the economic elite in Mexico in the first half of the twentieth century. *Bulletin of Latin American Research*, 32(2), 149–162.

Geo-Mexico, the geography and dynamism of modern Mexico (n.d.). Retrieved from www.geo-mexico.com

Ginzberg, E. (2014). The image of the limited good: A lesson on the striving for communal and human solidarity. *Journal of Law and Social Sciences*, 4(1), 20–33.

Gómez, C. F., & Rodríguez, J. K. (2006). Four keys to Chilean culture: Authoritarianism, legalism, fatalism and compadrazgo. *Asian Journal of Latin American Studies*, 19(3), 43–65.

Graham, C. (2011). *The pursuit of happiness: An economy of well-being.* Washington, DC: Brookings Institution.

History of Fairtrade (n.d.). Retrieved from https://www.fairtrade.net/about-fairtrade/history-of-fairtrade.html

Hofstede, G. (1980). *Culture's consequences: International differences in work-related values.* Beverly Hills, CA: Sage.

Hofstede, G., Hofstede, G. J., & Minkov, M. (2010). *Cultures and organizations: Software of the mind: intercultural operations and its importance for survival.* New York: McGraw Hill.

Hofstede, G. J. (2009). Research on cultures: How to use it in training? *European Journal of Cross-Cultural Competence and Management*, 1(1), 14–21.

Howell, J. P., De la Cerda, J., Martínez, S. M., Prieto, L., Bautista, J. A, Ortiz, J., Dorfman, P., & Mendez, M. (2007). Leadership and culture in Mexico. *Journal of World Business*, 42, 449–462.

Husted, B., & Serrano, C. (2002). Corporate governance in Mexico. *Journal of Business Ethics*, 37(3), 337–348.

Husted, B., & Allen, D. (2008). Toward a model of cross-cultural business ethics: The impact of individualism and collectivism on the ethical decision-making process. *Journal of Business Ethics*, 82, 293–305.

Javidan, M., House, R. J., Dorfman, P. W., Hanges, P. J., & De Luque, M. S. (2006). Conceptualizing and measuring cultures and their consequences: A comparative review of GLOBE's and Hofstede's approaches. *Journal of International Business Studies*, 37(6), 897–914.

King, R., Adler, M. A., & Grieves, M. (2013). Cooperatives as sustainable livelihood strategies in rural Mexico. *Bulletin of Latin American Research*, 32(2), 163–177.

Knight, A. (2013). War, violence and homicide in modern Mexico. *Bulletin of Latin American Research*, 32(1), 12–48.

Kras, E. (2000). The viable future of Mexico and Latin America: A new business paradigm. *International Journal of Public Administration*, 23(5–8), 1341–1358.

La Porta, R., Lopez de Silanes, F., & Shleifer, A. (1999). Corporate ownership around the world. *Journal of Finance*, 54(2), 471–517.

Latin-American Roundtable on Corporate Governance (n.d.). Retrieved from www.oecd.org/daf/ca/latinamericanroundtableoncorporategovernance.htm

Leunens, Y., Sañudo, M., & Schweigert, F. (2014). Dialogue: A pragmatic tool to actualize an ethics of cooperation. In L. Hammond Ketilson & M.-P. Robichaud Villettaz (eds.), *Cooperative' Power to Innovate: Texts Selected from the International Call for Papers* (pp. 123–135). Lévis: International Summit of Cooperatives.

Logsdon, J. M., Thomas, D. E., & Van Buren, H. (2006). Corporate social responsibility in large Mexican firms. *Journal of Corporate Citizenship*, 21, 51–60.

Mauss, M. (1990). *The Gift*. London: Routledge.

Mexico and NAFTA: Tariffs and tortillas (2008, January 24). Retrieved from www.economist.com/node/10566845

México en cifras (2015). Retrieved from www.inegi.org.mx/

Modelo de Gestión de Equidad de Género (n.d.). Retrieved from www.gob.mx/inmujeres/acciones-y-programas/modelo-de-equidad-de-genero-2003-2015

Morando, S. (2013). Paths to mobility: The Mexican second generation at work in a new destination. *Sociological Quarterly*, 54(3), 367–398.

Morris, T., & Pavett, C. (1992). Management style and productivity in two cultures (U.S. and Mexico). *Journal of International Business Studies*, 23(1), 169.

Muller, H. J., & Rowell, M. (1997). Mexican women managers: An emerging profile. *Human Resources Management*, 36(4), 423–435.

Murphy, D. S. (2006). Global leadership potential in Mexican firms. *Management Research News*, 29(3), 80–91.

Newman, K. L., & Nollen, S. (1996). Culture and congruence: The fit between management practices and national culture. *Journal of International Business Studies*, 27(4), 753–779.

Nicholls, A. (2010). Fair trade: Towards an economics of virtue. *Journal of Business Ethics*, 92, 241–255.

OECD Guidelines on Measuring Subjective Well-being (2013). Retrieved from www.oecd.org/statistics/oecd-guidelines-on-measuring-subjective-well-being-9789264191655-en.htm

Oyserman, D. (2006). High power, low power, and equality: Culture beyond individualism and collectivism. *Journal of Consumer Psychology*, 16(4), 352–356.

Petrick, J. A., Cragg, W., & Sañudo, M. (2011). Business ethics in North America: Trends and challenges. *Journal of Business Ethics*, 104, 51–62.

Pick, S., Contreras, C., & Barker-Aguilar, A. (2006). Violence against women in Mexico. *Annals of the New York Academy of Sciences*, 1087(1), 261–278.

Puppim de Oliveira, J. A. (2006). Corporate citizenship in Latin America: New challenges for business. *Journal of Corporate Citizenship*, 21, 7–20.

Rao, P. (2009). The role of national culture on Mexican staffing practices. *Employee Relations*, 31(3), 295–311.

Rocha González, J. M. (2011). Consejos de administración y gobernanza corporativa en México. *Revista Mexicana de Sociología*, 73(2), 261–295.

Ruiz, C. E., Wang, J., &Hamlin, R. (2013). What makes managers effective in México? *Leadership & Organization Development Journal*, 34(2), 130–146.

S&P Dow Jones Indices for Mexico (n.d.). Retrieved from http://eu.spindices.com/search/?query=Mexico&Search=GO&Search=GO

Schein, E. H. (2010). *Organizational culture and leadership*. San Francisco, CA: Jossey-Bass.

Schniederjans, M. J., Mahour Mellat, P., Nabavi, M., Subba Rao, S., & Raghu-Nathan, T. (2006). Comparative analysis of Malcolm Baldrige national quality award criteria: An empirical study of India, Mexico, and the United States. *Quality Management Journal*, 13(4), 7–21.

Sen, A. (1999). Economics, business principles, and moral sentiments. In G. Enderle (Ed.), *International business ethics. Challenges and approaches* (pp. 15–29). Notre Dame, IN: University of Notre Dame Press.

Shefner, J. (2007). Rethinking civil society in the age of NAFTA: The case of Mexico. *Annals of the American Academy of Political and Social Science*, 610, 182–200.

Smith, P. B., Huang, H., Harb, C., & Torres, C. (2012). How distinctive are indigenous ways of achieving influence? A comparative study of Guanxi, Wasta,

Jeitinho and 'Pulling Strings'. *Journal of Cross-Cultural Psychology*, 43(1), 135–150.

Steidel, A. G. L., & Contreras, J. M. (2003). A new familism scale for use with Latino populations. *Hispanic Journal of Behavioral Sciences*, 25(3), 312–330.

Stevenson, L. (2004). Confronting gender discrimination in the Mexican workplace: Women and labor facing NAFTA with transnational contention. *Women and Politics*, 26(1), 71–97.

Stiglitz, J. (2009). Progress, what progress? *OECD Observer*, 272(2), 27.

Stiglitz, J. (2012). *The price of inequality*. New York: W. W. Norton.

Stiglitz, J. E., Sen, A., & Fitoussi, J. P. (2009). *Report by the Commission on the Measurement of Economic Performance and Social Progress*. Paris, France: Institut national de la statistique et des études économiques.

Thaler, R. H., & Sunstein, C. R. (2009). *Nudge: Improving decisions on health, wealth, and happiness*. London: Penguin.

The World in 2050. Will the shift in global economic power continue? (2015, February). Retrieved from https://www.pwc.com/gx/en/issues/the-economy/assets/world-in-2050-february-2015.pdf

Thompson, D. (2013, August). Two concepts of corruption, Edmond J. Safra Working Paper No. 16. Retrieved from http://papers.ssrn.com/sol3/papers.cfm?abstract_id=2304419

Transparency International Corruption Perception Index 2014: Results (2014). Retrieved from https://www.transparency.org/cpi2014/results

US Relations with Mexico (2016, July). Retrieved from www.state.gov/r/pa/ei/bgn/35749.htm

UN Human Development Report for Mexico 2011 (2011). Retrieved from http://hdr.undp.org/sites/default/files/nhdr_mexico_2011.pdf

Velázquez, L., Marín, A., Zavala, A., Bustamante, C., Esquer, J., & Munguía, N. (2009). Mexico: An overview of CSR programmes. In S. O. Idowu & W. L. Filho (Eds.), *Global practices of corporate social responsibility* (pp. 273–283). Heidelberg: Springer.

Weisbrot, M., Lefebvre, S., & Sammut, J. (2014, February). *Did NAFTA help Mexico? An assessment after 20 Years*. Retrieved from www.cepr.net/documents/nafta-20-years-2014-02.pdf

World Happiness Report 2015 (2015). Retrieved from http://worldhappiness.report/wp-content/uploads/sites/2/2015/04/WHR15-Apr29-update.pdf

Zabludovsky, G. (2001). Women managers and diversity programs in Mexico. *Journal of Management Development*, 20(4), 354–370.

8 Ethical Business Cultures in Indonesia

Jane Maringka and Noor Rahmani

ABSTRACT

Indonesia is undergoing a transformation under a spotlight. Identified as one of the Next Economic Giants, the country has drawn tremendous interest from foreign business and investors. With Indonesia's increased participation in the global marketplace, and the growing influence of Western values and managerial practices, Indonesian culture continues to be a subject of considerable scholarly interest as well. However, research on business ethics is still scarce. Business entry to Indonesia remains challenging due to societal norms, cultural values, and expectations for standard business practices that differ from those held by businesspeople in Western societies. This chapter examines the deep and rich national history of Indonesia and the country's economy and discusses dimensions of national culture and its influence on ethical business environment. The current ethical business landscape is portrayed with the intention to give the readers insights on how to conduct successful business in Indonesia.

INTRODUCTION

Indonesia is located strategically in south-eastern Asia and comprises 17,000 islands. *The World Fact Book* (2015) lists Indonesia as "the world's third most populous democracy, the world's largest archipelagic state, and the world's largest Muslim-majority nation," with an estimated 255,993,674 people. From a 2010 census, it has been estimated that approximately 600 ethnic groups exist in Indonesia, with each group having its local culture and dialect, under Indonesia's national motto of Bhinneka Tunggal Ika, translated as "Unity in Diversity"

(Ananta et al., 2015). Although Indonesia is the world's most populous Islamic country (87.55 of the population is Muslim), it has maintained a significant presence of other religions (10% are Christian, 1% Hindu, 0.72% Buddhist, and 0.05% Confucian) (Ananta et al., 2015). All Indonesians speak Bahasa Indonesia as the official language.

In addition to its cultural diversity, Indonesia is blessed with natural resources and commodities, such as gold, copper, nickel, coal, natural gas, and oil. While initially an agriculturally based economy, Indonesia's mining industry has grown, and the country has now become a major exporter of various commodities. The Natural Resource Governance Institute (n.d.) noted that Indonesia supplies 20 percent of the world's tin and is the main producer of liquefied natural gas; however, a recent decline in production and increased domestic consumer consumption has made Indonesia a net importer of oil.

In the past few decades, Indonesia has made progress in its economic development and shows potential for continued growth. For example, the International Fund for Agriculture Development (2015) reported that the overall poverty rate decreased from 17 to 11 percent between 2004 and 2014, allowing Indonesia to become a middle-income country. The British Broadcasting Corporation (BBC) News Online Magazine (2014) identified Indonesia as an emerging economic giant. This assertion is consistent with a prediction from the Reserve Bank of Australia's report: "With plans for substantial infrastructure spending over the next several years and favorable demographics, the Indonesian economy is widely expected to continue to grow at a strong pace over the next decade" (Elias & Noone, 2011, p. 42). Additionally, unlike its predecessor, the new Indonesian government is under pressure to find ways to eradicate corruption and unethical business practices. The new president, Joko Widodo, elected in 2014, responded to such pressure by forming the Corruption Eradication Commission, an agency charged with enforcing the anti-corruption law. Even though the agency has experienced success in bringing some corrupt individuals to justice, a great deal of additional work is yet to be done.

While signs of reform are encouraging, the World Bank Group (2016) ranked Indonesia 91st worldwide in ease of conducting business, far below its neighbors Malaysia (23rd) and the Philippines (99th), suggesting that doing business in Indonesia remains relatively difficult compared to other countries. Indonesia continues to deal with unemployment, poverty, and corruption (Central Intelligence Agency, 2015). Joseph, Gunawan, Sawani, Rahmat, Avelind, and Darut (2016) noted, "In the Corruption Perception Index 2013, Indonesia rose seven spots from 114 in 2012's index to 107 in the 2013 edition" (pp. 2902–2903). According to the latest data, Indonesia is now ranked 88 out of 168 (Transparency International, 2015). It could therefore be implied that the Indonesian economy still suffers from endemic unethical business practices and corruption. Nonetheless, there is growing awareness and intolerance toward corruption and bribery as Indonesian business is realizing the importance of maintaining a good social image. Thus, there have been more efforts to expose acts of corruption. Whether Indonesia will be able to end its systems of patronage and corruption is yet to be seen.

HISTORICAL FACTORS THAT HAVE SHAPED THE SOCIOECONOMIC SYSTEM

To give some context to present-day Indonesia's business environment, it is perhaps best to look back at its history. Indonesia was home to many ancient kingdoms, the oldest of which was Kutai (located in East Kalimantan) in the 4th century AD (Aji & Achmad, 2014). These kingdoms were usually attached to a specific territory, where the local authority held power. Tradition held that the authorities would rule their own lands, despite the presence of a king.

Having been colonialized under the Dutch for 350 years shaped Indonesia's international, social, economic, political, and cultural environment, which had previously not been possible due to the large number of small territories. Prior to Dutch colonization, Indonesia was a rich spice producer, with many early trading partners including China, India, and Arabia. The spice trade was stable until, in the early 16th century, Portugal seized Indonesian harbors and built forts (Poesponegoro & Notosusanto, 1984). Then in 1596, Dutch companies started sending ships to the region, eventually forcing out the Portuguese. The Dutch were given authority to manage trade in the region and started a company known as Verneging Oost Indische Compagnie (VOC) or the Dutch East India Company (Poesponegoro & Notosusanto, 1984), often considered to be the world's first multinational company.

Through implementation of the *divide et impera* strategy (breaking the kingdom into smaller areas with less authority), the VOC gained influence in Indonesia by supporting various claimants seeking the throne, in return for concessions. This was achieved by loaning money to various local authorities with land as collateral, and when the debts were unpaid, the VOC gained concessions (Poesponegoro & Notosusanto, 1984). This era was characterized by the success of relatively incompetent leaders, who, in their own right, would not have done well had it not been for the support of external foreign parties, namely the VOC, which held monopolistic power in trading and politics over the islands (Poesponegoro & Notosusanto, 1984) and controlled relationships among the authorities. The Indonesian people did not welcome this practice, but their efforts to resist such changes were unsuccessful (Poesponegoro & Notosusanto, 1984). Such practices signaled the beginning of unethical behavior at the core of the business environment in the country.

Roughly around the 18th century, the Dutch had occupied almost all of Indonesia. They had established an agreement between themselves and various regional kings, with all appointments requiring the VOC's approval (Poesponegoro & Notosusanto, 1984). The Dutch maintained an indirect administration run by local officials, and Dutch agents supervised the cultivation of the land. This system facilitated corruption, as officials imposed taxes on farmers and impoverished them. Those who rebelled were unsuccessful (Kartodirdjo, 1987). After centuries of Dutch occupation, Indonesia was taken over by the Japanese between 1941 and 1945. However, on August 6, 1945, after the Allies bombed Hiroshima and Nagasaki, Indonesian politicians thought this was ideal timing to proclaim its independence, which occurred on August 17, 1945. This was followed by the ratification of a national constitution and the appointment of Soekarno as president of the Republik Indonesia (Poesponegoro & Notosusanto, 1984).

Between 1950 and 1959, Indonesia was ruled by a system of parliamentary democracy. At this time, there was effectively no indigenous middle class, and disruptive changes in government and economic problems gave the cabinet insufficient time to implement its economic programs (May, 1978). In March 1959, after the last cabinet resigned, President Soekarno declared the restoration of the 1945 constitution and decreed martial law, following the advice of Nasution, the Army Chief of Staff. This consolidated the power of Guided Democracy. Soekarno was appointed President for Life in May 1963 by the Majelis Permusyawaratan Rakyat (People's Consultative Assembly – Indonesian Parliament) (May, 1978). Believing that the Indonesian people's welfare could be protected by introducing the concept of socialism, Soekarno was inclined toward the leftist party and became an enemy of the army. The army, using martial law, took control of the country, banned strikes, broke up demonstrations, controlled the use of slogans, closed down newspaper offices, and ran the former Dutch estates (Grant, 1964). On October 1, 1965, eight generals and lieutenants of ABRI (Angkatan Bersenjata Republik Indonesia – Armed Forces of the Republic of Indonesia) were kidnapped and murdered. The murders were attributed to the PKI (Partai Komunis Indonesia – the Communist Party of Indonesia), and the event is remembered as the G 30 S PKI, meaning the 30th of September Movement of the Communist Party of Indonesia (May, 1978).

General Suharto (Commander of the Komando Strategi Angkatan Darat – Army Strategic Command) led the suppression and elimination of the PKI, with the active support of religious groups. Estimates of the numbers killed range from 500,000 (Cribb, 2002; Ricklefs, 2008; Vickers, 2013) to one million (Friend, 2003), and approximately 10,000 members of the Communist Party were arrested and exiled to Buru Island (May, 1978). This period remains largely uninvestigated, and nobody has yet been held accountable for the government-sanctioned mass murder of PKI members and other victims (Roosa, 2006). Following this struggle, Suharto was appointed as the second President of Indonesia by the Provisional People's Consultative Assembly (MPRS) in 1968, effectively concluding what, in effect, was a "creeping coup d'etat" by Soekarno (Roosa, 2006).

Suharto's 32-year-long rule had played a role in further oppression of the Indonesian public and corrupt political system. As president, he adopted policies that severely restricted civil liberties and instituted a system of rule that effectively divided power between his own Golkar Party and the military. Suharto responded to growing protests and social unrest by co-opting a few of his more powerful opponents, while criminalizing the rest. When the monetary crisis occurred in Asia in 1997, Indonesia became the country that was hardest hit. The final straw was the riots and havoc in 1997 and 1998, causing almost 5,000 casualties in Jakarta and other cities (Friend, 2003). Suharto resigned on May 21 and Habibie, the vice president, took over (Vickers, 2013).

During the post-Suharto era, Indonesia has been in a period of transition – an era known in Indonesia as *reformasi* (reformation), a more open and liberal political-social environment. In a review on Horowitz's 2013 book on constitutional change and demography in Indonesia, Caraway (2015) commented, "Indonesia has become a stable democracy in which parties govern by forming coalitions across ideological, cultural, and religious divides" (p. 561).

CHARACTERISTICS OF NATIONAL CULTURE

Many theorists have attempted to classify culture into different dimensions. The four most widely discussed frameworks in the business literature are those by Inglehart (1997, 2012), Hofstede (1980, 1997), Trompenaars and Hampden-Turner (1998), and Triandis (2001). This section will examine the characteristics of Indonesia's culture based on the dimensions proposed by these scholars.

Survival Values

Survival/self-expression values (Inglehart, 2012) relate to the level of materialism present in society. At one end of the scale, those societies described as having high self-expression values have large populations of individuals with considerable levels of wealth for whom quality-of-life issues, such as environmental protection, pluralism, and individual purpose, are prioritized, and in which individuals are typically less concerned with the struggle for economic and physical security. These societies have also been described as "post-materialist" (Inglehart & Baker, 2000). Inglehart (2012) proposed a global cultural map and displayed the United States, Great Britain, Australia, and much of Western Europe as countries with high self-expression values (factor score above 1). At the other end of the spectrum, those societies holding survival values typically have substantial portions of the population struggling to meet daily needs. Indonesia, with a score of –0.5, falls under this category. Generally, members of societies with survival values are focused on material needs and the accumulation of basic goods (Inglehart & Welzel, 2005).

Survival/self-expression values impact the ranges of behavior that are permissible in respective societies. Societies with high survival values are likely to perceive a wider range of behaviors that can be described as ethically "grey" and therefore acceptable, while in high self-expression value societies, there is typically a clearer differentiation between "right" and "wrong" and a narrower, widely held understanding of what ethical behavior is. The figure provided in World Values Survey (www.worldvaluesurvey.org/WVSContents .jsp?CMSID=Findings-) is a map showing the position of various countries on a dual-axis diagram, showing traditional–rational values and survival–self-expression values. The map shows Indonesia situated in the bottom-left quadrant, indicating stronger survival values; therefore, individuals in the society are less likely to identify ethical behavior and perceive a wider range of unethical behavior as acceptable, compared to individuals in a society with high self-expression values.

Particularism Dealing with Universalism Values?

Indonesia has been categorized by Trompenaars and Hampden-Turner (1998) as a particularist society. The opposite dimension is that of a universalistic society, defined as having standard rules to govern situations and to ensure equal treatment for all parties involved. Thus, based on this classification, Indonesians tend to value relationships more than rules. In some cases, rules are challenged, ignored, or bent for the sake of relationships. High levels of particularism in Indonesia, characterized by the prevalence of personal relations over rules and standards, hamper the establishment of a standard code of business ethics that would otherwise be the product of a universalist society.

Collectivism in Indonesian Society

The tendency of Indonesians to foster relations over rules and standards is a logical by-product of a collectivist society, where people are committed to being part of a group or community, and in return, the group takes care of them (Hofstede, 1980). According to the Hofstede Centre (n.d.), Indonesia has a low score on this dimension (14), which makes it a collectivistic society. Employees are expected to show loyalty and compliance toward organizations and to align their personal interests with those of the employers (Hofstede Centre, n.d.). Group interests are considered as more important than those of individuals (Koentjaraningrat, 1984). Similar to the concept of collectivism, Trompenaars and Hampden-Turner (1998) propose communitarianism, whereby Indonesians tend to put the group's interests above personal/individual needs. Personal independence or individual freedom is not considered as important as being part of a group or a community (Trompenaars & Hampden-Turner, 1998).

Offering a slightly different angle, Triandis (2001) dichotomized culture into individualism and collectivism and proposed that the aforementioned analysis would be more effective when performed at the individual level. While communities (societal level) can either be collectivist or individualist, individuals can exhibit situation-specific behaviors, which can be classified as allocentric or idiocentric. Allocentrics place emphasis on harmony, solidarity, social conformity, respect, self-sacrifice, and cooperation, while idiocentrics focus on personal achievement, independence, freedom, competition, and self-assurance (Markus & Kitayama, 1991; Triandis et al., 1995; Triandis & Suh, 2002). Triandis (2001) suggested that allocentric behaviors are more often found in collectivistic societies, and idiocentrics are more representative of individualistic societies. Thus, the majority of Indonesian people would fall under the allocentric category.

Applied to the Indonesian business context, the prioritization of personal relationships over merit-based decisions has resulted in a higher prevalence of nepotism. This also applies to group settings and employee–superior relationships. Rather than taking a stance and show disapproval of ethical standards violations, group members and employees tend to look the other way. This is in line with Rahmani (2014), who reported that when allocentric individuals are in organizations that embrace collective values, they tend to exhibit higher organizational commitment; on the other hand, in collective-based organizations favoring relationships over rules and standards, members are likely to comply voluntarily with requests to carry out unethical behaviors.

Power Distance

Subservience to superiors is measured using the metric of power distance, which is defined as the degree to which less powerful individuals of institutions and organizations within a country accept an unequal distribution of power (Hofstede, 1997). Indonesia scores high (78) (Hofstede Centre, n.d.) on the power distance continuum, suggesting a distance between superiors and employees within Indonesian organizations.

The Indonesian workplace is typically characterized by a strong hierarchical system and centralized governance (Hofstede Centre, n.d.). Employees are required to comply with instructions from their superiors. This system relates to Indonesians' concept of *hormat* (respect) (Magnis-Soeseno, 1991). All members of the society are expected to understand their roles and responsibilities and to uphold unity and harmony. People in higher positions should be respected and, in return, would reciprocate by displaying a paternal attitude (i.e., taking charge and providing protection). The behavior of those in high positions is perceived as the "right" behavior and should be accepted without question (Magnis-Soeseno, 1991).

Under the notion of *hormat*, rank-and-file Indonesians are admonished to eschew ambition, avoid competition, and behave politely toward people in higher positions. The desire for personal profit and power would lead to social dissension and disharmony, which must be avoided and minimized (Magnis-Soeseno, 1991; Mulder, 1983). Koentjaraningrat (1984) pointed out the local saying, *Asal Bapak Senang* (or often shortened as ABS), which can be translated verbatim: "as long as the father is happy." In Indonesia, subordinates would rather produce false reports or withhold information in order to avoid being criticized or punished by their managers and supervisors. In light of this issue, Koentjaraningrat (1984) cautioned that this inflexible power hierarchy has led to undesirable outcomes, such as corruption, inefficiency, and the absence of two-way communication between superiors and their subordinates.

An Ascriptive Society

As an ascriptive society, Indonesians place importance on individual status (i.e., family background, business connections, societal status, gender, and age) rather than on individual performance and personal success (Trompenaars & Hampden-Turner, 1998). Consequently, it is common for hiring, personnel, or promotion decisions in the workplace to be made based on societal status rather than on actual work performance (Trompenaars & Hampden-Turner, 1998). The concept of business ethics is a product of an achievement society, which highly values personal success and individual merits (Trompenaars & Hampden-Turner, 1998). It is therefore likely that enforcing business ethics in Indonesia can be a challenge.

A Diffuse Society

Besides the importance of status, Indonesia is characterized as a diffuse culture, implying blurred distinctions between private/personal and public/professional roles (Trompenaars & Hampden-Turner, 1998). This differs from specific-oriented cultures, where individuals normally compartmentalize relationships and uphold clear boundaries between work and personal relationships. In diffuse-oriented societies, the line between roles is less clear, and relationships with coworkers may be stronger and more personal in comparison to specific-oriented societies.

There is a large overlap between work and society involvement in a diffuse culture, as company leaders will also gravitate toward community leadership roles. For example, during the Suharto era, there was a policy that the wife of a senior government bureaucrat would become the head of the employees' wives' union (known as Dharma Wanita). This causes unethical business practices to expand from the workplace to the community. As the country has moved toward urbanization, this practice has waned, although it is still evident in smaller cities and rural areas.

Synchronous Time Orientation

Another key element to ethical behavior in business is the degree to which prior agreements or contracts are honored between parties. Indonesia is described as a synchronous time culture, which means that a lax attitude exists toward punctuality, scheduling, plans, and commitments (Trompenaars & Hampden-Turner, 1998). This is contrary to Western society, which favors a sequential time orientation and preference for time commitments, punctuality, and scheduled plans.

An Outer-Direction Culture

In comparison to societies with an inner-directed culture that is more likely to believe that they can develop their skills to control nature or their environment to achieve their goals, Indonesia is classified as an outer-directed culture. Whether at work or in relationships, outer-directed cultures typically focus their actions on others and avoid conflict (Trompenaars & Hampden-Turner, 1998). This implies that Indonesian people tend to prioritize harmony with nature and the environment, based on a core belief that they are limited by the environment and have no control over it. The implications of an outer-directed culture in Indonesian business are the projection of a more passive attitude toward its environment and any ethical business standards created by different cultures.

A Neutral Society

Indonesia is classified as a neutral society, compared to an emotional one (Trompenaars & Hampden-Turner, 1998). People in a neutral society go to great lengths to conceal their emotions and avoid emotional expression at work (Trompenaars & Hampden-Turner, 1998). This relates to the Indonesian cultural norm of *rukun* (harmony), which refers to the continuous effort of all individuals in society to remain calm in their interactions and to avoid matters of disagreement and social unrest (Magnis-Soeseno, 1991). *Rukun* includes maintaining visibly harmonious social relationships, regardless of inner feelings, or, in other words, a "harmonious social appearance" (Geertz, 1961). To be successful in Indonesian social life, one should have the ability to hide feelings. Disagreement, displeasure, disappointment, and anger are hidden from others in work settings. The influence of this culture on business practices is that it makes it less likely that unethical practices will be reported – even if a potential whistle-blower dislikes or disagrees with the unethical practices in question.

Uncertainty Avoidance

Uncertainty avoidance relates to the degree to which members of a culture actively avoid uncertain situations and how effective they are at dealing with the unknown future (Hofstede, 1980). Indonesia has a middle score on uncertainty avoidance (48), which implies that in comparison to other cultures, Indonesians are able to deal with a reasonable amount of uncertainty (Hofstede Centre, n.d.).

The reality of living in Indonesia is that life is ambiguous, and uncertainty is relatively high. Some well-written regulations exist, but enforcement is typically arbitrary, and thus, compliance is generally low. Personal connections allow individuals to circumvent regulations. Other regulations are either vaguely worded, and are thus prone to multiple interpretations, or they are subject to the desire by those in power to enforce or not enforce the rules, which creates uncertainty. This high level of uncertainty no doubt increases the frustration of people from other cultures with less uncertain regulatory frameworks.

RECENT CULTURAL CHANGES

Indonesian society and the Indonesian business environment have experienced dynamic growth since Hofstede's surveys were administered between 1967 and 1978. As a developing nation, Indonesia has been subjected to strong foreign influence. The influence of the United States is particularly strong due to Indonesia's adoption of a US-developed industrialization policy in the late 1960s and early 1970s. It is therefore likely that the cultural dimension scores have shifted.

In terms of economic development, continuous growth in Indonesia can be attributed, in part, to the 30 plus years of the Suharto era (with the exception of the monetary crisis). The implementation of policies focused on boosting private foreign investment and exports – as advised by Western-trained economists – resulted in an unprecedented socio-cultural transformation in the country. This strategy has played a large role in the country's economic transformation (Hollinger, 1996).

Heuer et al. (1999) noted statistically significant support for a narrowing cultural gap between Indonesian and US managers, compared to earlier findings by Hofstede. One indication of this is that economic growth in Indonesia has resulted in the adoption of Western management practices, such as greater individualism in the workplace and the promotion of individual creativity. Consistent with this view, Sumantri and Suharnomo (2011) performed a study of 108 employees in the Jakarta Stock Exchange (JSX) and reported changes in the scores of Hofstede's dimensions. From the collective-individualist approach, the score change provides validation to Hofstede's (1997) theory that cultural changes are affected by levels of social and economic development, as well as by the technological progress of a country; moreover, as a society becomes more sophisticated and modern, it moves from a collectivist/survival tendency toward an individualistic mindset.

Taken together, the works of Inglehart, Hofstede, Trompenaars and Hampden-Turners, and Triandis provide a snapshot of Indonesian culture. While the theories of culture discussed here may accurately describe the national culture at one point in time, caution should be exercised in generalizing Indonesia, which is still a culture in the midst of rapid change.

BUSINESS–GOVERNMENT RELATIONS

With the exception of the period between 1945 and 1959, and after the Suharto era, the Indonesian government has always followed an authoritarian, patrimonial, or authoritarian-paternalistic administration (Mas'oed, 1989). The democratic system, introduced as a result of Indonesia's independence in 1945, and persisting until 1959, was foreign to the Indonesian people and their cultural values. Thus, it eventually failed to work for the country (Benda, 1964). It has been argued that the authoritarianism often associated with Suharto's administration had existed prior to the Dutch hegemony. Traces of authoritarian political culture were evident in Soekarno's Guided Democracy regime after 1959, as well as the New Order regime of Suharto (Anderson, 1972; Benda, 1964).

During the Suharto era, Indonesia implemented a patrimonial administrative style (Muhaimin, 1991). This system resembles what Weber (1947) described as an authoritarian, bureaucratic, patrimonial system in which individuals and groups use power and authority for their own political and economic gain. Officials have authority over politics and governmental administrative functions, and decisions are made on the grounds of personal and political prerogatives. Relationships with officials take precedence over hard work, creativity, personal achievement, and honesty. Those who do not maintain close relationships with authorities cannot conduct successful business in Indonesia. Roepke (1982) referred to this as *social know-how* ability and proposed it as one of the most important factors in achieving success in Indonesian life, not only in business and entrepreneurship but also in government and the Indonesian military.

Purbasari (2006) hinted that during Suharto's regime, firms needed to be strongly connected with Suharto, his family, and/or his circle of friends in order to enter into highly profitable businesses and to secure their place in the market. This applied to almost all businesses and commodities, regardless of whether the business was local or international. Often, Suharto's family members were made business partners without any significant financial contribution to move the business forward, as was the case with his oldest son, Sigit Harjojudanto, who gained 20 percent ownership in PT Kekar Thames Airindo, an Indonesian venture seeking to gain access to the water supply.

Another example was presented by Koch (1996), who analyzed the case between PT Panutan Duta (a company owned by Suharto's oldest son, Sigit Harjojudanto) and Bre-X Mineral Ltd. (a mining company based in Calgary, Canada). Due to unforeseen circumstances, crucial contracts were withheld by Indonesia's general director of mining, and Bre-X Mineral Ltd.'s shares dropped by approximately

25 percent. Bre-X Mineral Ltd. formed an alliance with PT Panutan Duta and agreed to pay 10 percent of the shares, combined with a US$1 million per month contract for 40 months of technical support and administrative duties to overcome this barrier. Koch (1996) labeled the practice as an unethical tactic and cautioned that it would be disadvantageous for Indonesia in the long run, given the growing awareness of anti-bribery legislation around the world.

Since the fall of Suharto's regime, efforts have been made to eradicate corruption among public officials. The following constitution describes such an effort:

> The primary anti-corruption statute, which prescribes corruption as a substantive offence, is Law No. 31 of 1999 on the Eradication of Crimes of Corruption, as amended by Law No. 20 of 2001 (Indonesian Anti- Corruption Law). The primary objective of the Indonesian Anti-Corruption Law is to regulate and prevent public officials from committing corrupt acts. Articles 2 and 3 make it an offence to bribe to obtain profit for oneself, another person or a corporation or to abuse the authority, facilities or other means available as a result of one's rank or position in a manner that is detrimental to state finances or the national economy. The portions of the Indonesian Anti-Corruption Law that relate to bribery offences are Articles 5, 11, 12 and 13. (Fulbright, 2014, p. 66)

Providing insight into efforts to stop corruption in the post-Suharto regime, Schutte (2012) asserted that the purpose of the Anti-Corruption Law is to hold public officials accountable for corrupt practices and bribery and to treat such practices as criminal offences. To enforce enactment of the law, the government has formed the Corruption Eradication Commission (*Komisi Pemberantasan Tindak Korupsi*, or KPK). Since its launch, KPK has begun to gain the public's trust, respect, and support, as it succeeded in charging and incarcerating previously untouchable high-profile public officials for engaging in acts of corruption and bribery (Schutte, 2012).

A more recent case of unethical behavior is related to PT Freeport Indonesia (Freeport). Freeport's contract expires in 2021, and the company is seeking an extension, despite the fact that the terms of its contract clearly state that such an extension can only be negotiated starting in 2019. However, due to plans to commit to large capital to develop an underground mine at its Grasberg mining site (estimated at US$17 billion between now and the end of the 20-year extension), House Speaker Setya Novanto, former treasurer of the Golkar Party, was put under intense public scrutiny for allegedly offering help to extend Freeport's contract as a quid pro quo for free company shareholding in the name of President Joko Widodo and Vice President Jusuf Kalla. This was more than simply a corruption case, since it involves politics and an effort to implicate the administration in a bribery case, as well as an effort by Novanto to possibly enrich himself (Tempo.co, 2015). Novanto's actions were determined to be unethical, and under pressure from the government and the general public, he resigned from his position as Speaker of the House.

Arguably, one of the indicators of the extent to which business ethics are valued in a country is the degree of government involvement in terms of implementation and enforcement of ethical compliance (Schwartz & Weber, 2006). Given that financial survival and monetary gain take precedence over cultural, spiritual, and moral values, it can be inferred that government officials and businesspeople are also vulnerable to the temptations of ethical violations. Under these conditions, favoritism, nepotism, and bribery become common mechanisms for running business in developing countries, and personal relationships between business and politics provide protection for such practices (Purbasari, 2006). Acknowledging the legal dilemmas faced by interested foreign firms, Krarr (1995) referred to findings from the Hong Kong firm, Political and Economic Risk Consultancy Ltd., and noted that Indonesia – along with China and India – is among the countries with the highest corruption in Asia. Corruption has become a part of life in these societies, where money equates to power. There is nothing foreign businesses can do to legally defend against unethical practices. To be successful in Indonesia, foreign business must provide "payoffs" to tax officials and local authorities, even if the business has perfect returns. Moreover, even if the foreign business managed to find another approach, there is no guarantee that its competitors would not use money to win business favors (Kraar, 1995).

Blunt et al. (2012) reasoned and maintained that the fate of Indonesia remains to be seen – whether the country will move toward a true democracy or whether it will enter a danger zone of economic stagnation. The root of the problem is deeply embedded in the country's DNA in such a way that it will be difficult to eradicate in the short to medium term. In their view, patronage continues to be a salient feature of governance for the Indonesian state, and the combination of decentralization and mutually beneficial linkages of patronage and development assistance has formed a "patronage democracy."

CORPORATE SOCIAL RESPONSIBILITY IN INDONESIA

The new government is facing increasing pressure to act responsibly and become involved in adopting and implementing corporate social responsibility (CSR) in the post-Suharto era. Unlike its predecessor, the government is under scrutiny to regulate, enforce, and punish unethical and unacceptable business conduct and to simultaneously manage the stakeholders and the community (Achda, 2006; Joseph et al., 2016). The same applies to Indonesian business: for the first time, they are under scrutiny and are being held accountable for environmental damage and resulting social conflicts. It appears that as NGOs and the public become more sophisticated and environmentally conscious, demands for organizations to be more socially responsible will grow stronger every day. Failure to comply can hurt businesses – regardless how successful they are – as in the case of Asia Pulp and Paper (APP) (Dietrich & Auld, 2015).

In 2010, Greenpeace launched a global campaign with the message that APP – a well-known paper company founded in Indonesia with operations in Indonesia and China – was responsible for forest degradation and had no intention to phase out rainforest timber. Greenpeace was able to gain significant leverage by pushing international companies to sever ties with APP and to stop product purchases from the company and its subsidiaries. Financiers were forced to divest from APP, and the Indonesian government was moved to prohibit all forest clearing within existing concessions. In 2012, concurrent campaigns by the World Wildlife Fund (WWF) and Greenpeace successfully blocked the sale of APP's toilet paper brand Paseo in the United States. This and other campaigns against APP led to several contract cancellations by companies fearing prosecution under the US Lacey Act or European Union Timber Regulation. The last big Greenpeace campaign targeted the fast-food sector, leading several Kentucky Fried Chicken offices to cease their purchases from APP. Facing financial difficulties, APP had to examine its ethical conduct and come up with a new system for sustainability compliance. This effort would involve internal change (i.e., ethical training compliance and organizational cultural change) and more transparent relationships with the government (i.e., involvement in governmental policies and regulations) (Dietrich & Auld, 2015).

Considering its ingrained profit-driven mentality, Indonesian business and government are faced with a major challenge to adhere to CSR that goes beyond acts of kindness or benevolence. Various concerns expressed by community stakeholders must be given serious consideration and incorporated into the companies' policies and operation standards. In 2011, Mulkhan and Maulana reported that in comparison to other leading business countries in the world, CSR implementation, as well as CSR monitoring and reporting in Indonesia, has lagged behind. Sustainability reporting is still voluntary (National Center for Sustainability Reporting, 2015). In light of this, Mulkhan and Maulana (2011) encouraged the government to play a larger role in CSR enforcement. Creating new legislation to compel big companies to adopt CSR practices is a step in the right direction but is still insufficient. For successful integration, CSR policies would have to be facilitated, supported, assessed, and continually enforced in alignment with global standards.

MANAGERIAL CULTURE AND THE ROLE OF ORGANIZATIONAL LEADERSHIP

A study conducted by Sarwono and Armstrong (2001) examined the importance of micro-cultural differences on perceived ethical problems. The findings suggest that Indonesian-Chinese managers score higher in economic and values orientation, compared to Javanese and Batak managers, while Javanese and Batak managers score higher in religious orientation. This finding is consistent with the view that Chinese-Indonesians have dominated economic and business activity in Indonesia (Adidharta, 2015). Thus, Chinese-Indonesian culture should be considered when examining Indonesian business.

The family plays a central role in ethnically Chinese-Indonesian companies, which also affect operational and business management. There are advantages and disadvantages to this kind of management. One advantage is its flexibility and fast decision-making nature. However, this comes at the cost of insufficient standards of professionalism that can be expected from multinational companies, which are more structured and less family oriented. In the current era of modern globalization and technological advances, there is heightened pressure for Chinese-Indonesian business to adapt to professional business standards and to be less family oriented (Wijaya, 2008).

Given the predominance of Chinese-Indonesians in Indonesian business, native Indonesian business leaders are rare. Julius Tahija is among the few native Indonesians who had previously acted as the Managing Director of Caltex Pacific Indonesia, and later as Chairman of their Board of Commissioners. He also holds a Chairman role at Bank Niaga, Jakarta. These roles, as well as other prominent positions in the field of international business, have made him a well-known commentator on issues related to business ethics. The Rainforest Lake in the Zamrud area is an example of how he demonstrates ethical leadership and his stance around environmental issues. As the Managing Director of Caltex Indonesia, his geologists discovered a large oil reservoir beneath two unspoiled rainforest lakes in the Zamrud region, inhabited by a small indigenous tribe who subsisted on the lake. The company decided to mine the oil without causing further damage to the area. As Tahija (1993) asserted, "The additional expense was $8 million, but the profits covered the cost, and the local population continues to enjoy its traditional home" (p. 68).

The second example of his ethical decision-making involved whistle-blowing in Caltex. He was informed by a vendor that the accounts department would not release payments in accordance with the contractual terms unless bribes were paid. His response was to conduct an investigation in which he confirmed the information from the vendor. He took disciplinary action against those involved and issued a notice to all vendors, instructing them to contact him directly if they were not paid within two weeks of the due date of their invoices. Following this intervention, the problem disappeared in the organization (Tahija, 1993).

Based on his experience of leading large national and multi-national companies, Tahija (1993) suggested that Indonesian business have to pay attention to issues related to this discussion such as "environmental protection" and "promotion of an ethical business culture" (p. 65).

CSR AND BUSINESS ETHICS: POLICIES AND TRAINING

In Indonesia, issues surrounding CSR and business ethics can be found in company sustainability reports. It is difficult to gain insight into many Indonesian companies because such implementation is, at best, a voluntary formality. Some of the larger prominent companies, however, have begun to set new standards of business ethics and have described their efforts in public sustainability reports, which are published on their company websites. In this section, four leading companies will be presented as exemplary companies that are making significant efforts to successfully adopt and implement CSR ethics policies and training.

Ranked 230 in the Fortune Global 500 list of companies, PT Pertamina EP is an oil and natural gas corporation owned by the government. The company registered revenues of US$41,763 million (Fortune Global 500, 2016). This Jakarta-based company sets the standard and has defined its Work and Business Ethics (*Etika Kerja dan Bisnis* or EKB) as a set of rules of conduct that applies to all organizational members.

According to its 2015 sustainability report, starting in 2009, PT Pertamina began its implementation of the Good Corporate Governance (GCG) framework using the four principles of "Transparency, Independence, Accountability, Responsibility, & Fairness" (PT Pertamina, 2015, p. 65). The company stated that it aimed for "zero corruption incident and implementation of good corporate governance practice" (p. 63). To further ensure the successful implementation of GCG practices, the company implemented socialization training to enculture and educate its workers, conducted an annual assessment, and was among the few companies that publicly released its assurance statement (PT Pertamina, 2015, pp. 207–209).

The 2015 report indicated that complete integration of GCG into the company culture had been achieved and that GCG is "no longer regarded as something that is mandatory but has become a necessity, either by members of the organization who are in Top Management and by all levels of the organization's members" (p. 63). The report also mentioned that the company has gained respect for employing workers who refused to take bribes or gratuities. For its significant effort, PT Pertamina received numerous awards from the Eradication Commission (KPK) for "Control Unit Gratification."

The second company is Unilever, a prominent multinational company that has developed a code of ethics for its business operations around the globe (Crane & Matten, 2007). This code of ethics also applies to PT Unilever Indonesia Tbk, a part of the Unilever Group, which manufactures and distributes most Unilever brands (such as Surf, Close-up, and Clear) for the Indonesian community. Customized for local needs and conditions, the Code of Business Principles (CoBP) in PT Unilever Tbk requires adherence from all organizational members. All employees must incorporate CoBP into their internal and external daily interactions. Senior managers are responsible and are held accountable for providing detailed guidance throughout all business units, monitoring implementation within their units and teams, and presenting an annual report on CoBP compliance (PT Unilever Indonesia Tbk, 2015). The annual CoBP report is reviewed by the audit committee and Unilever executives. Any perception of code of conduct violation must be reported by following a specific procedure. Compliance with these principles or any other mandatory policies and instructions will not result in punishment or retribution (PT Unilever Indonesia Tbk, 2015).

PT Unilever Tbk publishes a sustainability report every two years to demonstrate its business impact on the economy, people, and environment. The fourth edition was published in May 2015 and states its quest as being "profitable in [the] growing market and at the same time having its environmental footprint and increasing its positive social impact" (p. 26). The report also describes anti-corruption training for all employees covering four aspects of CoBP, which include "Anti-bribery; Gifts and Entertainment; Avoiding Conflicts of Interest; and Contact with the Government, Regulators, and NGOs" (p. 23). The assurance statement is publicly released on page 84 of the sustainability record.

The third company is PT Telekomunikasi Indonesia Tbk (also known as Telkom Indonesia or Telkom) – the largest telecommunications services company in Indonesia and a semi-privatized, majority state-owned company. The company implemented its GCG framework to benefit its stakeholders, employees, and third parties, as well as to contribute to society and the surrounding environment. With regard to business ethics and corporate culture, Telkom states on its website that "the implementation of GCG has formed legal awareness and created employees who are sensitive to social responsibility and loved by customers" (Telkom Indonesia, n.d.). Telkom also promises to prohibit violations of ethics principles and the law for any business reasons or despite any pressure from any party.

Since the company announced its commitment to morals and ethics, Telkom has made significant efforts to enforce them. First, the company issued a code of ethics in accordance with the provisions of Section 406 of the Sarbanes Oxley Act (SOA) 2002, which applied to all organizational members, including board directors and other top executives (Telkom Indonesia, n.d.). The code provides protection to any whistle-blower who supplies information regarding any legal violations, unethical practices, or actions against the principles of good governance. The next step was to establish 2015 as the *Year of Corporate Culture Activation*, aiming to establish the Telkom Way and to set new values, a new philosophy, and a new code of conduct into its daily work practices through the Culture Agent Onboarding program. Company culture training was also provided to ensure successful implementation. To monitor and evaluate the progress of its program implementation and to assess its organizational members' understanding of the new corporate culture, Telkom conducts an annual assessment to measure topics such as "understanding corporate governance, business ethics, the integrity pact, fraud, risk management, internal control (SOA), whistleblowing, prohibition on gratuities, IT governance, ensuring information security and other integrated matters related to corporate governance practices." The survey is internally and externally audited through an SOA 404 audit process for best results (Telkom Indonesia, n.d.).

The fourth company is PT ODG Indonesia, a small, privately held company with revenues of approximately US$30 million, which works as a subcontractor in the mining and manufacturing sectors in Indonesia. Its customers have typically been top-tier Indonesian mining companies, as well as multinational construction companies. The company was previously a subsidiary of the US conglomerate Tyco International but was taken over in a management buyout in 2011 with the support of a private equity fund.

The reason for the buyout goes back to 2002, when Tyco's CEO and CFO had been embroiled in a scandal involving the improper use of company funds. As a result, the Securities and Exchange Commission (SEC) filed charges against them for artificially inflating their earnings and for not disclosing major financial information (Sorkin, 2002). In the wake of these revelations, the company brought in a new CEO and board, which then implemented worldwide ethical conduct training, an annual certification program for all existing employees, an ethical induction program for new employees, and a guide to ethical conduct. Management, and those employees dealing with external parties, also participated in the US Foreign Corrupt Practices Act (FCPA) awareness training and signed the compliance agreements. For sales staff, a "zero tolerance" policy was put in place, which made it clear that under no circumstances would payments, commissions, or incentives be paid to third parties in exchange for receiving product orders. In the past, the policy extended to third-party product distributors. However, after one distributor was caught violating the rules in 2009, the distribution program was shut down, as it became obvious that it was not possible to exert the same kind of control over third parties, even though the third parties received the same ethical conduct training and had signed the same compliance documents as the company employees.

Joseph et al. (2016) conducted a content analysis with 24 Malaysian and 34 Indonesian companies, respectively. Data were collected from annual and sustainability reports with the purpose of capturing policies and standard best practices concerning corruption. They reported that anti-corruption practices and whistle-blowing were the most often stated practices. Through a comparative analysis, the study also found that Indonesian companies revealed anti-corruption practices more often than their Malaysian counterparts on issues pertaining to "combating bribery (most reported), board and senior management responsibilities, responsible business relationships, external verification and assurance (least reported), and total disclosure" (p. 2902). When ranked, combating bribery was the most often reported, while external minimal verification was the least.

The state of CSR and business ethics in Indonesian business is yet to be seen. Whether it will serve as merely window dressing or a serious commitment is something worth continual examination. What is clear is that there is less tolerance for unethical conduct and sufficient external pressure for change. Some leading companies, including the four discussed in this section, have set the tone by making efforts to create a new workplace culture, beyond the issuance of new policies. These companies display their commitment by implementing training, ensuring transfer, assessing, and holding all organization members accountable in terms of (1) ethical compliance, auditing, and reporting; (2) business ethics values; (3) corporate responsibility toward the natural environment; and (4) sustainability.

CONCLUSION AND IMPLICATIONS FOR BUSINESS

Indonesia is undergoing a transition under the spotlight due to its high economic potential and prospects for growth. For academics, Indonesia's participation in the global marketplace, along with the growing influence of Western values, has made the country a subject of scholarly interest (Heuer et al., 1999; Hollinger, 1996; Joseph et al., 2016). However, there is little research on ethics in Indonesia, and what does exist is inconclusive. For foreign investors and multinational corporations, Indonesia has potential opportunities, as it is believed to be one of the upcoming economic giants (O'Neill, 2014). Still, business entry to Indonesia remains challenging due to societal norms, cultural values, and expectations for standard business practices that differ from those held by businesspeople in Western societies. Whether the "Western societal ways" are better or not is open to discussion and is beyond the scope of this chapter. Rather, the aim of this chapter is to provide a snapshot of the business ethics in Indonesia, which can only be understood by delving into the deep and rich national history that has shaped Indonesian culture and societal systems.

As in many other developing countries of Asia, business ethics in Indonesia are dealt with more informally, compared to the stricter rules and accountability commonly found in Western societies. However, external global pressure and insistence from the public for a more sustainable and environmentally friendly practice have put both the Indonesian government and well-established Indonesian businesses at risk of failing. Thus, they must take CSR more seriously and accept that it is more than an act of benevolence. There is real accountability to the community and the environment. Although still at a very early stage, efforts and initiatives have been observed and documented in some multinational companies and local corporations. This heightened awareness of responsible business ethics may signal new opportunities for businesspeople and foreign investors wishing to pursue business endeavors in Indonesia.

REFERENCES

Achda, B. T. (2006). The sociological context of corporate social responsibility development and implementation in Indonesia. *Corporate Social Responsibility and Environmental Management*, 13(5), 300–305.

Adidharta, S. (2015). Etnis china tionghoa masih nomor satu kuasai bisnis dan ekonomi Indonesia. *Kompasiana*. Retrieved from www.kompasiana .com/syaifud_adidharta_2/etnis-china-tionghoa-masih-nomor-satu-kuasai-bisnis-dan-ekonomi-indonesia_552985f2f17e61b07ed623ac

Aji, K. B., & Achmad, S. W. (2014). *Ensiklopedia raja-raja nusantara: Menyingkap tuntas riwayat hidup raja-raja nusantara*. Indonesia: Araska.

Ananta, A., Arifin, E. N., Hasbullah, M. S., Handayani, N. B., & Pramono, A. (2015). *Demography of Indonesia's ethnicity*. Institute of Southeast Asian Studies.

Anderson, B. R. O. (1972). The idea of power in Javanese culture. In C. Holt (Ed.), *Culture and politics in Indonesia*. Ithaca, NY: Cornell University Press.

Benda, H. (1964, May). Article review: Democracy in Indonesia. *Journal of Asian Studies*, 23(3), 449–456.

Blunt, P., Turner, M., & Lindroth, H. (2012). Patronage's progress in post-Soeharto Indonesia. *Public Administration and Development*, 32(1), 64–81.

British Broadcasting Corporation (2014, January 6). The Mint countries: Next economic giants? *BBC News Online Magazine*. Retrieved from www.bbc .com/news/magazine-25548060

Caraway, T. L. (2015, June 1). Book reviews: Comparative politics. *Perspective on Politics*, 13 (2), 561–563.

Central Intelligence Agency (2015). *The World Fact Book*. Retrieved from https://www.cia.gov/library/publications/the-world-factbook/geos/id.html

Crane, A., & Matten, D. (2007). *Business ethics: Managing corporate citizenship and sustainability in the age of globalization*. New York: Oxford University Press.

Cribb, R. (2002, August 1). Unresolved problems in the Indonesian killings of 1965–1966. *Asian Survey*, 42(4), 550–563.

Dieterich, U., & Auld, G. (2015, November). Moving beyond commitments: Creating durable change through the implementation of Asia pulp and paper's forest conservation policy. *Journal of Cleaner Production*, 107, 54–63.

Elias, S., & Noone, C. (2011, December). The growth and development of the Indonesian economy. *Reserve Bank of Australia Report*, 33–44. Retrieved from www.rba.gov.au/publications/bulletin/2011/dec/4.html

Fortune Global 500 (2016). Retrieved from http://beta.fortune.com/global500/list

Friend, T. (2003). *Indonesian destinies*. Cambridge, MA: Harvard University Press.

Geertz, H. (1961). *The Javanese family: A study of kinship and socialization*. New York: Free Press of Glencoe.

Grant, B. (1964). *Indonesia. Australia*. London: Penguin Books.

Heuer, M., Cummings, J. L., & Hutabarat, W. (1999). Cultural stability or change among managers in Indonesia? *Journal of International Business Studies*, 30(3), 599–610.

Hofstede, G. (1980). *Culture's consequences: International differences in work-related values*. Newburry Park, CA: Sage.

Hofstede, G. (1997). *Cultures and organizations, software of the mind, intercultural cooperation and its importance for survival*. New York: McGraw-Hill.

Hofstede Centre (n.d.). Retrieved from http://geert-hofstede.com/indonesia.html

Hollinger, W. C. (1996). *Economic policy under President Soeharto: Indonesia's twenty-five year record, Vol. XIV*. Washington, DC: United States Indonesia Society.

Inglehart, R. (1997). *Modernization and postmodernization: Cultural, economic, and political change in 43 societies*. Princeton, NJ: Princeton University Press.

Inglehart, R. (2012). *Values change the world: World values survey*. Retrieved from www.iffs.se/media/1931/wvs-brochure-web.pdf

Inglehart, R., & Baker, W. E. (2000, February). Modernization, cultural change, and the persistence of traditional values. *American Sociological Review*, 65(1), 19–51.

Inglehart, R., & Welzel, C. (2005). *Modernization, cultural change, and democracy: The human development sequence.* New York: Cambridge University Press.

International Fund for Agriculture Development (2015). Rural poverty in Indonesia. Retrieved from www.ruralpovertyportal.org/country/home/tags/indonesia

Joseph, C. J., Gunawan, J., Sawani, Y., Rahmat, M., Noyem, J. A., & Darus, F. (2016). A comparative study of anti-corruption practice disclosure among Malaysian and Indonesian corporate social responsibility (CSR) best practice companies. *Journal of Cleaner Production, 112,* 2896–2906.

Kartodirdjo, S. (1987). *Pengantar sejarah Indonesia baru: 1500–1900.* Jakarta: Gramedia Pustaka Utama.

Koch, G. (1996). The price of Third World business. *Alberta Report /Newsmagazine,* 23(49), 21–35.

Koentjaraningrat (1984). *Kebudayaan Jawa.* Jakarta: Balai Pustaka.

Kraar, L. (1995). How corrupt is Asia? *Fortune, 132*(4), 26–36.

Magnis-Soesono, F. S. J. (1991). *Sebuah analisa falsafi tentang kebijaksanaan hidup jawa.* Jakarta: PT Gramedia Pustake Utama.

Markus, H. R., & Kitayama, S. K. (1991). Culture and the self: Implications for cognition, emotion, and motivation. *Psychological Review, 98*(2), 224–253.

Mas'oed, M. (1989). *Ekonomi dan struktur politik orde baru, 1966–1971.* Jakarta, Indonesia: LP3ES.

May, B. (1978). *The Indonesian tragedy.* London: Routledge & Kegan Paul.

Muhaimin, Y. (1991). *Bisnis dan politik: Kebijaksanaan ekonomi Indonesia 1950–1980.* Jakarta: LP3ES.

Mulder, N. (1983). *Mysticism and everyday life in contemporary java: Cultural persistence and change.* Singapore: Singapore University Press.

Mulkhan, U., & Maulana, A. P. (2011). Peran pemerintah dalam kebijakan corporate social responsibility (CSR) dalam upaya. *Jurnal Ilmiah Administrasi Publik Dan Pembangunan, 2*(1), 274–281.

National Center for Sustainability Reporting (2015). *11th Indonesia sustainability reporting award 2010: Toward transparency and accountability.* Jakarta, Indonesia. Retrieved from www.ncsr-id.org/2015/12/21/sustainability-reporting-award-sra-2015-press-release/

Natural Resource Governance Institute (n.d.). Retrieved from www.resourcegovernance.org/our-work/country/indonesia

O'Neill, J. (2014, December 4). Who defines the next economic giants? *New York Times.* Retrieved from www.nytimes.com/2014/12/04/opinion/jim-oneill-who-defines-the-next-economic-giants.html?_r=0

Poesponegoro, M. D., & Notosusanto, N. (1984). *Sejarah national Indonesia iii.* Jakarta: PN Balai Bustaka.

Purbasari, D. P. (2006). *Political connection, trade protection and multinational corporations: Firm-level evidence of patronage in Indonesia* (PhD dissertation). Department of Economics, University of Colorado.

Rahmani, N. S. (2014). Cultural differences in organizational commitment. *American Journal of Management*, 14(1/2), 111–125.

Ricklefs, M. C. (2008). *A history of modern Indonesia since c. 1200* (4th ed.). Basingstoke, UK: Palgrave Macmillan.

Roepke, J. (1982). *Kewirausahaan dan perkembangan ekonomi indonesia, dalam bunga rampai masalah-masalah pembangunan.* Jakarta: PT Pustaka LP3ES.

Roosa, J. (2006). *Pretext for mass murder: The September 30th movement and Suharto's coup d'etat in Indonesia.* Madison, WI: University of Wisconsin Press.

Sarwono, S., & Armstrong, R. (2001). Microcultural differences and perceived ethical problems: An international business perspective. *Journal of Business Ethics*, 30(1), 41–56.

Schütte, S. A. (2012). Against the odds: Anti-corruption reform in Indonesia. *Public Administration and Development*, 32(1), 38–48.

Schwartz, M. S., & Weber, J. (2006). A business ethics national index (BENI) measuring business ethics activity around the world. *Business Society*, 45, 382–405.

Sorkin, A. R. (2002, September 13). 2 top Tyco executives charged with $600 million fraud scheme. *New York Times*. Retrieved from www.nytimes .com/2002/09/13/business/2-top-tyco-executives-charged-with-600-million-fraud-scheme.html?pagewanted=all

Sumantri, S., & Suharnomo (2011). Kajian proposisi hubungan antara dimensi budaya nasional dengan motivasi dalam suatu organisasi usaha. *Pustaka Universitas Pajajaran.* Retrieved from http://pustaka.unpad.ac.id/wp-content/uploads/2011/04/kajian_proposisi_hub_antara_dimensi_budaya_nasional.pdf

Tahija, S. (1993). Swapping business skills for oil. *Harvard Business Review*, 71(5), 64–77.

Telkom Indonesia (n.d.). Code of ethics and corporate culture. Retrieved from www .telkom.co.id/en/hubungi-kami/pt-telekomunikasi-indonesia-tbk/investor-relations/laporan-tahunan/tata-kelola-perusahaan/etika-bisnis-dan-budaya-perusahaan

Tempo.co (2015). Retrieved from http://nasional.tempo.co/read/news/2015/11/18/078720066/heboh-setya-novanto-melobi-freeport-hingga-pesawat-jepang

Transparency International (2015). Corruption by country/territory. Retrieved from https://www.transparency.org/country/#IDN

Triandis, H. C. (2001). Individualism-collectivism and personality. *Journal of Personality*, 69(6), 907–924.

Triandis, H. C., Chan, D.-S., Bhawuk, D. P. S., Iwao, S., & Sinha, J. B. P. (1995). Multimethod probes of allocentrism and idiocentrism. *International Journal of Psychology*, 30(4), 461–480.

Triandis, H. C., & Suh, E. M. (2002). Cultural influences on personality. *Annual Review of Psychology*, 53, 133–160.

Trompenaars, F., & Hampden-Turner, C. (1998). *Riding the waves of culture: Understanding diversity in global business*. New York: McGraw Hill.

PT Unilever Indonesia Tbk (2015). *Unilever 2013–2014 sustainability report* (Tech. Rep. No. 4). Retrieved from https://www.unilever.co.id/id/images/sustainability-report-2013-2014-en_tcm1310-484036_id.pdf

PT Pertamina (2015). *Sustainability report: Empowering resources for energy resilience*. Retrieved from www.pertamina.com/media/d2d30686-149d-4121-a63e-0dd6a776d1ee/SR_Pertamina_2015.pdf

Vickers, A. (2013). *A modern history of Indonesia*. Cambridge: Cambridge University Press.

Weber, M. (1947). *The theory of social and economic organization*. A. M. Henderson & T. Parsons (Trans.). New York: Free Press Glencoe.

Wijaya, Y. (2008). The prospect of familism in the global era: A study on the recent development of the ethnic-Chinese business, with particular attention to the Indonesian context. *Journal of Business Ethics*, 79(3), 311–317.

The World Bank Group (2017). Retrieved from: www.doingbusiness.org/data/exploreeconomies/indonesia

PART II **Building and Sustaining Ethical Business Cultures**

9 Building More Ethical Organizations: The Global Employee Perspective

Jack Wiley and Kelsey-Jo Ritter

ABSTRACT

Using the Ethical Perceptions Index, this chapter reviews employees' varying perceptions of ethical business practices across 22 of the world's largest economies. The chapter addresses two important research questions: *Do perceptions of ethical business practices relate to important organizational outcomes?* And, *How do we create and sustain ethical business practices?* In answering these questions, we draw on an extensive, globally representative sample of employees, and show that organizations operating with higher levels of ethics and integrity are more likely to succeed, both with respect to the way employees feel about their work environment as well as multiple indicators of organizational-level business performance. Finally, we explore the main drivers of ethical business cultures, and demonstrate that organizations that build a climate for diversity and inclusion, communicate transparently, codify and regulate important work processes, and hire and advance managers who act with a high degree of interpersonal justice, will score the highest on the Ethical Perceptions Index. We conclude by offering suggestions for leaders who seek to improve their organization's ethical standing amongst employees.

INTRODUCTION

Contemporary business organizations operate in an increasingly competitive global marketplace. Executives leading their organizations into new international markets, or expanding operations within existing markets around the globe, are naturally concerned about the successful implementation of organizational design features and elements of organizational culture they deem critical to the achievement of their business goals. Central to the thesis of this book is the notion that the strength of an organization's workplace ethics and integrity has earned a rightful position within the framework of various potent predictors of business success (Wiley, 2010).

Using a global database of employee work attitudes and a previously validated measure of an organization's ethical business culture, namely the Ethical Perceptions Index (Ardichvili, Jondle & Kowske, 2010), this chapter will first compare the strength of ethical business cultures across 22 countries, whose economies represent 80 percent of the world's GDP. From that foundation, the chapter will next establish the relationship between the strength of an organization's ethical business culture and employee engagement and performance confidence – work attitudes that have a known association with a variety of business success measures. The chapter will then explore those aspects of an organization's internal workplace environment that most contribute to employees' perceptions of ethical business practices. Armed with that knowledge, the chapter closes with recommendations for enhancing the strength of an organization's ethical business practices. Although we acknowledge that the extent to which employees perceive ethics and integrity in the workplace differs significantly from country to country, all organizations are capable of strengthening those perceptions. We maintain the point of view that organizations that do so position themselves for greater success in the future.

METHODOLOGY

The research results reported in this chapter are drawn from a multi-year, global survey of employee work attitudes. The data were collected by the Kenexa High Performance Institute (KHPI) as part of the WorkTrends survey program. (KHPI was the research and development function of Kenexa, an international human resources consulting company acquired by IBM in 2013.) The first author originated the WorkTrendsTM survey in 1985 to provide both normative data and a research platform for product and intellectual capital development. While initially developed as a survey of a representative sample of workers in the United States, the research initiative expanded to capture a representative sample of workers worldwide.

The data reported in this chapter were collected in 2011 and 2012. Table 9.1 displays the countries surveyed and their respective sample sizes. All countries, with the exception of Indonesia (n = 820) contain data from nearly 2,000 participants; country samples sizes range from 1,828 to 2,053 employees. Together, data from 42,527 participants were used for the research results reported here.

A market research firm recruited participants and administered the survey across the globe. In order to recruit participants, the research firm advertised online in order to develop a large database of volunteers willing to take an online survey. Volunteers "opted-in" to be considered, which allowed the research firm to ensure each person's demographic information was accurate. Subsequently, a panel of participants that was representative of each country's workforce demographics was randomly selected. This procedure helped ensure lower sampling error and higher external validity.

The Ethical Perceptions Index (EPI)

The Ethical Perceptions Index (EPI) was developed by the Center for Ethical Business Cultures (CEBC) and KHPI to capture employees' assessments of the strength of the ethical culture of their organizations, as indicated by their perceptions of senior management and coworker behavior, as well as organizational values and practices. Five items were developed that operationalize this definition. Employees indicated the

Table 9.1. *Sample Size*

Argentina	1,992
Australia	2,019
Brazil	1,999
Canada	2,014
China	1,898
Denmark	2,000
Finland	2,020
France	1,987
Germany	1,948
India	1,912
Indonesia	820
Italy	1,981
Japan	2,001
Mexico	1,990
Netherlands	2,000
Russian Federation	2,041
South Africa	2,013
Spain	2,009
Sweden	2,002
Switzerland	1,828
United Kingdom	2,053
United States	2,000
Total	**42,527**

extent to which they agreed or disagreed with each statement on a five-point Likert rating scale (1 = Strongly Disagree; 2 = Disagree; 3 = Neither Agree nor Disagree; 4 = Agree; and, 5 = Strongly Agree). By averaging employee responses across these five items, a picture of the ethical landscape of an organization can be painted.

- Where I work, ethical issues and concerns can be discussed without negative consequences.
- My organization's senior management supports and practices high standards of ethical conduct.

- My organization strives to serve the interests of multiple stakeholders (e.g., customers, employees, suppliers, and community), not just the shareholders.
- The behavior of the people I work with is consistent with my organization's mission, vision, and values.
- Where I work, people do not "get ahead" unless their behavior clearly demonstrates my organization's values.

To understand the determinants of an employee's ethical perceptions, we must understand how culture, and more specifically, *ethical culture* may be developed and assessed. Schein (1990) defines organizational culture "as (a) pattern of basic assumptions, (b) invented, discovered, or developed by a given group, (c) as it learns to cope with its problems of external validation and internal integration, and (d) that has worked well enough to be considered valid and, therefore (e) is to be taught to new members as the (f) correct way to perceive, think, and feel in relation to those problems" (p. 111). Schein further identifies three levels of culture: observable artifacts, values, and underlying assumptions.

While more direct observation and employee interviews are necessary for determining employees' values and shared assumptions (Schein, 2006), the EPI is useful for assessing formal and informal artifacts, and certain values. For example, asking employees to report on mission statements, reward systems, leadership, codes of ethics, and decision processes can provide information on the formal components of ethical cultures (Cohen, 1993). Further, the informal aspects of ethical cultures can be assessed through the employee reporting of unwritten rules or implicit behavioral norms, enduring stories, and role models (Cohen 1993; Schein 1990). These informal and formal artifacts of ethical culture are assessed with the five EPI items such that higher EPI scores reflect business cultures that are "based on alignment between formal structures, processes, and policies, consistent ethical behavior of top leadership, and informal recognition of heroes, stories, rituals, and language that inspire organizational members to behave in a manner consistent with high ethical standards that have been set by executive leadership" (Ardichvili et al., 2010, p. 446).

Researchers have demonstrated that countries may differ in their conceptualizations of ethical businesses – in other words, behavior that constitutes acting with integrity and fairness (e.g., Bailey & Spicer, 2007). In this globally representative sample, EPI scores were calculated using an employee's average score across the five items. The EPI scale demonstrated strong internal consistency ($\alpha = .82$). Among the countries surveyed, each was classified into categories of weak, medium, and strong ethical perceptions based on comparison of individual country scores to the global average. A country with weak ethical perceptions scored at least one standard deviation below the global average; a country with strong ethical perceptions scored at least one standard deviation above the global average. As shown in Table 9.2, employees in India and Sweden reported the strongest ethical perceptions; on the other hand, employees in Spain, Argentina, Italy, and Japan reported the weakest ethical perceptions.

A closer look at the country-level results reveals that emerging market countries (Brazil, Russia, India, China, Indonesia, South Africa, and Mexico) can be categorized as having moderate to strong ethical perceptions.

DO ETHICAL PERCEPTIONS PREDICT RELEVANT OUTCOMES?

Beyond the implicit importance of organizations operating well within ethical boundaries, our study explored the extent to which working for an ethical organization predicted meaningful outcomes by correlating the EPI with indexes of Employee Engagement and Performance Confidence.

Employers certainly desire engaged employees who will be motivated to go above and beyond the call of duty in service of the organization and its mission. Organizations that are fueled by engaged

Table 9.2. *EPI Scores across Sampled Countries*

Weak	Moderate	Strong
Spain	Mexico	Sweden
Argentina	Finland	India
Italy	United Kingdom	
Japan	Germany	
	Netherlands	
	Australia	
	Brazil	
	Canada	
	Switzerland	
	Indonesia	
	China	
	United States	
	Denmark	
	France	
	Russian Federation	
	South Africa	

employees are likely to enjoy superior performance as a result of both improved individual performance and team performance. Indeed, organizations with more engaged employees tend to report higher profitability and total shareholder return. In their meta-analysis of 42 studies, for example, Harter et al. (2002) document a significant link between business units with higher employee engagement and reports of the unit's profitability, productivity, and customer satisfaction. Additionally, engaged employees are more likely to be working for organizations with higher American Customer Satisfaction Index (ACSI) scores, Diluted Earnings per Share (DEPS), Return-on-Assets (R-O-A), and three-year Total Shareholder Return (3TSR) (Wiley, 2014).

Thus, the Employee Engagement Index (EEI) was designed to assess the extent to which employees are "motivated to contribute to organizational success, and are willing to apply discretionary effort to accomplishing tasks important to the achievement of organizational goals" (Wiley, 2014). The following listed items tap into four desired elements of engagement: pride, satisfaction, advocacy, and commitment (Macey & Schneider, 2008). Employees indicated the extent to which they agreed or disagreed with each statement on a five-point Likert rating scale. The Employee Engagement Index shows strong internal consistency ($\alpha = .90$).

- I am proud to tell people I work for my organization.
- Overall, I am extremely satisfied with my organization as a place to work.
- I would gladly refer a good friend or family member to my organization for employment.
- I rarely think about looking for a new job with another organization.

Are employees who work for highly ethical organizations more likely to be engaged, on average? Our representative, global data indicate the answer is yes. Specifically, scores on the EPI strongly correlate with EEI scores ($r = .65^{**}$)[1]. Thus, employees working for organizations with higher levels of ethical integrity are also more engaged – that is, more proud, satisfied, willing to advocate for, and committed to staying with their organizations.

We also considered the extent to which more ethical organizations – as perceived by their employees – are better positioned for overall business success. The Performance Confidence Index (PCI) was designed to assess employees' attitudes concerning their organization's future success and the quality of its products and services. A similar construct, Performance Excellence, has been shown to predict several relevant outcomes (Wiley, 2014). Employee ratings of their organization's Performance Excellence have been shown to predict the same business success indices as reported previously for Employee Engagement Index scores (ASCSI, DEPS, R-O-A, 3TSR). Put another way, measures of organizational effectiveness, such as the Performance Confidence and Performance Excellence indexes,

---

[1]   ** indicates the correlation was significant at $p < .001$.

indicate whether an employee feels she or he is on a "winning team." For each of the four following items, employees were asked to indicate the extent to which they agreed or disagreed with each statement on a five-point Likert rating scale. The scale demonstrated high internal consistency (α = .84).

Performance Confidence Index

- My organization's products and services are consistently innovative.
- My organization provides higher quality products and services than other similar organizations.
- I believe my organization has an outstanding future.
- My organization competes well against others in its industry.

When correlating the employee scores on the EPI with scores on the PCI, we see a pattern similar to the EPI x EEI relationship emerge. Employees who believe their organizations operate ethically are much more likely to report high Performance Confidence Index scores (r = .63**). Although these associations are based on cross-sectional data, which limits our ability to draw causal conclusions, the reported relationships are quite strong.

WHAT FACTORS ARE MOST STRONGLY ASSOCIATED WITH HIGH EPI SCORES?

Given the evidence that organizations operating with higher employee-perceived levels of ethical integrity are more likely to have both engaged employees *and* employees more confident of business performance, we sought to identify potential predictors of EPI scores.

Using multiple regression analysis, four unique predictors were identified from the WorkTrends survey: Diversity Climate, Transparent Communication, Managerial Interpersonal Justice, and Standardized Work Processes. Details regarding each scale are provided in the following sections; scores were obtained using the previously described Likert rating scales. Additionally, based on their scores being one standard deviation above or one standard deviation below the global average, the countries achieving the highest and lowest scores for each predictor (Diversity Climate, Transparent Communication, Managerial Interpersonal Justice, and Standardized Work Processes) are reported in the following sections.

Together, these four predictors explain 57 percent of the variance in EPI scores. Specifically, when all predictors are entered into the regression equation simultaneously, the unique, standardized coefficients for each variable are as follows: Diversity Climate (β = .23), Transparent Communication (β = .24), Managerial Interpersonal Justice (β= .16), and Standardized Work Processes (β = .13).

Given the strong relationships between these four predictors and the EPI, one avenue to improve the ethical standing of an organization is to develop within the organization each of the four EPI predictors: Diversity Climate, Transparent Communication, Managerial Interpersonal Justice, and Standardized Work Processes. Although a comprehensive review of such strategies is beyond the scope of this chapter, in the following sections we conceptually review the four predictors and offer a preliminary guide to ways in which organizations might benefit from these.

Diversity Climate

Diversity Climate has been explicitly defined as follows: "Employees' shared perceptions of the policies, practices, and procedures that implicitly and explicitly communicate the extent to which fostering and maintaining diversity and eliminating discrimination is a priority in the organization" (Gelfand et al., 2005, p. 104). The following six items reflect this definition; employees indicated the extent to which they agreed or disagreed with each statement on a five-point Likert rating scale. The scale demonstrated strong internal consistency (α = .91).

- All employees, regardless of gender, ethnicity, religion, sexual orientation, and culture have equal opportunities for advancement.
- My organization makes it easy for people from diverse backgrounds to fit in and be accepted.

- Diversity is very much a part of my organization's culture.
- My organization has a strong track record for recruiting people from diverse backgrounds.
- My organization enables people from diverse backgrounds to excel.
- The leadership at my organization is committed to diversity.

When referring to employee diversity, surface-level diversity such as gender, race, ethnicity, and age are most commonly considered (van Knippenberg et al., 2004). Researchers have reported mixed findings with regard to bottom-line indicators and attitudinal effects of increased demographic diversity within organizations. In many ways, researchers have suggested that diversity is a double-sided coin, presenting organizations with opportunity in the form of decision-making and innovation, but also the potential for increased conflict or reduced group performance (Guillaume et al., 2013; King & Gilrane, 2015).

However, in many cases, the presence of a strong diversity climate has been shown to moderate the impact of demographic diversity. For example, the presence of a strong diversity climate mitigated any negative effects of surface-level demographic diversity on intent to quit and organizational commitment and was linked to return on profit and firm productivity (Gonzalez & DeNisi, 2009). Others have shown that diversity climate is linked to decreased turnover intentions and higher retention and importantly benefits all employees, regardless of minority or majority status (Kaplan et al., 2011; McKay et al., 2007). And finally, stronger diversity climates have been shown to reduce racial-ethnic mean score differences in sales performance. That is, in businesses that have less supportive diversity climates, racial-ethnic disparities in sales performance of employees were largest (McKay et al., 2008).

Interestingly, as we see in Table 9.3, four out of five of the countries with the strongest diversity climates belong to the Anglo-Saxon group (Canada, United Kingdom, United States, and Australia). These countries are all fairly homogenous with regard to racio-ethnic diversity (Alesina et al., 2003). These countries have been previously

Table 9.3. *Diversity Climate*

Weakest	Strongest
Japan	Indonesia
Italy	Australia
Spain	United Kingdom
Finland	United States
	Canada
	India

grouped due to their cultural heritage and similar standing on two of Hofstede's cultural dimensions; the United States, Australia, and the United Kingdom represent cultures that are both highly individualistic and low in uncertainty avoidance (Jackson, 2001). Similarly, these countries are grouped as Anglo countries according to the GLOBE study criteria (Gupta & Hanges, 2004).

Establishing and Developing a Positive Diversity Climate

First, organizations should make a sincere commitment to the promotion and value of racio-ethnic diversity through the establishment of formal initiatives. For example, such initiatives may include targeted recruitment efforts in which the organization seeks to increase the diversity of the applicant pool and ultimately builds a more diverse employee profile. In addition, organizations can work to implement standardized systems for hiring, performance appraisal, and promotion that serve to minimize bias in reporting and increase perceptions of fairness. Social programs, such as networking and mentorship groups, can be designed to help minority employees feel more embedded within the organization.

Second, organizations should improve, when possible, the diversity of its workforce within management and higher-level positions. The visual representation of employee diversity in the upper echelons of management is important in many ways, including legitimizing the aforementioned diversity initiatives, in an organization's commitment to such efforts: *seeing is believing.*

And finally, and in line with the third predictor (Managerial Interpersonal Justice), organizations can focus on selecting and developing managers who are considerate, ethical, and supportive of their subordinates. (See Improving Managerial Interpersonal Justice for more details.)

Signal theory (Spence, 1974) suggests such strategies can send important messages to employees that the organization is both concerned about employee well-being and is committed to diversity and equality. For example, when employees are unsure of their environment, they look for signals to help them make sense of the situation. Signals that reveal the organization's commitment to diversity may cause employees to feel that rewards, assignments, and promotions now and in the future are more likely to be made in a nondiscriminatory way (Kaplan et al., 2011).

Transparent Communication

Successful communication between stakeholders, leaders, and employees is perhaps an implicit hallmark of successful organizations. And, in fact, about 10 percent of employees report their greatest desire from their organization is honest communication of information from management and from the organization in general (Wiley & Kowske, 2011). We define transparent communication as a free and honest exchange of information between employees and the organization. The following two items reflect this definition; employees indicated the extent to which they agreed or disagreed with each statement on a five-point Likert rating scale. The scale demonstrated strong internal consistency (ρ = .85).

- In my organization, there is open, honest two-way communication.
- Where I work, employees are kept well-informed about issues facing our organization.

Indeed, Ferrell and Herb (2012) reiterate that successful organizational functioning is contingent on "the communicative relationships among individuals within that organization because these relationships facilitate the dissemination of critical information and expertise that enables high performance" (p. 2). In 1974, Lawler et al. made similar remarks: "The communication pattern(s) used by the organization has an immediate impact upon the individual's life within that same organization" (p. 153). Thus, it is not surprising that when employees report more transparent communication practices, they are more likely to view their organizations as ethical. For example, if an organization's mission, vision, and values are not clearly communicated to employees, it is difficult for employees to discern whether the behavior of their managers and coworkers is consistent with these values.

One critical factor in the success of organizational communication efforts is the degree of trust that employees have in the communication and the source – especially when the source is their supervisor. When employees trust the communication, for example, they are likely to report higher job satisfaction (Muchinsky, 1977). Further, when leaders are transparent, they tend to be rated as more effective (Norman et al., 2010; Reave, 2005), yet recent work suggests this quality is in short supply, at least in the United States, where only 49 percent of employees agreed with the statement: "When my company's senior management says something, you can believe it's true" (Wiley & Kowske, 2011). In order for employees to gain trust in managers, researchers have argued and empirical evidence suggests that managers must appear skilled and competent, benevolent, and ethical (Mayer et al., 1995). More specifically, managers who are good at their jobs, who are concerned with the welfare of employees, and who uphold standards of integrity and fairness are more likely to be viewed as trustworthy by employees.

In Table 9.4, we see that employees in three emerging markets – China, India, and Indonesia – rank among the strongest in their ratings of transparent communication. Denmark is also included in this "strong" category. Alternatively, several countries are found to be relatively less likely to display transparent communication in their organizations: France, Italy, Spain, Argentina, Finland, and Japan.

Table 9.4. *Transparent Communication*

Weakest	Strongest
France	Denmark
Italy	Indonesia
Spain	China
Argentina	India
Finland	
Japan	

Improving Transparent Communication Practices
Given the increasingly virtual nature of organizations, employee working arrangements, and communication methods, it is important to consider how vital company information is disseminated. And further, organizations should consider the consistency of messages and behaviors that key information senders (leaders, managers, and senior members) convey to employees. Not only should information senders share the same vision and future for the organization but also these members should display behavior that is congruent with such information. Naturally, when this occurs, employees come to view these leaders as trustworthy.

Organizations may wish to conduct a communication audit to encourage employees to provide suggestions and feedback regarding the current communication systems and practices. For example, employees may report that messages fail to reach them or that the gatekeepers of information are unreliable or inaccessible (thanks to unruly internal servers or difficult, busy managers). They may fail to remember or comprehend a particular message because the announcement was not repeated or was lost in the chain of command. During economic downturns or company restructurings, employees may report that such news was delivered too late or that the severity or negative consequences of the information were underplayed. Perhaps especially in these times, employees appreciate direct and truthful communication. If the organization does conduct such a survey, the results and actions taken should be readily communicated to employees.

MANAGERIAL INTERPERSONAL JUSTICE

When managers act with interactional justice, they are likely to treat employees with fairness, respect, and dignity in their interpersonal relationships (Cropanzano et al., 2002). Importantly, while managers may be unable to influence directly other elements of employees' justice perceptions (e.g., fairness in pay or decision-making), they do operate with complete discretion in how they treat their employees (Scott et al., 2009). The downstream outcomes of treating employees with respect have been borne out in empirical research (Cropanzano & Mitchell 2005; Rockstuhl et al., 2012). That is, when supervisors treat their subordinates with fairness, they set the stage for high-quality leader–member exchange relationships to develop. This high-quality leader–member exchange has been shown to be a key mechanism for predicting job performance.

Interestingly, new research suggests that when managers (or organizations) expect employees to demonstrate ethical and fair behavior toward each other, but then fail to demonstrate such behavior themselves, the result can be even more harmful than poor manager behavior alone. That is, when employees viewed their managers as hypocritical (the manager expects interpersonal justice but then engages in undermining behavior), employees were even more likely to consider leaving an organization (Greenbaum et al., 2015).

The influence of interpersonal justice in the workplace is best understood within the tenets of both social exchange and equity theory. Social exchange theorists explain that in a relationship, each party's behavior toward the other engenders certain rules, obligations, and norms (Emerson, 1976) that evolve over time. Underlying employee interactions is the norm of reciprocity – positive behavior tends to be reciprocated with positive behavior, and negative behavior is likely to beget more negative behavior (Gouldner, 1960).

Managers acting with respect and dignity are likely to open doors for future positive exchanges, developing higher-quality relationships and fueling higher employee performance.

The following three items reflect managerial interpersonal justice; employees indicated the extent to which they agreed or disagreed with each statement on a five-point Likert rating scale. The scale demonstrated strong internal consistency ($\alpha = .92$).

- My manager treats employees fairly.
- My manager treats me with respect and dignity.
- My manager is trustworthy.

Table 9.5 provides information on the relative strongest and weakest ratings of managerial interpersonal justice across countries. Employees in Brazil, India, the United States, and Denmark report much higher levels of managerial interpersonal justice than their counterparts in Japan, Italy, and France.

Improving Managerial Interpersonal Justice

As employees look to managers as potentially key representatives of the organization, and as leaders and role models, it is not hard to see why (un)ethical management strongly influences employees' views of the ethical integrity of their organization. Researchers have well documented the effects of ethical management and leadership in reducing unethical employee behavior, counterproductive behavior, and work-group conflict (e.g., Mayer et al., 2009, 2013).

Yet in seeking to improve the ethical behavior of managers, organizations must recognize a wide sphere of impact: peers, leaders, written and unwritten rules, laws, and codes all influence employee behavior (Treviño et al., 2014). For example, in order to exert influence, organizational rules concerning ethical behavior must be closely tied to the actual climate and culture of the organization, with consistent enforcement and consequences for violations. Moreover, the presence of codes without consistent enforcement

Table 9.5. *Managerial Interpersonal Justice*

Weakest	Strongest
Japan	Denmark
France	United States
Italy	Brazil
	India

or support may actually be counterproductive (Kish-Gephart et al., 2010). One strategy for improving managerial ethics is to promote conversations concerning ethical behavior. Simply encouraging employees to ask if particular behaviors are ethical can help deter unethical behavior (Gino et al., 2009). In addition, organizations can develop managers to be more just and ethical through training programs that feature knowledge and skills-based information on interpersonal justice and improving fairness perceptions (Kiersch & Byrne, 2015).

From a prevention focus, organizations can seek to hire and promote more morally attentive managers. Those who have a stronger moral attentiveness – a tendency to notice and perceive morality in one's life and experiences – are more likely to remember and make note of ethics violations (Reynolds, 2008). Another trait that organizations may wish to consider is moral identity, that is, how an individual views him/herself with regard to moral traits, as a protective factor against self-serving behavior when holding a powerful position (DeCelles, et al., 2012).

REGULATED WORK PROCESSES

Regulated Work Processes refers to the extent to which organizations exhibit highly regulated and clearly defined work processes in the accomplishment of day-to-day work operations. The following three items reflect this conceptualization; employees indicated the extent to which they agreed or disagreed with each statement on a five-point

Likert rating scale. The scale demonstrated strong internal consistency (α = .84).

- Policies and procedures are strictly enforced.
- Rules and procedures precisely specify how my work is to be done.
- Work processes are clearly defined and documented.

Those familiar with classic organizational theory will immediately see a connection between regulated work processes and key elements of that early theory. The theory, mainly attributable to the work of German political scientist and sociologist Max Weber, contains various propositions regarding the ideal form of organization. Two dimensions that Weber extolled as predictors of organizational efficiency include (1) division of labor, i.e., the division of tasks performed in an organization into specialized jobs and departmental functions; and (2) delegation of authority, which describes very clearly the responsibility for tasks and functions over which a given employee has responsibility. Classic organizational theory thus places a premium on control by the organization of individual behavior (Landy & Conte, 2016).

For a variety of reasons, including especially the lack of consideration given to employee participation in decision-making, motivation, and leadership style, classic organizational theory has been superseded by more modern and humanistic theories of organization. Even so, previous analyses of the WorkTrends database revealed that more regulated industries are more likely to report more favorable EPI scores (e.g., healthcare products, business services, banking, and electronics and computer engineering; Jondle et al., 2009). Regulated industries may be likely to have normative reporting and auditing standards, such as those established in the United States by the Occupational Safety and Health Agency; the purpose of such standards might help employees and stakeholders truly appreciate the importance of maintaining ethical standards. Thus, organizational cultures with tighter decision-making controls leave less chance for individual actors to violate standards or norms for ethical behavior.

Table 9.6. *Regulated Work Processes*

Weakest	Strongest
Japan	Indonesia
Finland	United Kingdom
Argentina	China
Italy	India

In Table 9.6, we note that Indonesia, the United Kingdom, China, and India represent the countries in which employees are most likely to report regulated work processes – of note, several emerging markets are included here. Alternatively, Japan, Finland, Argentina, and Italy represent countries in which employees had the weakest perceptions of regulated work processes.

Improving Regulated Work Processes

One way for employers to improve the regulation of work processes is to ensure that information regarding appropriate behavior and performance standards are made known to all employees. Employees must be provided with relevant training and material that enables them to do their jobs correctly. Thus, employees must feel a strong sense of *role clarity*. Role clarity has been defined as the sense of certainty or predictability employees have concerning their job and role tasks, as well as the completeness and accuracy of information that is provided by role senders and their environments (Beehr, 1976; Rizzo et al., 1970). Often, role clarity is reduced when a large number of new employees are hired, changes are made to organizational hierarchy or technology, or employees take on tasks in other units of the organization.

These are the types of circumstances that reinforce the importance of continuous investment in employee training. Training is defined as "the systematic acquisition of knowledge (i.e., what we need to know), skills (i.e., what we need to do), and attitudes (what we need to feel) that together lead to improved performance in a particular environment" (Salas et al., 2006, p. 473). There are many ways in which training in work processes can be delivered, but the key to effective training is transfer-appropriate processing. Transfer-appropriate processing refers to the degree to which what employees learn in the training environment mirrors what is required of them in novel situations on the job (Morris et al., 1977). Practice and feedback are critical to employees learning how to properly implement policies, procedures, and processes deemed by the organization as critical to successful job performance.

Experience from within organizations also shows us that the successful implementation of work process regulation is likely to co-occur with other workplace factors. For example, when employees report that clear performance standards are set for product and service quality and that the organization recognizes productive people and excellent customer service, they are also more likely to report that structured work processes are in place. This is not surprising. An organization that has established clear performance standards for product and service quality is often the same organization that has engineered the processes by which these desirable outcomes are achieved. Further, inherent in an organization's decision to establish clear performance standards for product and service quality is a belief that accelerated success in the marketplace is dependent on the customer's experience with their products and experience. For organizations that have made such design decisions, it naturally follows that they would establish individual employee performance standards that would subsequently allow them to reward customer service excellence.

SUMMARY AND IMPLICATIONS

This chapter reviewed the strength of ethical business cultures across 22 countries, noting that significant differences between countries do indeed exist. Leaders who are considering establishing or expanding operations into diverse locations around the world, including emerging markets, should consider country-specific, employee-perceived ethical norms that may serve to enhance or potentially undermine their success. This is important because, across the globe, the strength of the ethical cultures of organizations is related to key work attitudes, such as employee engagement and performance confidence, which in turn serve as predictors of sustained business success.

The research outlined in this chapter clearly identifies four key drivers of a strong ethical culture: diversity climate, transparent communication, managerial interpersonal justice, and regulated work processes. Organizations whose employees rate these drivers favorably will be organizations whose employees also give high scores to the ethical business culture of their organization. Conversely, organizations whose employees view these drivers unfavorably will be organizations whose employees also see their organization's ethical business culture as weak.

What are the implications? Leaders desiring to strengthen the ethical business cultures of their organizations should first assess, using strategic employee surveys, the current perceptions of their employees vis-à-vis these topics. Regardless of what the survey results reveal regarding their current absolute or normative standing, organizational improvements can be achieved by holding leaders at all levels of the organization responsible for the following:

- Recruiting and retaining a diverse workforce; making sure it is easy for people from diverse backgrounds to fit in and be accepted; and ensuring that all employees have equal opportunities for advancement.
- Keeping employees well-informed about the issues facing the organization – both the good and the bad – and, as a result, engendering high levels of employee trust; and creating mechanisms for open and honest two-way communication, especially as it relates to employees being able to express concerns regarding ethical issues without fear of consequence.

- Selecting, developing, and advancing organizational leaders who treat employees fairly, and with dignity and respect, and thus further enhancing employee trust, an organizational characteristic foundational to a strong ethical business environment.
- Ensuring employees understand the organization's central mission and that the work processes by which the central mission is achieved are codified; and ensuring also that employees are properly trained for their day-to-day work operations and that superior performance in support of the central mission is properly recognized.

ADDITIONAL READING

Ardichvili, A., Jondle, D., Kowske, B., Cornachione, E., Li, J., & Thakadipuram, T. (2012). Ethical cultures in large business organizations in Brazil, Russia, India, and China. *Journal of Business Ethics*, 105(4), 415–428.

Brown, M. E., & Mitchell, M. S. (2010). Ethical and unethical leadership: Exploring new avenues for future research. *Business Ethics Quarterly*, 20(4), 583–616.

Folger, R., & Cropanzano, R. (1998). *Organizational justice and human resource management*. Thousand Oaks, CA: Sage Publications.

Herdman, A. O., & McMillan-Capehart, A. (2010). Establishing a diversity program is not enough: Exploring the determinants of diversity climate. *Journal of Business and Psychology*, 25(1), 39–53.

REFERENCES

Alesina, A., Devleeschauwer, A., Easterly, W., Kurlat, S., & Wacziarg, R. (2003). Fractionalization. *Journal of Economic Growth*, 8(2), 155–194.

Ardichvili, A., Jondle, D., & Kowske, B. (2010). Dimensions of ethical business cultures: comparing data from 13 countries of Europe, Asia, and the Americas. *Human Resource Development International*, 13(3), 299–315.

Bailey, W., & Spicer, A. (2007). When does national identity matter? Convergence and divergence in international business ethics. *Academy of Management Journal*, 50(6), 1462–1480.

Beehr, T. (1976). Perceived situational moderators of the relationship between subjective role ambiguity and role strain. *Journal of Applied Psychology*, 61(7), 35–40.

Cohen, D. (1993). Creating and maintaining ethical work climates: Anomie in the workplace and implications for managing change. *Business Ethics Quarterly*, 3(4), 343–358.

Cropanzano, R., & Mitchell, M. S. (2005). Social exchange theory: An interdisciplinary review. *Journal of Management*, 31, 874–900. doi: 10.1177/0149206305279602

Cropanzano, R., Prehar, C. A., & Chen, P. Y. (2002). Using social exchange theory to distinguish procedural from interactional justice. *Group & Organization Management*, 27(3), 324–351.

DeCelles, K. A., DeRue, D. S., Margolis, J. D., & Ceranic, T. L. (2012). Does power corrupt or enable? When and why power facilitates self-interested behavior. *Journal of Applied Psychology*, 97(3), 681.

Emerson, R. M. (1976). Social exchange theory. *Annual Review of Sociology*, 2, 335–362.

Ferrel, J., & Herb, K. (2012). Improving communication in virtual teams. Society for Industrial Organizational Psychology, Inc.

Gelfand, M. J., Nishii, L. H., Raver, J., & Schneider, B. (2005). *Discrimination in organizations: An organizational level systems perspective*. In R. Dipboye & A. Colella (Eds.), *Discrimination at work: The psychological and organizational bases* (pp. 89–116). Mahwah, NJ: Erlbaum.

Gino, F., Ayal, S., & Ariely, D. (2009). Contagion and differentiation in unethical behavior: The effect of one bad apple on the barrel. *Psychological Science*, 20, 393–398.

Gonzalez, J. A., & DeNisi, A. S. (2009). Cross-level effects of demography and diversity climate on organizational attachment and firm effectiveness. *Journal of Organizational Behavior*, 30(1), 21–40.

Gouldner, A. W. (1960). The norm of reciprocity: A preliminary statement. *American Sociological Review*, 25, 161–178.

Greenbaum, R. L., Mawritz, M. B., & Piccolo, R. F. (2015). When leaders fail to "walk the talk": Supervisor undermining and perceptions of leader hypocrisy. *Journal of Management*, 41(3), 929–956.

Guillaume, Y. R., Dawson, J. F., Woods, S. A., Sacramento, C. A., & West, M. A. (2013). Getting diversity at work to work: What we know and what we still don't know. *Journal of Occupational and Organizational Psychology*, 86(2), 123–141.

Gupta, V., and Hanges, P. (2004). Regional and climate clustering of societal cultures. In R. House, P. Hanges, M. Javidan, P. W. Dorfman, & V. Gupta (Eds.), *Culture, leadership, and organizations: The GLOBE study of 62 societies* (pp. 178–210). Thousand Oaks, CA: Sage.

Harter, J. K., Schmidt, F. L., & Hayes, T. L. (2002). Business-unit-level relationship between employee satisfaction, employee engagement, and business outcomes: A meta-analysis. *Journal of Applied Psychology*, 87(2), 268.

Jackson, T. (2001). Cultural values and management ethics: A 10-nation study. *Human Relations*, 54(10), 1267–1302.

Jondle, D., Shoemake, R., & Kowske, B. (2009). Assessing an ethical culture. *EvolveHR*, 3(2), 56–61.

Kaplan, D. M., Wiley, J. W., & Maertz, C. P. (2011). The role of calculative attachment in the relationship between diversity climate and retention. *Human Resource Management*, 50(2), 271–287.

Kiersch, C. E., & Byrne, Z. S. (2015). Is being authentic being fair? Multilevel examination of authentic leadership, justice, and employee outcomes. *Journal of Leadership & Organizational Studies*, 22(3), 292–303.

King, E., & Gilrane, G. (2015). Social science strategies for managing diversity: Industrial and organization opportunities to enhance inclusion, SHRM-SIOP Science of HR White Paper Series.

Kish-Gephart, J. J., Harrison, D. A., & Treviño, L. K. (2010). Bad apples, bad cases, and bad barrels: Meta-analytic evidence about sources of unethical decisions at work. *Journal of Applied Psychology*, 95(1), 1.

Landy, F. J., & Conte, J. M. (2016). *Work in the 21st century, binder ready version: An introduction to industrial and organizational psychology*. Hoboken, NJ: John Wiley & Sons.

Lawler, E. E., Hall, D. T., & Oldham, G. R. (1974). Organizational climate: Relationship to organizational structure, process and performance. *Organizational Behavior and Human Performance*, 11(1), 139–155.

Macey, W. H., & Schneider, B. (2008). The meaning of employee engagement. *Industrial and Organizational Psychology*, 1(1), 3–30.

Mayer D. M., Kuenzi, M,. Greenbaum, R., Bardes, M., & Salvador, R. (2009). How low does ethical leadership flow? Test of a trickle-down model. *Organizational Behavior and Human Decision Processes*, 108, 1–13.

Mayer D. M., Nurmohamed, S., Treviño, L. K., Shapiro, D. L., & Schminke, M. (2013). Encouraging employees to report unethical conduct internally: It takes a village. *Organizational Behavior and Human Decision Processes*, 121, 89–103.

Mayer, R. C., Davis, J. H., & Schoorman, F. D. (1995). An integrative model of organizational trust. *Academy of Management Review*, 20(3), 709–734.

McKay, P. F., Avery, D. R., & Morris, M. A. (2008). Mean racial-ethnic differences in employee sales performance: The moderating role of diversity climate. *Personnel Psychology*, 61(2), 349–374.

McKay, P. F., Avery, D. R., Tonidandel, S., Morris, M. A., Hernandez, M., & Hebl, M. R. (2007). Racial differences in employee retention: Are diversity climate perceptions the key? *Personnel Psychology*, 60(1), 35–62.

Morris, C. D., Bransford, J. D., & Franks, J. J. (1977). Levels of processing versus transfer appropriate processing. *Journal of Verbal Learning and Verbal Behavior*, 16(5), 519–533.

Muchinsky, P. M. (1977). Organizational communication: Relationships to organizational climate and job satisfaction. *Academy of Management Journal*, 20(4), 592–607.

Norman, S. M., Avolio, B. J., & Luthans, F. (2010). The impact of positivity and transparency on trust in leaders and their perceived effectiveness. *Leadership Quarterly*, 21(3), 350–364.

Reave, L. (2005). Spiritual values and practices related to leadership effectiveness. *Leadership Quarterly*, 16(5), 655–687.

Reynolds, S. J. (2008). Moral attentiveness: Who pays attention to the moral aspects of life? *Journal of Applied Psychology*, 93(5), 1027.

Rizzo, J., House, R., & Lirtzman, S. (1970). Role conflict and ambiguity in complex organizations. *Administrative Science Quarterly*, 15, 150–163.

Rockstuhl, T., Dulebohn, J. H., Ang, S., & Shore, L. M. (2012). Leader–member exchange (LMX) and culture: A meta-analysis of correlates of LMX across 23 countries. *Journal of Applied Psychology*, 97, 1097–1130. doi.org/10.1037/a0029978

Salas, E., Wilson, K. A., Priest, H. A., & Guthrie, J. W. (2006). Design, delivery, and evaluation of training systems. In Salvendy, D. (Ed.), *Handbook of human factors and ergonomics* (3rd ed., pp. 472–512). Hoboken, NJ: John Wiley & Sons, Inc.

Schein, E. H. (1990). Organization culture. *American Psychologist*, 45(2), 109–119.

Schein, E. H. (2006). So how can you assess your corporate culture? In J. Gallos (Ed.), *Organization Development: A Jossey-Bass Reader* (pp. 614–633). San Francisco, CA: Jossey-Bass.

Scott, B. A., Colquitt, J. A., & Paddock, E. L. (2009). An factor-focused model of justice rule adherence and violation: The role of managerial motives and discretion. *Journal of Applied Psychology*, 94, 756–769. doi: 10.1037/a0015712

Spence, A. M. (1974). *Market signaling: Informational transfer in hiring and related screening processes.* Cambridge, MA: Harvard University Press.

Treviño, L. K., den Nieuwenboer, N. A., & Kish-Gephart, J. J. (2014). (Un)ethical behavior in organizations. *Annual Review of Psychology*, 65, 635–660.

van Knippenberg, D. V., De Dreu, C. K. W., & Homan, A. C. (2004). Work group diversity and group performance: An integrative model and research agenda. *Journal of Applied Psychology*, 89, 1008–1022. doi: 10.1037/0021-9010.89.6.1008

Wiley, J. (2010). *Strategic employee surveys: Evidence-based guidelines for driving organizational success.* San Francisco, CA: Jossey-Bass.

Wiley, J. (2014). Using employee opinions about organizational performance to enhance employee engagement surveys: Model building and validation. *People and Strategy, 36*(4), 38.

Wiley, J., & Kowske, B. (2011). *Respect: Delivering results by giving employees what they really want.* San Francisco, CA: Jossey-Bass.

10 Good Ethics Is Good Business: The Case of Cargill

Emery Koenig

The following is the keynote address presented at the Building Ethical Business Cultures in Emerging Markets: Risks and Opportunities conference, September 25, 2015. The conference was convened by the Center for Ethical Business Cultures at the University of St. Thomas, Minneapolis, Minnesota, USA.

ABSTRACT

This chapter is based on the keynote address, presented by the author at *Building Ethical Business Cultures in Emerging Markets: Risks and Opportunities* conference. The conference was convened by the Center for Ethical Business Cultures at the University of St. Thomas, Minneapolis, Minnesota, USA, on September 25, 2015. The author at the time of the presentation was the Chief Risk Officer and Vice Chairman of Cargill, Incorporated. He is describing Cargill's business ethics and corporate social responsibility programs, and is sharing his experience in dealing with complex issues of doing business in various countries and cultures around the world.

Let me start with a real-life conundrum. In one of the countries where we operate, tax laws require us to pay value-added tax and then get refunded by the government. At times, the amount the government owes us on refunds can reach $80 to $100 million. This has a significant impact on our ability to run our business there!

As it turns out, there was one official who was making the decisions on how quickly we would get repaid. So when any of our leadership was visiting the country, each of us would pay this official a visit to ask, "Do you think we could get our money soon?"

One time, a few of our leaders paid this official a visit. And after asking when we could get our refund he said, "You know, it's funny. My son's soccer team needs a new fence and scoreboard for their field."

Okay, put yourself in our shoes. What would you do? $100 million for a fence and a scoreboard. And this is a positive thing for the community, right? Helping a kids' soccer team! We'll come back to this example later.

Cargill, Inc., is a privately held global corporation based in Minnetonka, Minnesota. It was founded in 1865. With more than $120 billion in annual revenue, it is the largest privately held corporation in the United States. Cargill has more than 150,000 employees in 67 countries (and only one-third of these employees are based on the US) and operates 70 different businesses in food, agriculture, financial and industrial products and services sectors. Today, about 75 percent of Cargill's capital investment is outside the US. After 150 years, the company is still owned by the family that founded it. The owners want a company that makes them proud to have their name on the door. Consequently, a commitment to doing business ethically is at the very core of all we do.

After 150 years our company still strives to operate under the founding premise that "our word is our bond." Consequently, a commitment to doing business ethically is at the very core of all we do.

There's a phrase that's come down through company lore: "Our word is our bond." In 1909, one of our leaders, John MacMillan Sr., was getting complaints about our barley trader in Duluth, that he wasn't doing a thorough enough job inspecting the barley he was buying, and it was causing us to misrepresent the quality of the product we were selling to customers. MacMillan wrote a sternly worded letter to this trader, reminding him, "We want to do exactly as we agree. There is one thing that we have always been proud of – our word is as good as our bond."

It sounds old-fashioned, because it is. But what does "our word is our bond" mean today in a complex, globally integrated market-place? What does it mean to do business ethically and how does it impact your ability to operate?

That's what I want to focus: how we keep that "our-word-is-our-bond" promise across 150 years, across 67 countries and across more than 150,000 employees. Two-thirds of our employees are located outside the US. Moreover, more than half our employees (and a significant portion of our assets) are in developing countries and emerging markets.

Given this global distribution, how does doing business ethically actually help us manage risk?

We have a lot to keep our eye on! When I was Cargill's chief risk officer, I would often tell people, "I sleep like a baby – I'm up every two hours!" We pay special attention to those risks that are high-impact with rapid speed of onset, where you can come into the office one morning and the whole world has changed.

But whether they're overnight game-changers or not, in nearly all of these areas, including with our customers, counterparties, employees or the communities where we work, our ability to operate is only as good as our ability to keep our word. In other words, good ethics is simply good business.

As the chief risk officer, I'm involved every day in evaluating the commodity and crisis risk exposures in our business, working with colleagues across the company to manage and mitigate risks, and to foster a culture where that orientation is instinctive. In this context, I believe an ethical culture is a powerful asset.

The best advice I ever got in my career was when somebody told me, "Cargill will never do anything to embarrass you, so don't you ever do anything to embarrass Cargill!" But as the leadership of the company, how do we make sure that the actions of one team or individual in Cargill won't embarrass the other 150,000 people we have working for us? After all, we share one balance sheet across the entire company, and one reputation as well. We each have the chance to enhance that reputation through our behavior, and we are each in a position to destroy it, too.

So with that in mind, how do we build an ethical culture?

It starts by putting in place what I call *essential infrastructure.* For instance, these are the seven Guiding Principles that make up our code of conduct:

- We obey the law.
- We conduct our business with integrity.
- We keep accurate and honest records.
- We honor our business obligations.
- We treat people with dignity and respect.
- We protect Cargill's information, assets and interests.
- We are committed to being a responsible global citizen.

Just seven sentences to guide the behavior of 153,000 people. But we want to be very clear about what we stand for, and what we won't stand for.

A lot of organizations probably have principles or rules like this. What makes them valuable, though, is not simply having them written down somewhere, but making them a vital part of your culture. Wrestling with them every day. As you'll see, we have plenty of chances to do this!

For example, think back to our opening conundrum about the tax refunds and the soccer field. Our Guiding Principles might seem simplistic in the abstract, but which ones come into play here?

We're talking today about doing business ethically in emerging markets, but in Cargill we don't think of these as values that we "bring" from the developed to the developing world. Rather, these are universal absolutes that do not vary, regardless of country, business, or circumstance, North and south, east and west – they're constant.

There also needs to be teeth behind these principles. Consequences for violations are real, material, and can include termination. We let go of a significant number of employees every year for violating these principles, and discipline even more.

HOW ELSE DO WE BUILD AN ETHICAL CULTURE?

We have a Business Ethics & Compliance Committee, which regularly examines real-life episodes drawn from the world of Cargill and clarifies how the team involved should have acted, especially in situations where things are not cut and dried. The committee publishes case studies based on these reviews that are available to all employees and promoted on our company intranet, so teams around the world can learn from both the tough choices and the mistakes of others.

We have required training globally for our Guiding Principles and code of conduct. This is translated into more than 20 languages. We also have a global ethics hotline, an anonymous way that employees can report situations where they either see a clear violation or just aren't sure about something.

We also call on employees to actively verify compliance. Every year, all of our salaried workers – roughly 35,000 – have to certify that they understand our principles and aren't aware of any situations that violate them. The rest of our employees go through this process every three years.

As you can imagine, operating in so many different countries, across so many different sectors, there can be gray areas. In my experience, it isn't the first mistake that gets employees in trouble. It's what they do after that mistake that proves far more damaging to their careers. Do they cover it up? Make other employees complicit to try and smooth it over? Or maybe they continue the behavior because they didn't get caught the first time.

To avoid these slippery slopes, we foster a culture of thinking out loud. We train our employees to communicate openly and ask questions if they're not sure about something. Generally, if they're uncomfortable talking about something, that's an even greater indication that there's a problem, and they need to get it out in the open.

The goal is always to encourage discussion. Our motto could be: "If you see something, say something." We had a case where a leader of a team that originates and exports commodities was falsifying export sales contracts to help an important supplier qualify for government subsidies. This person involved his entire staff – the controller, the commercial manager, the logistics manager – in this fraud. Unfortunately, the team members followed his instructions, knowing this was against the rules. They even misled their local lawyer about the true nature of the contracts.

Eventually, it was all uncovered. As I like to say, "You find out who's swimming naked when the tide goes out!" So we terminated the leader. But we also disciplined the team members who went along with him. Keeping quiet doesn't mean you're not culpable.

Another case where conversation could have prevented things from going downhill: We had a business that learned a major competitor was building a new plant nearby. They wanted to learn as much as they could about the plant's capacity, what products it would make, when it would be completed, etc. The business leadership challenged the sales and operations teams to learn as much as they could. So they started with publicly available data. Permits, zoning records, things like that. They talked with customers and suppliers about what they saw coming in the market. They drove by the construction zone to try and get a look at it.

Well, here's where things started to get off track. And if they'd stopped and had a conversation with their leaders about what they were really doing, it might have put a halt to it. But next they chartered a small plane to do a flyover of the plant under construction and take photos. Then they noticed that the perimeter of the construction zone, which had a "No Trespassing" sign, had a gap in the gate. So they drove through onto the competitor's property to take a look. When they turned around to leave, they'd been blocked in by someone who'd already called the police. They were arrested and, needless to say, we got some very irate phone calls from our competitor!

This is exactly why we encourage continuous conversation. Looking at public records, even driving by the perimeter of the construction on a public road were great ideas. When they got to the point where they were hiring a plane, they probably should have stopped and talked it over!

These episodes reinforce that the training we give our leaders is critical. Mentoring is a key way we help new leaders learn how to manage teams that often span geographies and cultural norms. All of us as senior leaders in Cargill regularly coach new managers to help them with this, because it's not always easy.

When I first went to work in Switzerland in 1992, my wife and I went to a Swiss enculturation class to learn more about what it takes to lead a team cross-culturally. What I learned was straightforward: keep things simple, make expectations clear, build trust and emphasize ethics, all while focusing on respect and integrity for the individual and keeping in mind the patriotism that all people have for their home country.

If the trust isn't there, it taxes the organization. This carries significant costs with it. For instance, in some cultures, it's impolite to bring bad news. I had an instance where a team in Latin America just could not give me the true picture of a bad situation. It was getting worse and worse, but the numbers weren't telling the story because of some wonky macroeconomic conditions in the domestic market. It took a major disruption in the currency of this country for the real economic condition of the business to emerge.

These aren't just issues in developing countries, by the way. Americans, for instance, are notoriously bad at handling candid feedback. Even when they ask for it! So you need to equip leaders to handle situations cross-culturally while still staying anchored to our core values.

Because complex situations will arise. Once you're already in the thick of a situation, you can't try to lay a foundation at that point. As our executive chairman Greg Page puts it, "You cannot talk your way out of a situation you've behaved your way into!"

Let's take a look at a few more real-life Cargill examples and what lessons we learned from those situations. These are situations where the rubber really meets the road.

Iraq: In the 1990s, Iraq and the UN started a food-for-oil exchange program many of you may have heard of. Because of the corruption that infiltrated this program, Cargill simply said we wouldn't participate in it.

When the program ended some years later, the Iraqi Grain Board was instructed to come to us to buy wheat, because we were perceived as being ethical as a result of refusing to participate earlier. A great opportunity for us that underscored the value of ethics, but the story didn't end there.

A while later, we were accused of corruption when some of the Baghdad flour mills where we were delivering wheat were reloading it out the back of the facilities at night and claiming the shipments had never arrived from us. This demonstrates that you can face extra scrutiny when you come in as an outsider, especially in an environment like Iraq where there is zero trust in anything or anyone. At times, it's just easier to blame the outsider than local players.

Ivory Coast: We entered this market 16 years ago, in part because of our desire to be an end-to-end player in the cocoa and chocolate supply chain. More than 60 percent of the world's cocoa is grown in just two countries: Ivory Coast and Ghana. So we need to be there if we want to be in cocoa.

Since we entered that market, there have been two civil wars. It's been a difficult, sometimes violent place to do business. Things can move very slowly for stretches of time. As one of our African colleagues puts it, "If you don't have patience, you will learn to have it. If you do have patience, you will lose it!"

But over time, people have realized that our word truly is our bond. This is priceless in Africa. It creates better relations with external stakeholders, who see us as a dependable, consistent partner who's there for the long haul. Suppliers love us because it lowers their costs, and the government respects us for doing what we say we will, and listens to our opinion. It also helps us attract and retain top local talent. When we were forced to close our operations in the country because of the war, we continued to pay our employees and support them in other ways. As a result, almost immediately after hostilities ceased, our operations were up and running again very quickly, unlike some of our competitors.

Another example of the business value of good ethics: Cocoa is a cash business, but we don't like to use cash for security reasons. However, paying by check in Ivory Coast is very hard, because it often takes more than a week for the check to clear through a bank and for a supplier to get their money. Because we're perceived as being ethical, honoring our obligations (i.e., we won't default), we are the only company in Ivory Coast that can issue a check for cocoa, and anyone with a check from us can get cash immediately over the counter. This is a huge competitive advantage!

Truck Weights: This one is very much a gray area at times. In many countries where we operate, there are laws on the books that dictate how much trucks can weigh when they're transporting goods like agricultural commodities. But in some of these countries, regular practice is to overload trucks beyond the legal weight of the truck.

To further complicate the issue, we aren't always the ones bearing the legal or commercial responsibility for loading trucks coming in and out of our plants, as customers will send their own vehicles or ones from a third party and have us load them in fulfillment of procurement contracts. In other words, we aren't the responsible party according to the law. So although we wouldn't ever fill our own trucks over weight in violation of a local law, how do we handle a situation where our actions could be construed as helping another party to break the law?

This is a $75 million global issue for us, with implications for competitiveness (paying for two trucks instead of one), safety (accidents) and environmental impacts (more fuel to run more trucks), as well as ethics. Many times, although a local law may state one thing, how it is put into practice is very different. We need to hold true to our Guiding Principles, yet as the saying goes, "It doesn't help to be the best-looking horse going into a glue factory!"

We had an ongoing leadership debate about this issue a few years ago. The obvious guidance we gave our businesses was that they were never allowed to break the law themselves. As for the grayer area where we were not the legally responsible party, we asked our local teams to bring their influence to bear in getting the existing laws enforced and followed evenly across the board. Doing so was the harder choice, and it threatened some of our commercial relationships. But we felt it was important, even when we didn't bear the legal responsibility for compliance, to help move the industry in a positive direction. In fact, we were able to get meaningful changes made in two very large countries.

South Korea: Recently we settled a case with the Korea Fair Trade Commission for allegations that we and 10 other companies engaged in price collusion on animal feed from 2006 to 2010. The case centered on industry meetings that our employees attended where prices were discussed.

This was a disappointing case for us. Although we believe we never made agreements on pricing, we know it was inappropriate for our employees to stay at those meetings once pricing came up. They should have gotten up and left, and that's what we instruct people to do.

But it also illustrates the risk when you transplant other companies into your own culture via acquisition, rather than what we refer to as "growing your own timber" – growing businesses and individual careers internally. The Korea case was an example of a business we had largely absorbed through an acquisition. To mitigate this risk, we often embed experienced senior Cargill managers in newly acquired companies at the highest level to help establish the right expectations and behaviors.

In this case, we did terminate 41 out of about 7,000 employees globally who came with the acquisition, some at a very senior level.

This is in addition to self-selected departures as a result of us making our expectations about ethical conduct clear. In one instance, we did training for new employees on our Guiding Principles after the deal was finalized, and the next day, the entire night shift for one plant in Central Europe didn't show up for work! We made our expectations clear, and they simply didn't want to work in that environment. But this does help us to avoid risk, and it's not just reputational. We had a significant theft problem at that plant and it got much better after the night crew resigned!

India: Another issue we often face is in obtaining government permits in many countries where we operate. Our businesses are routinely told by officials that the permitting process for new facilities could be sped up considerably if we would just make "facilitation payments."

For example, in India, a colleague and I led a project to build a palm oil refinery on the east coast in the state of Orissa, which is the second poorest state after Calcutta. Building the plant required 53 permits. Each one of those came with a request for a bribe in order to get the permit. It took us a lot of extra time and a lot of extra relationship building, but we didn't pay one dollar to anyone and we eventually got all the permits we needed. It may require more effort, but it can be done.

Incidentally, when I went to visit the plant, we were celebrating 1 million man-hours without a lost time accident. Can you imagine? One million hours with no one getting hurt. This is in a region where the value of human life can be tragically low. There was a facility being built next to ours in another industry, where 117 people were killed during construction and nobody blinked an eye. But here we were, sending our employees home every night in the same condition that they arrived in the morning. Eventually, the public port nearby started to adopt our safety policies, which was great to see. So in many cases, doing the right thing is simply a choice.

We don't just focus on the internal side when it comes to ethics, as important as that is. Our ethical behavior has to carry through to our activities outside our front door.

We have a broad commitment to corporate responsibility that includes four main focus areas. One, we've already talked about at length, and that's conducting our business with integrity. Let me talk a little bit more about the others.

Everywhere we operate, we try to enrich the communities where we live and work. This includes school-building programs in Vietnam and Ivory Coast, programs to support women entrepreneurs in India, Zambia and Honduras, contributing expertise to food banks in Canada and the US.

We also believe that a key part of working to feed the world is empowering farmers to grow their best crops: to feed their families, their neighbors and world markets. We have farmer training programs in more than 20 countries to help producers raise their productivity, conserve resources and increase their livelihoods.

We have global partnerships with NGOs like CARE, the Nature Conservancy, World Wildlife Fund, TechnoServe and World Food Programme to strengthen food security, education and environmental stewardship.

Increasingly, our commitment also focuses on operating sustainable supply chains. This can be difficult, given the length and complexity of those supply chains in many cases. But to paraphrase Greg Page, in a world where people want to know where their food comes from and how it was produced, it's the responsibility of the middleman to account for all the links in the chain before us and all the links after us.

In the past year, we've undertaken the development of a new company-wide strategy on sustainability, to take action in the areas where we think we can have the greatest impact. The four areas we identified are land use (including deforestation), water use, climate change and farmer livelihoods.

All of these efforts unite with our business purpose of nourishing people, lifting them out of poverty as we work to raise standards of living around the globe. This means that our work "on the clock" and our work "off the clock" are in lock step.

The simple truth is: You can't bifurcate and be one person with a certain set of core values in life and then come into work and adopt a totally different set of values. This is why we put the "who" before the "what" in terms of hiring. Hiring based on a person's inclination to act ethically is more important to us than just domain expertise. We can train you to do a job, we can provide an ethical environment for you to work in, but we can't make you an ethical person!

As a result of all this internal and external work, what benefits do we realize? These can be summarized in five bullet points:

- Cost avoidance
- Moving at the speed of trust
- Customer preference
- Employee engagement
- Freedom to operate

Let's start with the simple stuff and build up to the really crucial ones. First, there's *cost avoidance*. That includes litigation, fines and other penalties for noncompliance, either from governments or from counterparties.

Second, we *move faster*, at what I like to call "the speed of trust," because we know that as a rule, we can take our colleagues at their word and trust that they're doing the right thing. As I've said, a lack of trust creates drag, friction, and this taxes the organization.

Third, we win and keep the *support of our customers*. We are a key supplier to major consumer brands. They entrust us every day with their brand equity and reputations when they choose to source from us. They know they won't end up in the newspaper for something unethical or illegal that we've done.

Fourth, we *engage our employees* and *attract strong recruits*. Employees want to know they aren't going to be embarrassed by the company they work for. And they want to work for organizations with a "noble purpose" whose values are aligned with their own. This is especially true of the younger generation entering the workforce. Simply getting a paycheck doesn't cut it anymore.

Fifth, it helps us maintain our *license to operate*. We are a guest in the 67 countries and thousands of communities where our plants and offices are located. Being appreciated as a responsible organization that operates with integrity underpins our ability to do business in each of these places. It also helps us pursue new opportunities, being welcomed into new markets and expanding in existing ones.

All of these add up to a strong brand and reputation as a company you want to work with, one that will help you thrive, whether you're a customer, an employee or a community. It also adds up to a company all of us, including our employees, our leadership team and our family owners, can be proud of.

So as you can see, it isn't easy to maintain a commitment to ethical business. I joked earlier that I'm up every two hours, but really, I sleep pretty good at night. If you're acting unethically, you can forget sleep! A colleague once quoted Confucius to me: "He who is pure of heart, need not fear a knock on his door at midnight."

No, in the end, we believe it's simply better to do business this way in the long run. The world is increasingly complex, with murky areas in virtually every geography, and yet we also know that demands for corporate accountability and transparency are rising.

Nothing stays hidden in today's environment, and as we like to say, "In a world where nothing stays hidden, you better have nothing to hide!"

So to go back to our original conundrum with the soccer facilities, what do you think we did?

I'll tell you what we were prepared to do, after much debate. We weren't prepared to buy one official his fence and scoreboards. What we were willing to do was to build new fences and scoreboards for every soccer field in the city!

II Ethics and Culture: Challenges for Businesses Operating in the Global Economy

Douglas Jondle and Alexandre Ardichvili

INTERVIEWS CONTRIBUTED BY DEON ROSSOUW,
MARTHA SAÑUDO, NOOR RAHMANI, AND THOMAS
THAKADIPURAM

On April 24, 2013, Rana Plaza, an eight-story commercial building on the outskirts of Dhaka, capital of Bangladesh, came tumbling down, taking with it 1,135 lives and injuring some 2,500 more. The collapse of Rana Plaza was labeled "the worst disaster in garment industry history" (Greenhouse & Harris, 2014).

Numerous serious issues preceded the collapse of the building. First, the building was built on unstable soil, and this problem was only compounded by poor-quality construction practices and materials. Second, proper building permits for the construction of the building had never been obtained. Third, three floors of additional factory space were added to the building in blatant disregard of the original building permits. Fourth, visible cracks in the concrete walls of the building were ignored by owners and managers, who forced workers on the day of collapse to work despite fears of imminent disaster.

Implicated in the tragedy were 41 persons, including the owner of Rana Plaza, his parents, and owners of factories located in the building, as well as more than a dozen officials from various government entities. The charges included murder, which carried a death sentence if convicted (Associated Press in Dhaka, 2015).

Customers in developed countries have grown accustomed to purchasing fashionable clothing that is both cheap and of high quality. To meet the demand, Western companies have increasingly been moving the manufacturing of garments to emerging market countries like Bangladesh, where labor is cheap but the quality of work is traditionally high.

> They [Western companies] liked doing business in Bangladesh because of the high quality of goods at low prices. Their reputations, however, were at severe risk by staying in Bangladesh as more factories would certainly have problems and the safety issues were extensive. But pulling out would be met with more criticism for abandoning the country and the only means for many women (who make up 80 percent of the garment workers) to support their families and learn new skills. The cost of fixing the safety issues might be astronomical and some factory owners could be resistant to change. The Bangladeshi government did not possess the capacity, will or means to fix the issues, and the U.S. government was imposing trade sanctions. Finally, international unions were eyeing this as an opportunity to organize workers to make demand on wages and other labor issues around the world and had backing on Capitol Hill.
>
> The situation was, no doubt complex (Duty, 2015).

So what, if anything, resulted from this disastrous accident that fostered change in the mind-set of those using the international marketplace to source goods, those creating the goods, and those consuming the goods? Solutions are never easy or simple – or are they? If you want to know what one group of businesses did to address the serious issues highlighted by this tragedy to help remedy the problem, see the outcome at the end of the chapter.

A goal of this book was to bring to light the ethical challenges facing companies doing business in emerging market countries. In many academic works, the voices of practitioners are discounted or all too often silent. However, it is their experiences, trials, and tribulations that write the epitaphs to ethical challenges and breakdowns encountered in the global marketplace. That is why we have included a chapter specifically devoted to the practitioner, and the stories they tell of dealing with ethical challenges in emerging markets and beyond.

We also wanted to understand the cultural challenges of conducting business ethically in the global economy regardless of the country of origin of the company. Do companies based in emerging market countries have the same issues as companies from developed Western countries? Are ethical challenges universal? Are ethical business practices transferable? As discussed in the Introduction, we were interested in answering the following questions: Will norms that shape current acceptable business behavior be challenged by the growing influence of stakeholders within emerging market countries? What competing values and behaviors will business practitioners/ executives have to reckon with as they conduct business globally? How can we design compliance and ethics programs that reflect the influence of competing cultural and societal norms?

To address these and other important questions, the editors of this book designed a unique knowledge-sharing event that brought together the academic authors of the country-specific chapters and around 50 executives from large Minnesota-based business organizations and law firms (Best Buy, Cargill, Target, Medtronic, St. Jude, Toro, General Mills, Carlson, Wells Fargo, Oppenheimer Wolff & Donnelly, Robins Kaplan, Fredrikson & Byron, and others). The participants met on September 25, 2015, at the invitation of the Center for Ethical Business Cultures (Minneapolis, MN) for a two-day conference called "Building Ethical Cultures in Emerging Markets: Risks & Opportunities." No papers were given. All sessions were interactive, with active participation by attendees. Thus, this event provided the academics and practitioners with a forum to exchange ideas and reflect on the ethical and cultural challenges business practitioners are facing when operating in emerging markets.

After the conference, one of the editors of this volume conducted follow-up conversations with two US executives from the participating companies (one a large multinational company [US1] and the second a major US retailer [US2]) and also obtained from them supplementary materials (texts of relevance to these conversations). In the same period of time, the editors and several of the chapter authors interviewed executives from emerging market companies that operate internationally. The interviewees included an Australian expatriate executive working for a foreign-owned company based in Indonesia (ID) and operating throughout South-East Asia; an executive of a large South African company (SA) operating in 17 countries in Africa; an executive from a large multinational consumer products company headquartered in Mexico (MX); and an executive from an Indian subsidiary of a US multinational corporation (IN) responsible not only for the Indian market but also for operations in several other Asian countries.

All data were gathered with the understanding that names of individuals and the identity of the companies that they work for would not be divulged. We asked our interviewees for their opinion about ethical business challenges, risks, and opportunities facing their companies, industries, and countries. When talking about ethical business practices and challenges, we also included issues related to corporate responsibility and sustainability. Reflecting on opportunities and barriers, we asked the participants to consider the regulatory environment, as well as societal and cultural issues, and business norms.

Interviews were conducted in person or by Skype, ranged from 30 to 70 minutes, and were recorded. The interviews were based on the following open-ended questions:

1. What are top challenges in the area of business ethics, corporate social responsibility (CSR), and sustainability, faced by businesses in your country?
2. What are the business ethics, CSR, and sustainability challenges faced by your company?
3. What are examples, stories, illustrating your responses to the above questions?
4. What are the main business ethics-related issues that your company has to deal with when operating in other countries?

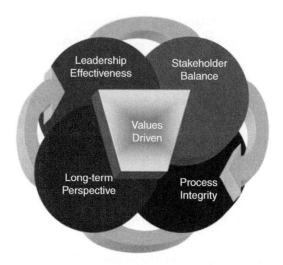

FIGURE 11.1. The CEBC Model of Ethical Business Cultures © 2016
Center for Ethical Business Cultures.

If the respondents did not provide sufficiently detailed responses
to these questions, the interviewers asked further, probing questions.
An example of such a follow-up request is: Discuss governmental
regulations, business norms, or cultural factors that have the most
significant impact on business ethics, CSR, and sustainability.

The two authors of this chapter have independently analyzed
transcripts of the conference presentations and transcripts of individual interviews and related documentation. We have used the Center
for Ethical Business Cultures (CEBC) Model of Ethical Business
Cultures (MEBC) (Figure 11.1) as a conceptual tool for analyzing and
presenting themes that emerged from the interview data.

The CEBC Model of Ethical Business Cultures

CEBC has been conducting research and consulting on issues of ethical business culture and behaviors for more than 35 years. Business
leaders from the Minneapolis/St. Paul business community created
CEBC in 1979. The center was created with the mission to assist
"business leaders in creating ethical and profitable business cultures

at the enterprise, community, and global levels" (Center for Ethical Business Cultures, 2017).

The effort to first develop a model of ethical business cultures was the brainchild of James (Jim) A. Mitchell, former CEO of IDS Life Insurance and retired executive vice president of marketing and products for the American Express Company. During his tenure as CEO of IDS Life, IDS became the fastest-growing and most profitable large life insurance company in the United States. As an executive business fellow at CEBC, Jim authored the center's monograph, *The Ethical Advantage: Why Ethical Leadership is Good Business*. In the monograph he outlines a three-element model of ethical business culture based on his personal beliefs and experiences as an executive. The three elements of his model are (1) effective leadership, (2) stakeholder balance, and (3) process integrity. While it was an effective tool for conversations with the current business members of the center, and for consulting and training purposes with business organizations, the model was not based on systematic research, and the center felt a growing need to conduct well-designed research studies aimed at validating the model, or developing a new, research-based model instead. Thus, in order to create an empirically validated model, the decision was made to conduct, first, a qualitative study to theorize a model of ethical business cultures and, second, a series of quantitative studies involving the development of a survey instrument to be used with various populations of business students and managers to test and validate the hypothesized model.

While Jim's model is based on his personal business experiences and beliefs, the genesis and subsequent evolution of the Model of Ethical Business Cultures (MEBC) is a reflection of a large number of business leaders' experiences, representing diverse industries with contributions from the academy. A qualitative analysis of interviews with close to 70 business executives and prominent business ethics academics resulted in a theoretical model of five characteristics (Ardichvili et al., 2009). Validation through a series of quantitative studies followed, resulting in affirmation of the MEBC's five characteristics: (1) Values Driven, (2) Leadership Effectiveness, (3) Stakeholder Balance, (4) Process Integrity, and (5) Long-term Perspective (Jondle et al., 2014). Figure 11.1 shows the five elements of the model. As can be seen from the figure, the Values-Driven element is at the center of the model, indicating that this is the linchpin of the whole system.

Driven by this ideal of respect for all stakeholders, the CEBC, formerly the Minnesota Center for Corporate Responsibility, created the Minnesota Principles (a codex of ethical behavior for global business) (Ryan, 2005). Out of the Minnesota Principles grew the Caux Round Table Principles for Business, developed as a "transcultural set of ethical norms [for business]" (Goodpaster, 2007, p. 71). Therefore, "it is no accident that the [MEBC represents] a platform ... which corporate conscience is indelibly part of. By focusing on the five characteristics of an ethical business culture [in the CEBC Model], organizations have specific directions to take in building and sustaining their organizational culture based on ethical principles" (Jondle et al., 2014, p. 37).

Values-Driven

The linchpin or keystone of the model is the Values-Driven element. It represents an organization's quintessence – its ability to survive and thrive. "Values provide the structural integrity that delimits [ethical business] culture ... which in turn imparts knowledge, experience, and expectation that influences leadership's impact on the business operationally and socially" (Jondle et al., 2014, p. 38). Usually linked to an expression of an organization's mission and vision, organizational values must become a strategic focus of that organization in order to be most effective in guiding expected behavior. The intended outcomes of creating the statement of values will only be realized if the essence of what they represent is embedded and then expressed through all aspects of an organization's core business functions and processes. The organizational values must become institutionalized. "They must be aligned to foster a high performance culture and flow freely and systemically throughout the organization to become the genesis of operational norms (i.e., codes of conduct and ethics) that drive desired behavior" (Ardichvili et al., 2009, p. 449).

Again, no one set of values is identified as the "right" set. Two key features of this element of the model are (1) that an organization has a set of values it espouses and (2) that those values foster a nurturing environment that is based on integrity and transparency. At the minimum, the organization discerns and chooses right versus wrong as defined by laws, regulations, and social standards and norms. What sets a values-driven organization apart from other organizations is its ability to reach for higher standards in the gray areas, when all options or decisions seem right. Such an organization embraces its unique set of organizational values to establish guidelines of acceptable behavior by its employees and other agents acting on its behalf, such as vendors and subcontractors. In short, the values of an organization epitomize its consciousness and are responsible for sustaining an ethical culture. Furthermore, when organizational values are aligned with the core business functions, an environment is created that fosters employee engagement and congruence and drives company longevity.

Leadership Effectiveness

The next characteristic of an ethical business culture is Leadership Effectiveness. A business operating in a global economy must have effective leadership. Thus, "effective leaders lead effective organizations" (Jondle et al., 2014, p. 40). As illustrated in previous chapters, the margins for error are too small and the costs too high to have people in charge who do not understand the complexities and dynamics of culture and cultural diversity.

"The bottom line for leaders is that if they do not become conscious of the cultures in which they are imbedded, those cultures will manage them. Cultural understanding is desirable for all of us, but it is essential to leaders if they are to lead" (Schein, 2004, p. 15). So too is an understanding of cultural diversity. Business leaders in a global economy must recognize the value of diversity to fully capitalize on the potential benefits that the global economy has to offer.

As a business leader, as you look at yourself in the mirror each morning, you should ask, "who am I and what kind of person do I want to be?" Effective leaders running an ethical organization are those who "walk the walk" *and* "talk the talk." They are the ones who know that ethical culture starts at the top of the organization ("tone at the top") and only trickles down to every nook and cranny as the message is delivered, over and over again. The building and sustaining of an ethical business culture results from a leader's persistent commitment to do what is right beyond the letter of the law. Ethical leaders lead by example, applying high ethical standards by exemplifying organizational values both in their personal and professional lives. They act as role models of the organization's ethical culture, exhibiting prototypical ethical judgment and decision-making. They do what they say and have the ability to articulate the meaning of the values not only to employees but also to all stakeholders that the company interacts with. They demonstrate behavior that employees and others notice and want to emulate.

Effective and ethical leaders are known for being fair and open and not "shooting the messenger" who bears bad news. They are characterized as being non-retaliatory while placing high value on stakeholder reciprocity. In other words, they expect ethical treatment in return for ethical behavior, from top management to line employee, from company to all stakeholders. An ethical leader expects ethical behavior and conduct to be part of everyday life within the organization, permeating all business functions and processes.

Stakeholder Balance

A business culture primed on being ethical performs at a level where constituents are identified most broadly and holistically. It is not enough to list owners and employees as the sole stakeholders of an organization. Many more groups of stakeholders need to be taken into account, including, but not limited to, customers, suppliers, the community, competitors, and the environment. The MEBC model "provides a framework by which an organization can foster a discussion on the role of various stakeholders.... It reinforces the notion that the purpose of business is to service the community of stakeholders. It is not restricted [to] or defined by stockholder needs" (Jondle et al., 2014, p. 40). Key to the model's notion of stakeholders is the belief that the active sphere of community expands to encompass the whole global community of humans. Paramount to this notion is the expressed belief that the organization's participation in the global community is linked to its ability to demonstrate to the world that it is a good corporate citizen and worthy of participating as a benefactor of the global economy.

The identification of each stakeholder introduces new tensions and opportunities for misalignments within the frameworks of the organization's business functions and processes that may impact on the decision-making process. This, in turn, can create distortion and imbalance in the business continuum, resulting in moral lapses and ethical breakdowns, even for the best of companies. Thus, the third characteristic of ethical business cultures is Stakeholder Balance.

Process Integrity
The imbedding of ethical practices within all aspects of the company, or the institutionalization of an organization's mission, vision, and values, is crucial to creating and sustaining an ethical operational business culture. The fourth characteristic of the MEBC is Process Integrity.

This characteristic speaks to how an organization hires, fires, evaluates, compensates, rewards, and disciplines its employees, and how it treats customers and vendors, interacts with regulators, and engages with the community at large. It is where, in an ethical business culture, all agents of the firm are compelled to do what is right and not just what is easy. This includes making decisions from time to time that will result in short-term losses but in the long haul have the potential for greater pay back.

Inherent in the institutionalizing of ethical cultures are the challenges associated with alignment of the stated values with the values in practice. The key to success is alignment between the values embossed in gold on the company lobby walls and prominently stated in the company's code of conduct and the values that are actually practiced at all levels, from the boardroom to the shop floor. This includes establishing desired behavior standards and aligning all the business systems predicated on the company's values. In turn, this will help reduce confusion and allow for transparent decision-making by the people closest to the issues. In encouraging the desired behavior, such alignment must be accompanied by a system to monitor behavior. This monitoring system is needed not just to identify violations of desired behavior but also to provide the crucial feedback needed to improve the processes.

Of course, in real life perfect alignment or harmony are elusive. However, the goal is to constantly strive for perfection at all times and to focus decisions on the long-term gains and not to dwell on short-term fixes or losses. In addition, when it comes to ethics training or any other aspect of the institutionalization of ethics, it goes without saying that it is not enough to go through the motions or to just check the box.

Long-term Perspective

The Long-term Perspective is the final characteristic of the CEBC model of an ethical business culture. In simple terms, it is about focusing decision-making on a long-term horizon and reestablishing the purpose of business. It implies that an organization is striving to set goals to achieve the common good for its community of stakeholders and sets in motion the potential for redefining the purpose of business.

A business culture displaying this characteristic is not a culture that revolves around instant gratification or snap judgments. It is not about making easy money. The author (Jondle) is reminded of a story recounted by a president of a large medical technology company. The board and senior management of his firm were interested in acquiring another company. The said company was doing quite well with its product line and would have contributed nicely to the bottom line of the acquirer. Still, there was some underlying noise with regard to one of the product lines that could spell trouble if proven true. After long and sometimes divisive conversations between management and board members, the decision was reached not to purchase the said company. Several years later, the company in question was facing numerous class-action lawsuits against its product that would eventually lead to its bankruptcy. Sacrificing short-term gain while exercising prudent decision-making in the long run was the right decision.

Note that in Figure 11.1 the circumferences of the five characteristics of the MEBC are overlapping. This is quite deliberate. Through these interfaces the model illustrates how an organization's success in achieving its long-term objectives is indelibly intertwined with its ability to manage its operational culture. It defines how things are done day-to-day, year-to-year within the organization, but ultimately it illustrates the impact ethical decisions have on long-term survivability. Holding it all together are the corporate values. As we have discussed before, values, processes, leadership, and a company's behavior toward its internal and external stakeholders are forever linked.

What follows is a conversation based on the thoughts and comments of business leaders from various multinational companies who conduct business ethically in the global economy. It is through their personal experiences that we demonstrate how the MEBC comes to life in practice.

Practitioners' Perspective – Values-Driven
All our interviewees stated that their companies placed significant weight on the value of corporate values and culture in general. Values present themselves as the guiding principles that define the organization, how it wants to be seen as an actor in the greater community,

and how its employees are to behave, as well as its expectations in performance from all the other stakeholders that interact with the company.

US1, US2, and MX pointed out the importance of culture and the values that define it. They felt there were universal values that might or might not be listed as specific corporate values but nevertheless are factored into establishing desired behavior within the workings of the corporation such as "never to be dishonest, not to lie, not to spy, not to get involved in disloyal competition, not to pay money for others to speak well of our company" (MX).

Interviewees from South Africa (SA) and the United States (US1) stressed the need for and the role of core values in fostering an ethical culture within their corporations, and the need to communicate them widely and continuously to employees. Importantly, this included providing related training. Not only is there a need to reinforce corporate values within the corporation but also it is important or necessary to make sure all stakeholders that interact with the company are aware of those values and just what they mean. As pointed out by SA, in high-context cultures many cultural assumptions about the right behavior go unstated and are implied. However, this presents a problem for an organization operating internationally. To make ethical expectations clearer, it is necessary to state what company values are, and it is necessary to communicate them in such a way that they can be understood by representatives of various cultures, regardless of their cultural assumptions.

Going beyond corporate values, an important theme touched on by many of the participants was the tension between corporate values and local cultural customs. How do you reconcile the demands of corporate and local cultures, or address challenges in reconciling corporate values, norms, policies, local norms, regulations, and cultural assumptions? Which principles or values apply in different situations? How do you honor local values while abiding by your own corporate values and country laws and regulations? A ubiquitous and chronic conundrum or challenge when conducting business in your hometown is only compounded when moving operations to nonsimilar lands. Our interviewees constantly drew wisdom and confidence from their organizational core values in meeting these challenges: "So you need to equip leaders to handle situations cross-culturally while still staying anchored to our core values" (US1). US1, MX, SA, and ID pointed out the need to understand local cultural contexts and to act consistently according to their own company values, while also being able to communicate these values to local partners and employees in a culturally appropriate manner. An example of these cultural clashes relates to gift giving. SA pointed out that gift giving is "not foreign to our culture. But when this becomes pervasive. Our rules are stringent about this" (SA). Likewise, MX stated: "A main ethical challenge is to understand to what extent should we adapt to other countries' ways of doing things ... we found in Columbia they had a culturally embedded Catholicism, similar to the Philippines ... when our director went to the Philippines to explore the business opportunities, he was taken to pay visits to various authorities, and these included the Catholic Cardinal."

These issues become all the more relevant – as well as challenging and potentially a liability – in societies where people's choices and behavior are mostly determined by the specificity of relationships they have with others, rather than driven by universal rules or principles. Consider the following quote: "Indonesia is not a rules-based culture, and it is more situational and not litigation-based society, like Australia. Also, safety rules are the other difference: the government-level regulations, like OSHA in the US or similar legislation and government agencies in Australia, are not playing a major role. All safety-related standards are created and enforced by companies themselves" (ID). This is driven, in part, by the fact that basic human needs are not being met in some of these countries. In the chapter on Indonesia, it was correctly pointed out that self-actualization or global warming are not the main priority in a country where more basic needs have not been satisfied. In addition, age and respect for the older generation play an important role in shaping behavior in organizations, for an example: "[I]n a meeting, young people will not speak up if older people are present. So we try to directly address younger people to get their opinions" (ID).

Conflicts between organizational values and norms of the local culture are further highlighted by an example shared by the Indonesian (ID) interviewee and relate to a reluctance to bring up problems or to even confront problems when they surface. Managers must constantly encourage the sharing of issues, which result in serious "implication for whistleblowing and reporting of ethical violations" (ID). In many countries, hotlines – while normal protocol for US companies – are viewed with apprehension and distrust. In India, since the culture is hierarchical and paternalistic, leaders are even more powerful and play a very important role in shaping many aspects of an organization's culture and the behavior the organization wants to encourage. For example, "managers may be reluctant to give feedback to top executives; on the other hand, coaching by outside consultants may work better" (IN). An implication of this reluctance to provide feedback or point out problems for attempts to instill a culture of ethics in an organization is that nepotism and harassment could go unchallenged.

Discussing the challenges that operating in other African countries present for their company, respondent SA stated: "[I]t is not sufficient to understand cultures of other countries. The question is how to realistically implement the corporate rules of behavior while taking into account local cultural assumptions." It is important that companies find something that people can relate to in terms of their own value systems and traditional ethics. Using this as a reference point, SA gave an example of discussing issues of corruption with local employees in West Africa. A story was created centered on the common local practice of "groups of individuals pulling the net with fish out of the water." As participants think about this activity and the storyteller reminds them that "all people in the village participate, everybody shares," they are asked, "[I]s there foundation for corruption in such a situation?" The response was "not really. So you don't have the culture of corruption historically. It is something that was brought in later." That's how you build the culture of ethics, from the bottom up, by using culturally recognizable stories and examples that participants can relate to in ethics discussions.

Leadership Effectiveness

Someone needs to be at the helm of the ship, guiding it in times of good weather and reacting with good judgment during periods of bad weather and severe storms. Marshaling a company through good and bad times requires a management team that is both able and willing to make sound judgment based on good information and that knows how to listen to all points of view and understands that a change of course may be needed as new information becomes available and relevant to the situation at hand.

As pointed out in the US1 interview, both at home and abroad, an important requirement is that leaders at all levels need to "[m]odel an ethical culture as part of earning trust" of members of organization's numerous global teams. This requirement "reinforces the top-to-bottom nature of accountability in the organization" (US1). Likewise, SA pointed out "[t]he central role of leadership in creating ethical culture" in his company and further elaborated on this: "[L]eadership is the heart of everything. What do you expect leaders to do? Walk the talk. Every single day you have to live, sleep, eat ethics. And there is always a discussion of ethics. Who I am, what are my values. Make it a habit to talk about ethics." The IN interviewee pointed out an important feature of leadership in Indonesia (and, we must add, this applies to many other emerging market economies): that the role of leaders in setting the tone for ethical behavior may be even more important than in Western countries. Because of the paternalistic and hierarchical nature of the country's culture, leaders in India are even more powerful and unchallenged. Therefore, their modeling of ethical behavior is even more critical.

As already pointed out, leadership of a company is crucial to its success and to its ability to be sustainable in the long run. It is also obvious that the challenges placed on leadership are compounded when it is asked to manage operations outside the familiar operating range that is its domestic market. So how do businesses prepare their leaders for operating in the complex environments of the emerging markets? What challenges do multinational corporations face in their development of competent, empathetic, and ethical leaders?

The main challenge, as pointed out by one of the respondents, is to develop leaders who have sufficient understanding of and commitment to company values, the ability to understand the local cultural specificity of countries in which they operate, and who are able to successfully reconcile these (often clashing) value systems while doing their work in a consistently ethical manner. This task is complicated by the fact that, in most cases, leaders operate not just on the interface of two cultures (the culture of the headquarters of the multinational corporation and the culture of the host country) but also in multiple cultures at the same time. All of the executives we talked to are responsible for a number of countries in the regions where their companies operate.

Leadership development is a critically important component of such preparation. However, as pointed out by one of our interviewees, training based on Western models may not work with local leaders, and other Western approaches, like 360-degree feedback, may not work either, due to the reluctance to provide feedback to superiors and the perception of leaders as all-powerful beings who cannot be wrong and already know everything. In such conditions, coaching and individual consultation by outside consultants may work better. For example:

> The training we give our leaders is critical. Mentoring is a key way we help new leaders learn how to manage teams that often span geographies and cultural norms. All of us as senior leaders regularly coach new managers to help them with this, because it's not always easy … keep things simple, make expectations clear,

build trust, and emphasize ethics, all while focusing on respect and integrity for the individual and keeping in mind the patriotism that all people have for their home country. (US1)

Stakeholder Balance

As implied in the term "Stakeholder Balance," organizations often face problems of misalignment, or the existence of tensions between interests, wants, and needs of various stakeholder groups. It becomes a balancing act, sometimes precariously aligned, that often creates a no-win situation. And the problem becomes compounded when, in addition to its more familiar domestic stakeholder groups, an organization deals with numerous new groups of stakeholders, as found in foreign markets.

In our interviews, participants focused on one specific cluster of stakeholder groups that seemed particularly important for organizations that have a significant footprint in emerging market countries. These stakeholder groups included a wider range of various sections of the community-at-large than would normally be expected for a Western company's domestic stakeholder network.

Our interview with US1 revealed a strong emphasis on CSR within the company, viewing business ethics and CSR as tightly interconnected: "Our ethical behavior has to carry through to our activities outside our front door." Further, the interviewee emphasized that their broad commitment to corporate responsibility includes four major areas. The first is a general principle of conducting business with integrity. The second is the organization's and its employees' commitment to enriching the communities where they live and work. They listed numerous examples, including both the work in developing countries (e.g., building schools in Vietnam and Ivory Coast and programs in support of women entrepreneurs in India, Zambia, and Honduras) and the work with disadvantaged members of the community in developed countries (e.g., contributing resources and employees' expertise to food banks in Canada and the United States).

Society as a stakeholder was a recurring theme within the discussions on the role of business in the global economy. Because government is not always responsive to social needs, MX and US2 professed a need for the corporation to participate in the "promotion of civic culture." Interviewees gave examples of what this might entail, for example, "not supporting any individual politician or party in secret" (MX). This, in turn, was extrapolated to an aversion to payment of bribes and corruption in general, a theme echoed by SA and US1.

As an illustration of a commitment to stakeholders beyond the traditional group of employees, customers, and owners, one of our US participants (US1) is running farmer training programs in more than 20 countries, aimed at making them more productive and able to conserve resources. In addition, US1 has global partnerships with numerous nongovernmental organizations (NGOs) (e.g., CARE, the Nature Conservancy, and World Food Programme) aimed at strengthening food security, supporting environmental programs, and offering training and education.

SA devoted a significant part of their interview to discussing the importance of working with local communities to promote their livelihood and well-being. They connected their work with local communities to the issues of sustainability.

On the other hand, ID pointed out that CSR in general is not as important in Indonesia, since there are other concerns, perceived to be of a more pressing nature, and local companies rarely invest in large CSR projects, contributing mostly to minor local projects, disaster relief, etc. In general, CSR programs are mostly pursued by large multinational corporations.

MX stressed the importance of sustainability in defining business ethics, and linked it to service for the common good of the community. "Sustainability ... means that the neighbors of our plants should love our company and that there is a secure neighborhood not vulnerable to criminal acts or to violence." This was, again, linked to corruption and suggests that perhaps government was failing in its job to provide a secure society. Therefore, "sustainability is ... a broad concept which is much related to a good society in which there is room for a sense of community." Through their charitable foundation, the company would focus on issues that were of "high importance to Mexican society." These included water sustainability, education, nutrition education, and smoking cessation.

Process Integrity

Process Integrity is a key element of the MEBC. All aspects of the MEBC are important, but it is in the institutionalization of company values throughout all its business functions and processes that the ethical culture of a company takes hold, is built, and is sustained. Think of it as the factory where things are built. This is where the essence of ethical culture is first captured and redirected into action as embodied in its leadership. This is where corporate values are transformed into operational norms, allowing all employees to become active participants, engaged with the processes and functions of the business. Fully engaged employees can make the most of their vantage points by critiquing and providing feedback on what works or does not work within the bowels of the company.

MX felt that business ethics "must be an integral part of every area of the company." US1 emphasizes what they call "putting in place the essential infrastructure" for business ethics. This includes communicating to all employees the principles of the code of conduct, and "making them a vital part of your culture.... Wrestling with them every day." The company does not look at it as "values that we 'bring' from the developed to the developing world. Rather, these are universal absolutes that do not vary, regardless of country, business or circumstance." And a key element in the institutionalization of values is to make sure employees understand that there are consequences for misbehavior, "consequences for violations are real, material, and can include termination." To assist in reporting misconduct in the workplace, a global ethics hotline is provided to employees for both pointing out clear ethical violations and bringing up situations in which the employees may not be sure whether there is a cause for concern.

But beyond the threat of termination, it is important for the company to provide a pathway that avoids the pitfalls or temptations of misconduct so common in business. Here, the goal is to "foster a culture of thinking out loud." The "thinking out loud" mentality elicits an evolving ethical culture that begins to express ethical behavior normatively, which relies on training employees to openly communicate with each other, including when they observe misconduct in the workplace. It gives the employee permission to freely ask questions "if they're uncomfortable talking about something, that's an ... indication that there's a problem, and they need to get it out in the open." This becomes even more important when operating in so many different countries. Ambiguity becomes more the norm, where operating in the gray areas becomes more prevalent and worrisome and where people left alone or isolated are willing or forced to take steps that they might not normally take. "It isn't the first mistake that gets employees in trouble. It's what they do after that mistake that proves far more damaging to their careers. Do they cover it up? Make other employees complicit to try and smooth it over? Or maybe they continue the behavior because they didn't get caught the first time. The goal is always to encourage discussion. 'If you see something, say something'" (US1).

Measurement and feedback were themes raised by several of our participants. SA felt that "in a culture where transactions are based on unwritten rules, there is a need for a clearly articulated system for measuring performance and success." This involves incentivizing employees to produce desirable outcomes through ethical behavior, as articulated by the company values. To help with discussions of ethical issues arising within the workplace, US1 has a Business Ethics & Compliance Committee, which regularly discusses real-life cases. It discusses how the involved individuals or teams should have acted to meet the requirements of the organization's guidelines for ethics. The committee pays special attention to situations where there is significant ambiguity about the possible decisions and actions. Based on these reviews, case studies are written and disseminated to employees from all globally dispersed company locations, via the intranet.

As important as it is in the home country, ethics training remains a keystone to the institutionalization of an ethical business culture when operating in the global marketplace. In fact, when operating internationally, it becomes even more crucial that a united front is presented when training employees on the company values, principles, and code of conduct. In US1, organizational "pamphlets on the [principles] have been translated into more than 20 languages and distributed globally." Beyond the training, salaried employees are asked to annually certify that they know and understand the principles and that they are not aware of any violations of those principles. Non-salaried employees participate in certification every three years.

Long-term Perspective

The key to the Long-term Perspective is in how the company manages its everyday operation. Do they have their eye on the distant horizon, or on the hill across the pond next door? A prime example of short-termism is managing the company's financial affairs from quarter to quarter, listening only to the expert voices of financial analysts who know your company only through your financial statements, rather than engaging in dialogue with company employees, customers, the environment, and other stakeholders.

Both SA and MX made it clear that emphasis on "long-term sustainability is at the center of [the] company's operating philosophy, and they perceive ethics and sustainability as being the same" (SA). Both assumed that sustainability is much more than environmental sustainability and involves long-term sustainability of the company's products and services, as well as sustainable development of local communities. SA is trying to make sure that in all decisions made by employees, they consider ethical concerns and questions, such as "how to ensure sustainability. How do we interact with the environment? What [is] our imprint on the world? What is the impact of our decisions on communities?" Ethics conversations with managers and employees involve discussions of the difference between short-term successes and long-term sustainability: "This is not about short-term success. We want to be here in 100 years. We want to build [an] ethical value system for the company. Everything you do, must not destroy the longevity of the company."

The issue of reputation surfaced as important to the discussion on long-termism. At US1, ethical considerations are related to a "long-term view of company's reputation and risk management." If company reputation, which is not always so tangible a concept, is damaged through ethical breakdowns, there exists the real potential for highly deleterious outcomes. Ethical breakdowns result in lost goodwill, and customers will punish you by switching to competitors. Furthermore, there is always a real likelihood that the government will impose fines and restitution. All managers, in all countries, go through ethics training that emphasizes the need to use "the organization's ethical decision-making model, that shows how any local decision and action is linked to company's long-term reputation and success" (US1).

As is evident from the previous conversations with global business leaders, the problems – and solutions to those problems – faced when doing business in the global economy can be seriously perplexing. However, solutions do exist. Companies need to be creative and flexible in their evolution and be willing to modify processes that have a real potential to foster rewarding outcomes.

So back to the Rana Plaza. In light of the problems facing the international garment industry in general, and particularly in Bangladesh, business leaders from a host of companies met and created a solution that was creative and resulted in beneficial outcomes. What follows is the experience of one of the participants in a meeting of representatives of the US garment industry in New York City. The meeting was convened in response to the accident at Rana

Plaza, and its purpose was to form a coalition as a solution to the deteriorating working conditions in the Bangladesh garment industry in general.

Following the accident at Rana Plaza, representatives

> from at least 15 major retail and apparel manufacturing companies, including Walmart, Gap, Li & Fung, the Children's Place and others... The goal of the discussions was to determine how Western corporations should respond and assess what action we could take to begin improving the standards of safety in Bangladesh apparel factories. Several of these companies had just returned from Europe, where they had failed to reach an agreement with a safety accord that was forming between mostly European retailers and international trade unions. (Duty, 2015)

The participants, who represented competitors in the marketplace with both common and competing interests, had it in mind to come together to create a "successful coalition seeking to make true impact [with] clear alignment on its goal and strategies." Through their discussions, the group, known as the Alliance for Bangladesh Worker Safety (the Alliance), came together to promote one goal that provided an unobstructed path to improving "the level of safety in Bangladeshi ready-made garment factories." The laser-beam focus on this one goal provided the Alliance with the ability to meet certain milestones on schedule, such as "conducting immediate inspections, transparency, worker training, remediation and capacity building." In addition, the coalition established open and transparent channels of communication between members that included frequent calls between members, monthly updates, and scheduled member meetings. All were intended to provide avenues for members to provide input and ask and answer questions.

A key component contributing to the success of the coalition, beyond the alignment of its goal and strategies, was the understanding by members that to be successful they needed to have in place measurements or key performance indicators that allowed the

Alliance to assess progress in achieving its goal. Having performance metrics in place not only allowed the coalition to assess what was or was not working but also provided a tool that could be used to "hold the coalition accountable, increasing the likelihood of success."

Once the Alliance established an efficient working relationship among members, it proceeded to expand its circle of stakeholders to include "partnerships with the US, European and Bangladeshi governments, NGOs, trade associations and local labor leaders.... These additional parties have enhanced the discussion by bringing new ideas, challenging assumptions, and helping implement solutions." As an example, "the partnership with the NGO Phulki, led to creation of a help line that is a reliable, responsive channel through which workers can report imminent risks to health and safety."

"Looking back, it is clear that success in raising safety standards in Bangladesh has thus far stemmed from [the creation of] the right coalition of partners with tight alignment around a goal and strategies.... the Alliance and other like-minded coalitions can and will make real social impact for the betterment of all" (Duty, 2015).

REFERENCES

Ardichvili, A., Mitchell, J., & Jondle, D. (2009). Characteristics of ethical business cultures. *Journal of Business Ethics*, 85, 445–451.

Associated Press in Dhaka. (2015, June 1). Rana Plaza collapse: dozens charged with murder. *The Guardian*.

Center for Ethicial Business Cultures. (2017, June 13). CEBCGLOBAL.org.

Duty, D. (2015, July 16). Building successful coalitions for greater social impact. TriplePundit.com.

Goodpaster, K. (2007). *Conscience and corporate culture*. Malden, MA: Blackwell.

Greenhouse, S., & Harris, E. (2014, April 21). Battling for safer Bangladesh. *New York Times*.

Jondle, D., Ardichvili, A., & Mitchell, J. (2014). Modeling ethical business culture: Development of the Ethical Business Culture Survey and its use to validate the CEBC Model of Ethical Business Culture. *Journal of Business Ethics*, 119, 29–43.

Ryan, L. (2005). Codes of ethics. In P. Werhane & E. Freeman (Eds.), *The Blackwell encyclopedia of management: Business ethics* (2nd ed., pp. 80–83). Oxford: Blackwell.

Schein, E. (2004). *Organizational culture and leadership* (3rd ed.). San Francisco, CA: Jossey-Bass.

Epilogue

Douglas Jondle and Alexandre Ardichvili

Economies of individual countries can no longer exist in a vacuum and function in isolation from the global marketplace. Likewise, it is hard for any individual business organization to avoid playing in the arena called "globalization" if they hope to maximize their chances of surviving in today's economy. As the success of business organizations is increasingly dependent on their participation in global markets, consumers have grown accustomed to the benefits of globalization with the expectation of high-quality and inexpensive goods available anytime and anywhere, on demand.

The need to actively participate in global marketplace transactions is associated with numerous challenges of operating in an unfamiliar territory. One of the most daunting tasks is overcoming cultural barriers and figuring out how to conduct business with integrity, without violating either national culture norms or company values and codes of conduct. We believe that long-term success in the global marketplace depends largely on the existence of a sustainable business culture that is built on a solid foundation of ethical values and processes. Having such a strong, values-based culture is crucial for success in domestic operations, and it is even more important when operating in other countries, where the organizational and national cultures of the headquarters clash, inevitably, with host country cultures and local customs.

This book has focused on the challenges of building and sustaining ethical business cultures in emerging economies. We have included eight country-specific chapters covering Brazil, Russia, India, China, South Africa, Mexico, Indonesia, and Turkey. We have exposed the challenges and risks associated with conducting business ethically in the context of diverse national cultures and norms.

Chapters 9 through 11 discuss ways of building and sustaining ethical business cultures by providing perspectives from employees and business leaders from across the globe. Employee perceptions of ethical business cultures were communicated through survey data that were subsequently linked to employee engagement and performance metrics, while business leaders' stories were captured through interviews and personal reflections.

In this conclusion, we share lessons and observations based on our reading of the chapters. We will focus on two important areas. First, we will compare the information presented in the eight country-specific chapters in order to identify challenges and opportunities for developing ethical business cultures that are common to all or the majority of the countries discussed in this book. Second, we discuss lessons learned from the surveys of employees' perceptions of ethical cultures and specific examples shared by business leaders from around the globe.

COUNTRY PERSPECTIVES: CULTURAL, NORMATIVE, AND REGULATORY CHALLENGES TO BUILDING ETHICAL BUSINESS CULTURES

As demonstrated in Chapters 1–8 of this book, Western ethical business ideology is prevalent worldwide. At the same time, the rate and extent of adoption of Western standards varies greatly from country to country (Ardichvili et al., 2012). According to Michaelson (2010),

> A fundamental question of global business ethics is, "When moral business conduct standards conflict across borders, whose standards should prevail?" Western scholarship and practice tends to depict home country standards as "higher" or more "restrictive" or "well-ordered" than the "lower" standards of emerging market actors. As much as the question appears culturally neutral, many who ask it do so with a culturally-specific lens shaped by prevailing conditions of Western economic strength. However, the

dominant economic powers of the future are not likely to be the same North American and Western European markets that have reigned supreme in the recent past. As corporations increasingly re-examine their political roles in global governance, we need also to re-examine the moral authority of global ethical norms so they do not merely reflect the dominant ideologies of the most economically powerful market actors. (p. 237)

Indeed, "the indigenous multinational corporations from [emerging market countries] are gaining increasing presence and influence in global trade" (Ardichvili et al., 2012, p. 425), and in doing so they are following multiple pathways in establishing ethical norms based on cultural and institutional conditions inherent within countries' cultures, social norms, and behaviors. However, an alternative hypothesis is that the acceptance of a more universal set of ethical business values is a natural outcome of the evolution of organizational forms in business, helped along by globalization and advances in information technology (Ralston, 2008).

While the authors of country-specific chapters were given latitude to draw upon their personal perspectives and expertise in exploring culture and business ethics in their countries, all provided a macro-analysis of the business climate within their country and discussed the role of normative frameworks and characteristics of national cultures in shaping ethical business cultures. Our comparison of individual country chapters revealed a number of common themes. In the following pages we will discuss four major themes that are prominent in the majority of the chapters and have direct implications for both the theory and practice of developing and promoting ethical business cultures at a national and organizational level. The following four subsections discuss how ethical business cultures are influenced by national cultures; informal networks and relationships; religion and indigenous philosophies; and institutional frameworks (including the role of government, regulatory frameworks, and political structures).

THE ROLE OF NATIONAL OR ETHNIC CULTURES IN SHAPING ETHICAL BUSINESS CULTURES

All eight country chapters discussed dimensions of national cultures, based on Geert Hofstede's framework (Hofstede et al., 2010). In Table E.1, we provide a comparison between the dimensions of cultures of these countries and the United States.[1]

As can be seen from the table, the most striking differences between the United States and the eight emerging market economies are on the Power Distance (PDI) and Individualism (IND) dimensions: the majority of the eight countries have high PDI and low IND scores, while the United States has low PDI and extremely high IND. Note that South Africa (SA) is an outlier among the emerging market countries, having scores that are rather different from the rest of the emerging market group (although still different from the US scores).[2]

As was explained by Hofstede et al. (2010), a high PDI score means that people accept hierarchical structures, large differences in power between different layers of the society, and significant income inequality. In high PDI societies, employees tend to avoid questioning decisions made by their superiors and are not comfortable with empowerment-oriented management approaches. An important implication for business ethics, and for creating and maintaining ethical business cultures, is that in a high PDI society it is difficult to expect employees to be willing to report ethical violations committed by their superiors. And, as pointed out by Sañudo (Chapter 7),

---

[1] We are using the United States as a comparison point, as just one example of a Western developed nation culture, being fully aware that there are significant cultural differences even between countries that share the same Anglo-Saxon cultural heritage. For example, the Hofstede scores for the United Kingdom, the United States, Canada, and Australia differ on a number of dimensions. And scores for France or Germany will be even more divergent.

[2] Note that Hofstede's scores for SA should be interpreted with caution. His sample included mostly white South Africans, and therefore, the SA country scores, especially those on individualism, could have been different if a larger sample, more representative of the majority black population, was included.

Table E.1. *Comparison of Select Hofstede's Scores for the Eight Emerging Market Countries and the United States*

Dimension	Brazil	Russia	India	China	South Africa	Mexico	Turkey	Indonesia	United States
Power distance	69	93	77	80	49	81	66	78	40
Individualism	38	39	48	20	65	30	37	14	91
Masculinity	49	36	56	66	63	69	45	46	62
Uncertainty avoidance	76	95	40	30	49	82	85	48	46
Long-term orientation	44	81	51	87	34	24	46	62	26
Indulgence	59	20	26	24	63	97	49	38	68

Source: The table was created by the authors using data from https://geert-hofstede.com/cultural-dimensions.html.

"inequality makes it easier for people to rationalize their own corrupt behavior" (p. 171).

High levels of Individualism (as opposed to Collectivism) mean, among other things, that individuals will not have long-term commitment to the members of their "in-group" (an in-group could be a clan, an extended family, a tightly knit group of co workers, or any other group toward which an individual feels especially strong loyalty). In cultures where in-group membership is of central importance, promotion and compensation decisions, performance assessment, and decisions related to long-term business strategies are based on considerations of loyalty to the in-group, and performance considerations are given lower priority.

An implication for business ethics is that loyalty to the in-group may override considerations of larger societal good and individuals will be more likely to apply situational ethics decision rules rather than adhere to universal norms of ethical behavior. Giving preferential treatment to members of one's in-group may be considered unethical in a universalist and rule-based society, like the United States. In contrast, in collectivist countries, characterized by strong in-group orientation, not being supportive of one's in-group will be considered unethical. In addition, considerations of group harmony and consensus in groups, and conflict avoidance, will result in employees' reluctance to raise ethical issues.

As can be seen from the table, there are significant differences in cultural dimensions, not only between the emerging markets and the United States but also among the eight emerging market countries. For example, Brazil, Russia, Mexico, and Turkey have high levels of Uncertainty Avoidance (UAI), while scores for India, China, South Africa, and Indonesia are low or moderate. According to the Hofstede Centre, cultures exhibiting stronger UAI tend to maintain more rigid codes of behavior and may be more intolerant of unorthodox ideas. This is done in order to create more structure in life and to combat anxiety that is associated with facing an unknown future. In such cultures, change is perceived more as a threat than opportunity, and innovation may be viewed with suspicion and caution. An implication for building ethical business cultures is that the change efforts required to institutionalize cultures of ethics will face significant resistance. And the rate of adoption of CSR and sustainability initiatives could be low as well, since these initiatives will be perceived as conflicting with established organizational routines and norms.

Space limitations do not allow us to provide a detailed analysis of the differences between the eight countries on each of the Hofstede dimensions. However, we would urge the reader to review corresponding parts of the country chapters, and visit the Hofstede Centre website,[3] to make comparisons between country scores and draw their own conclusions.

Our final observation regarding the role of national culture in shaping ethical business cultures is that several of the countries in our sample are so large and culturally diverse that any country-level generalizations should be made with caution. India, for example, is comprised of dozens of ethnic groups, and different parts of the country have distinctly different regional subcultures. Russia has, in addition to the majority Russian population, millions of citizens who are ethnically different from Russians. Many of these ethnic groups live in their own autonomous regions, and some of these regions have the status of autonomous republics. In Brazil, while ethnic diversity is not as pronounced (the exception being large immigrant groups living in several major cities, for example, millions of ethnic Japanese living in Sao Paulo), the country has a wide spectrum of racial diversity. In addition, different parts of this vast country also have distinctive local subcultures (for example, there is a striking contrast between the fast-paced business culture of the south and a more relaxed pace of life in the northeast).

---

[3] https://geert-hofstede.com/countries.html

THE ROLE OF RELIGION AND INDIGENOUS
PHILOSOPHIES

Five chapters (on China, India, Turkey, Indonesia, and Russia) devote substantial space to a discussion of the influence of religion and moral philosophies on business in general, and business ethics in particular. In China, as pointed out by Li (Chapter 4), the Confucian value system "includes a set of moral and ethical codes, such as trustworthiness, propriety, altruism, filial piety, and having a sense of shame" (p. 88) and has a strong influence on all aspects of business behavior. In fact, after decades under the Communist regime, when Confucianism was out of favor, the country is moving to a new stage where Confucius and his moral teachings are widely promoted by the ruling elite as a means of strengthening the business ethics and socially responsible behavior of the new generation of business leaders and employees.

Thakadipuram (Chapter 3) shows that in India the influence of religion on business is more complex than in any other country in our sample. Multiple major religions are present (among them, Hinduism, Islam, Sikhism, Jainism, and Buddhism), each bringing its own set of moral codes and beliefs. However, Thakadipuram points out that despite the variety of indigenous ethical beliefs, there is at least one prominent idea common to many Indian religious and philosophical systems that is especially important in the context of business ethics. This is the concept of *dharma*. Among other meanings, dharma is interpreted as ethical and social responsibility and encompasses a comprehensive set of ethical and moral values and codes of conduct.

Chapters on Turkey and Indonesia elaborate on the role of Islam in these predominantly Muslim countries, showing that Islam offers a comprehensive value system governing all aspects of social life and business activities. Thus, the chapter on Turkey shows that the Qur'an has specific verses that address standards of business behavior, prohibiting "unjust, unfair, and unethical business."

It is important to point out that, as indicated by Coskun and Akdere (Chapter 6), it would be premature to assume that there is always a direct and strong relationship between religion and ethical business cultures in a Muslim country. As a result of secularization and globalization, businesspeople often tend to discriminate between religious values and business practices and believe that the "business world has its own rules."

Likewise, the chapter on Russia demonstrates that it is impossible to understand the ethical business culture of that country without considering the role and influence of the Russian Orthodox Church, since for many Russians Orthodoxy defines their entire way of life. And, similar to the chapter on Turkey, the chapter on Russia shows that there is often a gap between high moral values, as prescribed by religion, and the day-to-day behavior of business people: "The Orthodox often tend to believe that there is such a deep divide between the temple and the marketplace that overtly pious behavior can easily co-exist with unethical conduct in business" (Ardichvili, Chapter 2, p. 37). However, the author also points out that recent years have witnessed a revival of interest in applying Orthodox principles in the business sphere, and numerous articles in business publications discuss the role of religious principles in shaping rules for business ethics conduct.

THE ROLE OF INFORMAL NETWORKS
AND RELATIONSHIPS

Another important theme that emerged from our analysis is the role of informal networks and relationships in business in general, and in business ethics in particular. These issues were discussed to some extent in most of the chapters and were given special attention in chapters on China, Brazil, Russia, Turkey, and Indonesia.

Thus, as pointed out by Li (Chapter 4), in China the normative institution of *guanxi* plays a central role in regulating individuals' behavior both in private life and in the workplace. Li defines guanxi as "interpersonal relationships based on a common background or existence of direct particularistic ties" (p. 90) and explains that guanxi results in the formation of tightly knit, relation-based networks. Similar concepts and practices exist in Russia, India, Brazil, Turkey, and many other countries of the developing and emerging market world. As pointed out by authors of several chapters, in and of themselves these informal network relationships are not unethical and could be regarded as an important prerequisite of doing business. However, their existence creates conditions for unethical behavior, corruption, and bribery. Foreign businesspeople who are new to working in societies dominated by such relationship networks find it difficult to figure out the subtle nuances of rules for establishing and maintaining such networks in order to distinguish between the legitimate use of networks and bribery and corruption. Furthermore, it is hard for foreign businesspeople to establish such networks with local counterparts, and attempts to break into tight-knit networks may lead to inadvertently straying into gray or even overtly unethical areas, especially when gift giving and reciprocal favors are used.

THE ROLE OF GOVERNMENT AND POLITICAL PARTIES

Another important theme is the role of governments and governmental regulation, and, in some cases, of the dominant political parties. Thus, in China and Russia the role of government in regulating all aspects of business is much stronger than in the rest of the countries covered in this book, or in the developed countries of the West. In addition, in China, the Communist Party still plays the key role in shaping institutional frameworks for business transactions. As Li points out, "China remains an autocratic country under the leadership of one party. China's economic reform is a government-driven initiative; the government has been and will continue to play a significant role in governing and regulating the market" (Chapter 4, p. 97).

In Russia, another form of autocratic rule has emerged, with an exceptionally powerful presidency, supported by an elite group of oligarchs and security apparatus. The legislative framework of the country is less powerful, and businesses do not have the same level of legal protection as in the West or a number of emerging market democracies.

In India, while the government is not nearly as centralized and powerful as in China or Russia, it still has a much stronger regulatory role in the business sphere than is the case in most developed countries, or in emerging market countries like Brazil, Indonesia, or Mexico. In addition, the legacy of the British Raj, and of a long period of post-independence rule by successive socialist-leaning governments, resulted in the creation of a cumbersome system of regulations and massive bureaucracy.

Finally, the chapters on South Africa, Brazil, Indonesia, and Mexico point toward common struggles faced by young democracies that are combatting the negative trends resulting from their colonial legacies and/or military dictatorships, alongside complex influences of globalization and their expanding role in international trade.

The implication of the previous discussion for business ethics is that, despite differences in political systems and legislative structures, all countries in our sample are facing significant barriers to the creation of ethical business cultures. These barriers are created by excessive bureaucracy and power of the government (and of dominant parties) and/or by weaknesses of the regulatory frameworks. In many cases, a combination of powerful bureaucracies, vague or cumbersome business legislation, and the lack of enforcement leads to corruption and bribe taking by government officials. At the same time, in order to counter government interference or the inefficiency of legislative frameworks, businesspeople are forced to rely mostly on informal networks to accomplish their business goals.

Building and Sustaining Ethical Business Cultures

In Part II of the book, we offer a lens through which to view and assess ethical business cultures at the corporate level. While Chapters 1–8 focus on the challenges of building and sustaining ethical business cultures, Chapters 9–11 provide, first, an understanding of employees' perceptions of the ethical cultures of their organizations and, second, specific examples shared by business leaders from around the globe.

Employees' perceptions of ethical business cultures were examined using the Ethical Perception Index (EPI) (Chapter 9). With more than 42,000 respondents from 22 countries, a map of ethical perceptions by country was created and compared to employee engagement and performance confidence metrics.

Four drivers of strong ethical cultures, common to the majority of the surveyed countries, were identified: (1) diversity climate, (2) transparent communication, (3) managerial interpersonal justice, and (4) regulated work processes. The authors of the research concluded that in businesses wanting to build and sustain an ethical business culture while operating in the emerging markets and more generally in the global economy, management must

- make a concerted effort to recruit and retain an inclusive and diverse workforce that fosters an environment conducive to equal advancement opportunities;
- provide frequent and transparent communication to employees regarding issues involving the organization, and create a climate within the organization that is accepting of open-door policies and free of fear of retaliation;
- hire and train managers who "walk the walk" and "talk the talk," as it pertains to building and sustaining ethical business cultures; and
- take to heart the institutionalization of organizational values throughout all processes and functions of the organization as it builds and sustains an ethical business culture.

The business leaders' perspectives were discussed in Chapter 11. This discussion was anchored by the application of the Center for Ethical Business Cultures' (CEBC) Model of Ethical Business Cultures (MEBC) (Ardichvili et al., 2009; Jondle et al., 2014). The analysis of the interviews of six business practitioners representing companies from the United States, Mexico, South Africa, India, and Indonesia was conducted using the five characteristics of the MEBC: (1) Values Driven, (2) Leadership Effectiveness, (3) Stakeholder Balance, (4) Process Integrity, and (5) Long-term Perspective.

Anecdotal evidence from major multinational corporations was overlaid onto the MEBC, an empirically validated model of ethical culture, in such a way that a usable roadmap is provided for action within organizations through the telling of stories. All interviewees shared the theme of the importance of creating and sustaining ethical business cultures within their companies and maintaining the same high standards of ethics regardless of where in the world business took them. Furthermore, the interviewees agreed that ethical business conduct is important not because governments legislate ethical behavior but because it is just good business. It is good for the bottom line, and it is good for employee morale and engagement. Having an ethical business culture creates a pathway to differentiation in a crowded marketplace, providing a competitive advantage when trying to win over customers, regardless of where they might live.

REFERENCES

Ardichvili, A., Jondle, D., Kowske, B., Cornachione, E., Li, J., & Thakadipuram, T. (2012). Ethical cultures in large business organizations in Brazil, Russia, India, and China. *Journal of Business Ethics*, 105, 415–428.

Ardichvili, A., Mitchell, J., & Jondle, D. (2009). Characteristics of ethical business cultures. *Journal of Business Ethics*, 85, 445–451.

Hofstede, G., Hofstede, G. J., & Minkov. D. (2010). *Cultures and organizations: Software of the mind.* New York: McGraw Hill.

Jondle, D., Ardichvili, A., & Mitchell, J. (2014). Modeling ethical business culture: Development of the Ethical Business Culture Survey and its use to validate the CEBC Model of Ethical Business Culture. *Journal of Business Ethics*, 119, 29–43.

Michaelson, C. (2010). Revisiting the global business ethics question. *Business Ethics Quarterly*, 20(2), 237–251.

Ralston, D. (2008). The convergence perspective: Reflections and projections. *Journal of International Business Studies*, 39, 27–40.

Index